FEMINIST PERIODICALS 1855-1984

FEMINIST PERIODICALS
1855-1984

An Annotated Critical Bibliography of British, Irish, Commonwealth and International Titles

David Doughan

Denise Sanchez

THE HARVESTER PRESS

First published in Great Britain in 1987 by
THE HARVESTER PRESS LIMITED
Publisher: John Spiers
16 Ship Street, Brighton, Sussex

© David Doughan and Denise Sanchez, 1987

British Library Cataloguing in Publication Data
Doughan, David
   Feminist periodicals, 1855—1984 : an
   annotated critical bibliography of
   British, Irish, Commonwealth and
   international titles.
   1. Feminism—Periodicals—Bibliography
   I. Title II. Sanchez, Denise
   016.3054'2'05   Z7962

   ISBN 0-7108-0992-1

Printed in Great Britain by
Biddles Ltd, Guildford and King's Lynn

THE HARVESTER PRESS PUBLISHING GROUP
The Harvester Group comprises Harvester Press Ltd (chiefly publishing literature, fiction, philosophy, psychology, and science and trade books); Harvester Press Microform Publications Ltd (publishing in microform previously unpublished archives, scarce printed sources, and indexes to these collections) and Wheatsheaf Books Ltd (chiefly publishing in economics, international politics, sociology, women's studies and related social sciences).

Contents

Foreword

This book is intended as a guide to feminist periodicals for
those working in women's studies (particularly feminist history),
or related fields. Our aim has been to identify, describe and
locate titles we consider useful, with annotations where necessary
to help researchers assess the relevance of a periodical to their
own needs (NB: length of annotation is not necessarily any
indication of a periodical's importance, or vice versa). The
majority of locations imply a London-based researcher, using
mainly the British Library Newspaper Library at Colindale, the
Fawcett Library, the Feminist Library and Information Centre, and,
as a last resort, the British Library at Bloomsbury (British
Museum); however, many of these periodicals are held in other
libraries both in Britain and throughout the world, and even more
are available in microform. The titles listed are mainly British,
though we have included a number of Irish and Commonwealth
magazines (mainly those which are held in British libraries). All
periodicals listed are at least principally in the English
language.

The question of what makes a periodical "feminist" is, to put
it mildly, open to debate, and we have not always been consistent
in our inclusions and exclusions. Our tendency has been to
interpret "feminist" extremely broadly for titles up to about 1960,
including not only a number of titles which are far more
philanthropic than feminist in intention, but a number of papers
campaigning for the repeal of the C.D. Acts which are only
feminist in that the campaign itself was of enormous feminist
significance. After about 1960, however, the sheer quantity of
material has led us to exclude most periodicals which do not define
themselves at the minimum as committed to improving the social,
legal and economic position of women in relation to men.
Nevertheless, there are two broad classes of exceptions to this.
At all dates, we have included those few periodicals whose explicit
purposes is to oppose feminism, as being a matter of legitimate

concern to those studying feminism. Finally, we have included a fair number of false drops, i.e. titles which look feminist, but which, on examination, turn out to be anything but. Our own experience in this area leads us to believe that a considerable amount of researcher's time, energy and general psychological well-being can be preserved by indicating which paths lead only to a dead-end.

While we have made every effort to be accurate and thorough in our coverage, readers should bear in mind that this is the first serious attempt to produce a bibliography in this field, so that, despite ourselves, we are likely to have made errors both of commission and of omission. We apologise for these in advance; we should be most grateful to anyone who discovers such errors, or who can amplify the information we have given in a useful way, if they would let us know in order that we may be able to amend any future edition. All information used will be acknowledged.

This work began as two independent pieces of research, which we have brought together for publication, so individual responsibility is easier to define than is usual with a collaboration of this sort. David Doughan was responsible for items 1-236, and the indices; Denise Sanchez was responsible for items 237-920; the rest is joint effort. The material was typed by Jenny Curtis; the editor was Edward Elgar.

Acknowledgements

We should like firstly to thank those collectives and editorial bodies which replied to Denise Sanchez's questionnaires, and especially the collectives of Spare Rib and Outwrite. We are also grateful for the help of the staffs of the Feminist Library, the British Library at Bloomsbury (British Museum) and the British Library Newspaper Library. David Doughan's colleagues at the Fawcett Library and City of London Polytechnic have been not only tolerant but helpful. Leonore Davidoff and Jane Lewis made constructive comments at an early stage of writing; and many readers of the Fawcett Library were extremely generous in sharing their experience and expertise in specialised areas. These have included Elizabeth Sarah, Mary Stott, Jill Craigie, Anne Kramer, Cheris Kramarae, Martha Vicinus, Rosemary VanArsdel, Jane Lidderdale, Les Garner, Sheila Jeffries, Annemarie Turnbull, Sally Alexander, Jill Liddington, Jo Vellacott, Sybil Oldfield, Eugene Black, Brian Harrison . . . . and many others.

Dale Spender has been a constant source of information and inspiration.

Introduction

Periodicals in general are often under-estimated as a source for the social sciences, particularly history. Through them can be seen the development of political and social movements, their shifts of attitude and emphasis, and their changing preoccupations and styles. Equally importantly, they are excellent means of determining what happened when (and where), and who was seen to be involved - hence valuable sources for biography, prosopography and networking (among other approaches).

Even those who do value periodicals tend to assume that they are mainly a nineteenth-century Victorian-Edwardian form of discourse, whose significance has been seriously curtailed by such mass media as radio and television - and it is true that the Quarterly Review and Fraser's have long since disappeared, and even the Spectator is not what it was. This, however, does not mean that periodicals as such have declined in importance, though their form and emphasis may have changed. Indeed, a glance at the contents of this bibliography give the impression rather that the feminist periodical, at least, is essentially a late-20th century form; less than a quarter of the entries are for periodicals which began publication before 1950. Casual observation would tend to reinforce the impression that this trend is not peculiar to feminism, but is common to most areas of political discourse, particularly on the Left.

Still, it is especially true that the feminist press deserves far more attention than it receives. Women in any case have tended to be ignored by, or written out of, conventional secondary sources, and feminist movements, however influential, are usually overlooked or discounted both by contemporary writers (mainly, though not only, men) and by historians (again, largely thanks to and overwhelming male presence). This places an even greater importance on what women themselves have written, whether it is a working-out of ideas or an account of what women are doing or have done. Feminist periodicals in particular show women writing for women in a variety of ways for some fairly diverse political ends, for a period of well over a century. The periodicals and their contributors have been numerous and diverse, and identifying them has been less a question of investigative ingenuity than of sheer plod.

Investigative ingenuity, however, comes into its own when trying to find out who has received the message that these papers are disseminating. Certainly by the mid-19th century some degree of literacy at minimum seems to have been widespread among women, and, following the advent of compulsory schooling, it became nearly universal by the early 20th century. So these periodicals have been at least in theory available to women of all classes. Unfortunately, circulation figures are often difficult to obtain, the more so the farther back in time they are sought. When they are available, they indicate considerable diversity. While some are predictably tiny (e.g. Merseyside Women's Liberation Newsletter with only 70 copies), and some, such as the Freewoman have made a virtue of their tiny circulations by claiming to be too advanced for all but the creme de la creme, others have had circulation of which few "mainstream" political magazines would be ashamed. Spare Rib's 27,000 + puts it nearly in the same league as the venerable New Statesman; in its heyday, Time and Tide was even more popular, albeit at the expense of its feminist commitment; and Frederick Pethick Lawrence claimed a peak circulation of 50,000 for Votes for Women. Again, when a paper appears as the organ of a particular society, it may reasonably be assumed that all members of that society will at least have seen it, if only on its way from mailbox to waste-paper-basket; but in some cases, it is also apparent that some periodicals of this type have achieved some readership outside their parent society. The major suffrage papers of 1907-1918 are a notable example of this: the Common Cause, the Vote, Votes for Women and the Suffragette were the organs of their own suffrage societies, but were also sold on the street, at meetings and elsewhere by activists, as well as in the offices of the appropriate society, and by subscription. Just how many copies were sold informally is difficult to ascertain, but the figure for Votes for Women cited above is well in excess of the highest estimates of membership of the W.S.P.U.

Yet however briskly some feminist papers may have sold, there is no record to date of a skilful entrepreneur making a fortune out of one (Time and Tide at its peak probably came nearest to this). Far more typical is the struggle even to cover printing or reprographic costs, despite the fact that very few of the collectives which have produced these periodicals have ever been paid for their trouble (Spare Rib is one notable exception). This constant shortage of funds has had obvious effects on the format, content and frequency of publications; their very existence is precarious, and some have died out after only a few issues (occasionally, after just one issue) for sheer lack of womanpower. Even when they do manage to keep going, they are usually slim, and either mimeographed or lithographed (conventional typesetting has been beyond the means of all but a few groups since the early 1930s). One traditional method by which the mainstream magazines cover costs is by carrying advertisements, and some feminist periodicals have resorted to this, though not without misgivings (see Swanwock, 1935), since there can be a marked divergence between editorial text and advertising copy. The Women's Penny Paper and its successors are notable past examples, together with the suffrage papers already mentioned (though it is interesting to note that many commercial advertisers in the latter explicitly express their support for women's suffrage). The U.S.A. feminist magazine Ms is the most notorious contemporary example of this conflict between principle and profit. To date, Spare Rib and Outwrite seem to be the only major feminist periodicals which have managed to attract advertising which brings in some money without compromising them politically (most contemporary periodicals carry no paid advertising at all). Spare Rib is also one of the very few feminist magazines which has managed to get accepted by a commercial distributor, and therefore can be bought in "non-alternative" newsagents.

Because of the problems associated with advertising, most feminist periodicals have had to survive on sales or subventions - usually a combination of the two. Reader loyalty plays a considerable part especially in the survival of many current titles, most of which are constantly appealing not only for subscriptions but also for donations (which they often get). Sometimes the readers take part in such fundraising activities as discos or jumble sales, or pass the hat round at friendly

conferences. Many newsletters have been saved by their readers'
generosity. Another method of financing periodicals which has been
surprisingly frequent, given the lack of women who are wealthy in
their own right, seems to have been direct subsidy out of the
funds of one woman, notably in such cases as Woman's Opinion
(1874), Woman's Signal, Shafts, New Freewoman, Women Speaking and
the Vote. This last is a particularly interesting case, since it
was the organ of the Women's Freedom League, and might have been
assumed to be financed by the League, had not its true position
been revealed by the sudden and intestate death of its sponsor,
who was not even officially part of the editorial staff (see item
99). This, of course, raises the possibility that similar covert
subventions may have been made in order to keep other papers going.
Unfortunately, it would take a major research effort even to
attempt to test this hypothesis.

Another piece of information which can be revealing is the
price. With periodicals which are no longer current, establishing
this can be difficult, especially when covers have been removed
for conventional library binding. At first sight, most of the
periodicals listed in this bibliography appear to have been quite
cheap. Notable exceptions have been such relatively fat magazines
as the English Women's Journal, and the Englishwoman, and more
recently such academic journals as Feminist Review or Women's
Studies International Forum. All of these, by their size and
style, assume not only a high level of academic education in their
readers, but also a willingness and ability to pay heavily for
this sort of material. Even some of the apparently cheap
newsletters, which aim only to cover production and distribution
costs, may seem poor value for money to women who are not
committed feminists and who are used to receiving a greater number
of pages for an equivalent price in commercial women's magazines.
Some publications do their best to avoid "selling feminism" and do
not charge at all (e.g. Women Come Together), but this sort of
effort is obviously very difficult to keep up. Certainly all this
would seem to indicate a readership which is very committed, or
very well-off - sometimes both. In older publications this
impression is often reinforced by internal evidence, such as the
correspondence on the Servant Question in the English Women's
Journal, or the type of clothing advertised in Votes for Women.
However, other periodicals do appear to be addressed at least
equally to working-class women (and even sometimes produced by

them), such as Shafts, Women's Union Journal, Working Women's
Charter Campaign, etc., and current feminist periodicals
increasingly identify themselves with working-class women.

The readership which these periodicals have consciously
sought has varied. Some periodicals define their intended
readership quite explicitly. For example, many recent titles are
restricted to women only (and have been indicated as such in
annotations). These are usually available on subscription only, or
are kept on restricted access in feminist bookshops. Their
collectives hope that deliberate limiting of availability will
encourage women to express their ideas more freely. Other recent
periodicals have targeted their readership by sexual preference
(e.g. Sappho, Move, Sequel), while others have been intended at
least primarily for members of a particular organisation or
participants in a political campaign, such as the organs of the
Women's Social and Political Union, the Girls' Friendly Society,
the National Housewives' Register, the Socialist Workers' Party,
Women in Publishing, the National Abortion Campaign, etc.. However,
many have been less precise about their target readership (e.g.
"for women and the working class"), and some have given no
explicit indication of their intended audience. Again, internal
evidence can help; Time and Tide, for instance, was obviously
expected to be read by sympathetic men as well as women; it also
had an increasing number of male contributors, and was not always
averse to printing material which conflicted with its general
"line" (a relatively small, but influential, number of feminist
periodicals have at various times attempted to provide a forum for
their readers' divergent opinions, in addition to their other
functions). Time and Tide was also one of the very few feminist
periodicals which set out with the avowed aim of propagandising
the uncommitted; the vast majority of papers seem to assume a
pre-existing commitment to feminism, or at least to the
organisation which they represent.

Many more points could be made about these periodicals which
would be true of at least some of them, if not others — because
they are very diverse, in form, content, outlook, politics, style,
etc.. Even over the past 20 years or so, when feminism has come to
be identified with a general left-wing outlook, the range of
political lines has included hard-line Communists (Link), orthodox
Labour Party women (Focus), middle-of-the-road S.D.P. supporters

(<u>Women for Social Democracy</u>), various sorts of anarchists
(<u>Libertarian Women's Network</u>, <u>Zero</u>, <u>Child-care Bulletin</u>), animal
liberationists (<u>Sequel</u>), spiritual ecologists (<u>Women for Life on
Earth</u>), matriarchalists (<u>Arachne</u>), <u>Roman Catholic Feminists</u> . . . .
as well as those who reject any label or who cannot be neatly
pigeonholed.

In arranging these periodicals chronologically, we have found
ourselves telling a story. It is only one part of the much larger
story of the feminist movement, and we are aware that its content
is affected both by the fact that it is based on just one variety
of source material and by the way it is told (we are particularly
conscious that some at least of the annotations may seem
excessively magisterial and judgemental; this is partly due to
compression, and we apologise in advance). We are also conscious
that it is not very coherently told, and are apprehensive that it
may have errors of fact. Nonetheless we think that it is a hopeful
story, and one that is worth telling. We hope it will continue for
many generations to come.

David Doughan
Denise Sanchez
April 1985

Abbreviations

BL   British Library Newspaper Library Microfilms,
            Colindale Avenue, London NW9 5HE, England
BM   British Library Reference Division, Department of
            Printed Books, British Museum, Great Russell Street,
            London WC1, England
Bodleian   Bodleian Library (of the University of Oxford), Oxford,
            England
BWTA   British Women's Temperance Association
C   British Library Newspaper Library (for address see BL)
C D Acts   Contagious Diseases Acts
DA   Datamics, Inc., 120 Liberty Street, New York NY 10006,
            USA
DORA   Defence of the Realm Act
F   Fawcett Library, City of London Polytechnic, Old Castle
            Street, London E1 7NT, England
Flic   Feminist Library and Information Centre, 1st Floor,
            Hungerford House, London WC2, England (formerly Women's
            Research and Resources Centre)
Harvester   Harvester Press Microform Publications Ltd., 17 Ship
            Street, Brighton, Sussex BN1 1AD, England
IDC   Inter Documentation Company BV The Netherlands,
            Hogewoerd 151-153, 2311 HK Leiden, The Netherlands
LC   Library of Congress Photoduplication Service, 10 First
            Street, S.E., Washington DC 20540, USA
MF   Microform Ltd., Main Street, East Ardsley, Wakefield,
            West Yorkshire WF3 2AT, England (N. American
            distributor:Clearwater Publishing Co., Inc., Room 400,
            1995 Broadway, New York NY 10023, USA)
MML   Micro Media Ltd., 144 Front Street West, Toronto,
            Ontario, Canada M5J 2L7
NUWSS   National Union of Women's Suffrage Societies
OM   Oxford Microform Publications, 19a Paradise Street,
            Oxford OX1 1LD, England
TUC   Library of the Trades Union Congress, Congress House,

Great Russell Street, London WC1, England

UM   University Microfilms International, 300 North Zeeb Road
Road, Ann Arbor, MI 48106, USA

WSPU   Women's Social and Political Union

Format of Entries

Item number. "Uniform" title with overall dates (-c. means that the periodical was still appearing at time of writing)

  T1:title as found on title-page

  T2, T3, etc.:variant forms of title, as far as possible in chronological order

  Ed.:editor, edited by

  Pub.:published by

  Frequency (weekly, monthly, etc.) (f.n.k.:frequency not known), date of first and last issue (or total number of issues) (n.i.c.:no indication of cessation)

  C:continues, succeeds

  C BY:continued by, succeeded by, merged with

  L:location (see abbreviations list)

  M:microform availability (publisher:see abbreviations list)

Note 1:Unless otherwise stated (immediately after title information), place of publication is assumed to be London.

Note 2:Locations are not necessarily exclusive; C, F and Flic are preferred, then other London libraries (except BM), then libraries outside London. BM is only given as a location when it appears to be either a unique or a "least incomplete" location, in which case a shelf mark is given.

1. SEMPSTRESS   1855
   T1:The Sempstress/Distressed Needlewoman's Home
   Monthly;October 1855 (n.i.c.)
   L:BM;PP 1423ab
   M:Harvester
Only one issue found. Philanthropic-reformist.

2. WAVERLEY   1856-1858
   T1:The Waverley journal:for the cultivation of the honourable,
   the progressive, and the beautiful
   T2:The Waverley:a working women's journal
   T3:The Waverley:a journal of literature, science and general
   information
   (Edinburgh;London) Glasgow
   Fortnightly;1856(?)-15 April 1858 (n.i.c.)
   L:C
   M:Harvester
Social reform, including much of feminist interest (and a serial
by Amelia B. Edwards). This is presumably the "very harmless but
very inefficient" paper referred to by Bessie Rayner Parkes
(Parkes, 1864) which she briefly "took control of" in 1857.
N.B. only issues 4 and 5 of 1858 found. T1 and T2, together with
bracketed place of publication, are from Harrison, 1977.

3. ENGLISHWOMAN'S REVIEW AND DRAWING ROOM JOURNAL   1857-1859
   T1:The Englishwoman's review and drawing room journal of social
   progress, literature and art
   T2:Englishwoman's review and home newspaper
   T3:The Englishwoman's review of literature, science and art
   Ed. E. Duckworth
   Weekly;21 April 1857-13 September 1859
   L:C
   M:Harvester
An "improving" magazine with little or no feminist content. Not to
be confused with item 8.

4. ENGLISH WOMAN'S JOURNAL   1858-1864
   T1:The English woman's journal
   Ed. Bessie Rayner Parkes and Mary Hays
   Monthly;March 1858-August 1864
   C BY:item 7
   L:Bodleian, F

M:Fawcett

The theoretical and practical source of organised feminism, emanating from the Langham Palace Circle. Contributors included Barbara Bodichon, Jessie Boucherett, Emily Davies, Isa Craig, Adelaide Ann Procter, Emily Faithfull, Maria Rye, etc.. It began as a general literary magazine with a feminist bias, but by late 1858 had already become a feminist magazine with some literary contributions (fiction, poetry, etc.). It consisted mainly of long articles, with shorter reviews, letters and notes on current events. Topics covered regularly included education, employment, married women's property, the legal disabilities of women, women's emigration, women artists, etc., etc., with women's suffrage getting its first mention in the last issue. This is the early British feminist movement working out its theoretical base in public, but away from such general reforming bodies as the National Association for the Promotion of Social Science. Circulation never more than about 500, but readership probably much greater. For the journal's history in detail, see Parkes, 1864.

5. BRITISH WORKWOMAN   1863-1896
   Tl:The British workwoman:out and at home
   Monthly;November 1863-December 1896
   L:BM;PP 1103c
   M:Harvester
Extremely misleading title. "Improving", religious stories and poems, with occasional sermonising philanthropic articles. Not even faintly feminist.

6. VICTORIA MAGAZINE   1863-1880
   Tl:The Victoria magazine
   Ed. Emily Faithfull. Pub. Victoria Press
   Monthly;bi-monthly;October 1863-June 1880
   L:Bodleian (incomplete, but far and away best found)
General and literary (fiction, poetry etc.) women's magazine, with strong feminist emphasis, and detailed notes on topics of feminist interest, e.g. suffrage, married women's property, education, employment, etc.. Reported activities of the Victoria Discussion Society. A very useful complement to items 4, 7 and 8. For further information, see Fredeman, 1973.

7. ALEXANDRA MAGAZINE   1864-1865
   Tl:The Alexandra magazine and English woman's journal

T2:The Alexandra magazine and woman's social and industrial
advocate
Ed. Susannah Meredith
Monthly;September 1864-December 1865
C:item 4
C BY:item 8
L:Bodleian
M:UM

The English woman's journal in the process of becoming the
Englishwoman's review. Later editors of the latter regarded all
three as being one continuous publication, and referred to them
accordingly.

8. ENGLISHWOMAN'S REVIEW 1866-1910
   T1:The Englishwoman's review:a journal of women's work
   Quarterly;January 1866-July 1869
   T2:The Englishwoman's review of social and industrial questions
   New series
   Ed. Emilia Jessie Boucherett (1870); Caroline Ashurst Biggs
   (1871-1889); Helen Blackburn and Antoinette M. Mackenzie (1889-
   1902); Antoinette M. Mackenzie (1903-1910)
   Quarterly;bi-monthly;January 1870-July 1910
   C:item 7
   L:BM, Bodleian, Fawcett (incomplete)
   M:UM

In direct line of descent from items 4 and 7, this differs from
both in being mainly a current awareness bulletin, with few long
articles, theoretical or otherwise, but very many short notices of
feminist activities and relevant events. It is thus an invaluable
aid to researchers throughout the whole of its long life (though
contents lists vary in helpfulness). Its standpoint is classic
"bourgeois" constitutional feminist. Recurrent topics include
employment, education, suffrage, married women's property,
protective/restrictive legislation, legal and constitutional
rights and disabilities, etc., etc.. In 1869, an abortive attempt
was made to merge this publication with item 11 q.v..

9. WOMAN'S WORLD 1868
   T1:Woman's world:dux foemina facti
   New series
   Ed. Mr Charles Jones
   Monthly;May-December 1868 (v.2 begins November:"Part VII, part

XIV from commencement")
C BY:item 10
L:BM;PP 6004p
M:Harvester

General women's magazine, with very mild feminist leanings (the
Latin subtitle means approximately "Woman leads the action").
"Serial" stories were published in four parts in one issue, with
no other indication by format or otherwise that a "monthly" issue
was really four weeklies bound together. Of interest mainly
because of its successor.

10. KETTLEDRUM 1869
    Tl:Kettledrum:with which is united Woman's world:a magazine
    of art, literature, and social improvement:dux foemina facti
    Monthly;January-June 1869
    C:item 9
    C BY:item 11
    L:as for item 9
    M:Harvester

Like its predecessor, but with much more definite feminism.
Contributors include Josephine Butler and Jessie Boucherett.

11. NOW-A-DAYS 1869
    July 1869?
    C:item 10
    C BY:item 8
    L:none found

This was projected as a successor to both items 10 and 8, "but
Now-a-days was ephemeral, of a day" (Englishwoman's Review, 1900).
Only one issue seems to have been published, and even that appears
to have vanished without trace; it was advertised in item 10 as
appearing from July 1869, with contributors including Josephine
Butler, Jessie Boucherett and Elizabeth Wolstenhome (Elmy). It was
definitely intended to supersede items 10 and 8 (see for example
Josephine Butler letters 3401 and 5208 in the Fawcett Library),
but for various reasons did not get beyond issue n°1.

12. WOMEN'S SUFFRAGE JOURNAL 1870-1890
    Tl:Women's suffrage journal:official organ of the National
    Society for Women's Suffrage
    Ed. Lydia Becker
    Manchester

Monthly;March 1870-August 1890

L:BM, Fawcett

M:Fawcett

The first specialised British suffrage periodical, with
considerable detailed campaign information, it nevertheless
covered other contemporary feminist issues, e.g. married women's
property. Very much Lydia Becker's paper, and died with her. Quite
usefully indexed.

13. SHIELD 1870-1970

T1:The shield:the Anti-Contagious Diseases Acts Association's
weekly circular

T2:The shield/National Association for the Repeal of the
Contagious Diseases Acts.

Ed. Josephine E. Butler

South Shields

Weekly;7 March 1870-20 July 1886

T3:The shield:the official organ of the British branch of the
Federation for the Abolition of the State Regulation of Vice

T4:The shield:the official organ of the Association for Moral
and Social Hygiene

T5:The shield/Josephine Butler Society

London

Eds. include Alison Neilans, Margaret Schwartz

Monthly;quarterly;irregular;May 1897-November 1970

L:BM, Fawcett

M:IDC

The specifically feminist paper of the campaign against the C.D.
Acts and state-regulated prostitution in general, it ceased in
1886 on the repeal of the Acts, but was revived in 1897 because of
attempts to extend the application of state-regulated prostitution
in India to Britain. Thereafter it continued as a feminist voice
within the social purity movement, frequently taking a strong
specifically feminist stand, e.g. over the provision for
prostitution of the Defence of the Realm Act after 1914. Very much
a single-campaign periodical, with much useful campaign information
and exhortation, but little theoretical analysis or coverage of
other feminist issues. First series complicatedly (but quite
usefully) indexed.

14. WOMAN 1872

T1:Woman:a weekly journal embodying female interests from an educational, social, and domestic point of view

Weekly;27 January-27 July 1872

C BY:Social review (not listed)

L:C

M:Harvester

General social reform; little specific feminism.

15. WOMEN'S EDUCATION UNION 1873-1882

Tl:Journal of the Women's Education Union/National Union for
Improving the Education of All Classes

Ed. Emily Shireff and George C. T. Bartley

Monthly;January 1873-June 1882

L:BM;PP 1215f

M:Harvester

Considerable information on education in general, but especially
girls' schools, the Girls Public Day School Company, and the
Teachers' Registration Society. For further information see
Ellsworth, 1979.

16. WOMAN'S OPINION 1874

Tl:Woman's opinion:representing the social, domestic and
educational interests of women

"edited, printed, and published by Mrs Amelia Lewis"

Weekly;fortnightly;24 January-18 April 1874

C BY:National Food and Fuel Reformer (not listed)

L:C

M:Harvester

Fairly strong feminist; pro-suffrage, anti-C.D. Acts, etc.. Amelia
Lewis was an elusive woman who was very visible in feminist
circles in the 1870s, but seems to have disappeared without trace
thereafter. She was much involved in food and fuel reform, and was
the inventor of the "People's Stove".

17. WOMEN'S ADVOCATE 1874

Tl:Women's advocate

Ed. T. J. Haslam

Dublin

Irregular;April-July 1874 (3 issues;n.i.c.)

L:BM;1866 a 16(5)

M:Harvester

Apparently Ireland's first feminist paper. Very thin; only one
article per issue. For further information, see Owens, 1984.

18. WOMEN AND WORK   1874-1876

   T1:Women and work:a weekly industrial, educational and
   household register for women
   Ed., pub. and printed by Emily Faithfull at the Victoria Press
   Weekly;6 June 1874-26 February 1876 (n.i.c.)
   L:C
   M:Harvester

Mainly a practical guide to employments for middle-class women,
but included reports on different trades and skills (e.g.
shoemaking, sewing-machining, compositing) as well as some items
(and polemic) and general feminist concern.

19. WOMAN'S GAZETTE   1875-1879

   T1:Woman's gazette:or, news about work
   Ed. Louisa M. Hubbard
   Monthly;October 1875-September 1879
   C BY:item 28
   L:BM, Fawcett

Another practical guide for "genteel" women seeking employment,
together with general information about women's work.

20. NATIONAL LEAGUE JOURNAL   1875-1883

   T1:The National League Journal:a monthly record of the Working
   Men's National League for the Repeal of the Contagious
   Diseases Acts.
   T2:The National League Journal:a monthly record of the
   movement for the repeal of the Contagious Diseases Acts
   Pub. Dyer Bros.
   Liverpool
   Monthly;August 1875-December 1883 (n.i.c.)
   L:C (incomplete), F
   M:IDC

Originally a men's equivalent of item 13, then took a more general
line.

21. MEDICAL ENQUIRER   1875-1883

   T1:The medical enquirer:a quarterly journal and review:the
   organ of the National Medical Association for the Abolition of
   the State Regulation of Prostitution
   Liverpool
   Quarterly;March 1875-September 1883
   L:F

M:IDC

Self-explanatory.

22. ENGLISHWOMAN'S YEAR BOOK   1875-1916

    T1:The year book of women's work

    T2:The Englishwoman's year book

    Ed. L. M. Hubbard to 1898; thereafter Emily Jones, G. E. Mitton

    Annual

    L:BM;PP 2493ma, F (incomplete)

    M:MCA

Annual directory first of work opportunities for women, then of
women's (not just feminist) societies, clubs, etc.. Very useful
reference work, particularly in the 20th century.

23. FRIENDLY LEAVES   1876-1917

    T1:Friendly Leaves/Girls' Friendly Society

    Monthly;January 1876-June 1917

    C BY:item 135

    L:BM;PP 358ha

The first magazine of the Girls' Friendly Society of the Church of
England. Mainly philanthropic; some mention of rescue and
preventive work among prostitutes, covertly referred to.

24. WOMEN'S UNION JOURNAL   1876-1890

    T1:Women's union journal:organ of the Women's Protective and
    Provident Association

    T2:Women's union journal:organ of the Women's Trade Union
    League

    Quarterly;February 1876-October 1890

    C BY:item 51

    L:F, TUC

    M:F

The original periodical of the pioneer woman printer and trade
union organiser Emma Paterson; much about women workers, with
increasingly socialist leanings, though little connection at this
stage with the concerns of "bourgeois" constitutional feminists.
Printed by Women's Printing Society.

25. METHODIST PROTEST   1876-1883

    T1:The Methodist protest:the organ of the Wesleyan Society for
    Securing the Repeal of the Contagious Diseases Acts

    Monthly;January 1876-October 1883

```
        L:F
        M:IDC
Self-explanatory
```

26. MIDLAND COUNTIES ELECTORAL UNION 1877-1886
    T1:Occasional paper:issued by the Midland Counties Electoral
    Union for the Repeal of the Contagious Diseases Acts relating
    to Women
    Birmingham
    Monthly;irregular;January 1877-February 1886
    L:F
    M:IDC
Self-explanatory.

27. GFS ADVERTISER 1880-c.
    T1:GFS advertiser
    T2:Girls' Friendly Society Associates' journal and advertiser
    T3:GFS workers' journal
    T4:GFS review
    Monthly;January 1880-c.
    L:BM;PP 1103f
Another Church of England magazine devoted to the moral welfare of
young women.

28. WORK AND LEISURE 1880-1893
    T1:Work and leisure:the Englishwoman's advertiser, reporter
    and gazette
    Ed. Louisa M. Hubbard
    Monthly;October 1880-December 1893
    C:item 19
    L:C, F
    M:UM
Fairly straight continuation of item 19, with slightly more
philanthropic emphasis.

29. PERSONAL RIGHTS JOURNAL 1881-1903
    T1:Journal of the Vigilance Association for the Defence of
    Personal Rights
    T2:Personal Rights journal/National Association for the
    Defence of Personal Rights
    Monthly;January 1881-January 1903
    C BY:Individualist (not listed)

                               9

L:C, F

M:Harvester, IDC

Originally an anti-C.D. Acts paper, with much feminist involvement
with prominent contributions by Elizabeth Wolstenhome Elmy;
however, after the break with the National Vigilance Association
in October 1886, it moved to more general libertarian issues (e.g.
anti-vaccination, anti-vivisection), and the feminist content
rapidly disappeared.

30. SENTINEL   1881-1889

   T1:The sentinel:a monthly journal devoted to the expansion and
   advancement of public morality and to the suppression of vice
   Monthly;May 1881-July 1889 (n.i.c.)
   L:F
   M:IDC

A C.D. Acts journal with an increasing social purity emphasis.

31. INDIA'S WOMEN   1881-1957

   T1:India's women:the magazine of the Church of England Zenana
   Missionary Society
   T2:India's women and China's daughters
   T3:Looking east at India's women and China's daughters
   Monthly;January 1881-June 1957 (n.i.c.)
   L:BM;PP 982b
   M:UM (as "Looking east")

As much social/philanthropic concern for Indian and Chinese women
as proselytising. See also item 36.

32. SCHOOLMISTRESS   1881-1935

   T1:The schoolmistress:a weekly paper specially devoted to the
   interests of those engaged in female education
   Weekly;1 December 1881-4 September 1935
   C BY:Teachers' world (not listed)
   L:C

Little feminism; occasional articles in later issues by Winifred
Holtby.

33. GATHERER   1882-1883

   T1:The gatherer/ed. Mrs Rawlinson Ford; sub. ed. Isabella
   C. Ford
   F.n.k.;March 1882-January 1883 (n.i.c.)
   L:F

Generally progressive, literary, feminist, albeit small. Printed
by Women's Printing Society. Contributions by Walter McLaren.

34. FRIENDLY WORK   1883-1917
    T1:Friendly work:published under the sanction of the Central
    Council of the Girls' Friendly Society
    T2:The girls' quarterly:a paper for workers:with which is
    incorporated "Friendly work"
    T3:Friendly work for friendly workers
    Monthly;Quarterly;January 1883-June 1917
    C BY:item 135
    L:BM;PP 358ha
Another Girls' Friendly Society paper.

35. BRITISH WOMEN'S TEMPERANCE JOURNAL   1886-1892
    T1:The British women's temperance journal:the official organ
    of the British Women's Temperance Association
    Monthly;January 1886-September 1892
    C BY:item 56
    L:BM;PP 1138mb
The first British feminist temperance paper, dealing with the
evils of drink particularly affecting women, e.g. domestic
violence.

36. DAYBREAK   1886-1918
    T1:Daybreak:illustrated magazine of the Church of England
    Zenana Missionary Society
    T2:Homes of the East
    Monthly;April 1886-January 1918
    L:BM;PP 982bd (for T1);PP 982bda (for T2)
See also item 31.

37. PIONEER   1887-1898
    T1:The pioneer:being the organ of the Social Purity Alliance
    and the Moral Reform Union
    T2:The pioneer of social purity:being the organ of the Social
    Purity Alliance
    Monthly;quarterly;February 1887-July 1898 (n.i.c.)
    L:F
    M:IDC
Social purity with a feminist slant; some contributions by
Josephine Butler.

38. WOMAN 1887

    Tl:Woman

    Weekly;1 June-20 July 1887

    C BY: <u>Nursing notes</u> (not listed)

    L:C

    M:Harvester

Fairly strong feminist: nursing notes, midwifery, British Women's
Temperance Association, Women's Co-operative Guild, pit-brow
women, etc..

39. LINK 1888

    Tl:The link:a journal for the servants of man/Law and Liberty
    League

    Ed. Annie Besant and W. T. Stead

    Weekly;4 February-1 December 1888

    L:C

    M:BL

Libertarian, with slight feminist emphasis. Considerable coverage
of Bryant and May matchgirls' strike; contributions by E. Nesbit
and Josephine Butler.

40. DAWN 1888-1896

    Tl:The dawn:an occasional/quarterly/sketch of the progress of
    the work of the British, Continental and General Federation
    for the Abolition of State Regulation of Vice

    Ed. Josephine Butler

    Quarterly;May 1888-October 1896

    L:BM, F

    M:IDC

Held a watching brief on prostitution laws in Britain, with a more
active concern for the situation in Europe and India. See also
items 13 and 71.

41. WOMAN'S TRIBUNE 1888

    Tl:The woman's tribune:the organisation of the unrepresented
    and the chronicle of the Women's Liberal Federation

    One issue only (9 August 1888)

    L:C

Nothing at all about women, let alone the Women's Liberal
Federation.

42. WOMEN'S PENNY PAPER   1888-1890

   Tl:The women's penny paper:the only paper in the world
   conducted, written [printed and published] by women
   Ed. Helena B. Temple
   Weekly;27 October 1888-27 December 1890
   C BY:item 46
   L:C, F
   M:UM (as "Woman's herald")

Lively and uncompromising feminism; the most vigorous feminist
paper of its time. Contents included interviews with prominent
feminists, and regular reports from a variety of women's
organisations, e.g. BWTA, WLF, Primrose League; from May 1890 the
Central National Society for Women's Suffrage was given a column
of its own. The paper was printed by the Women's Printing Society
to 22 March 1890, thereafter by the National Press Agency.
Newspaper (but not broadsheet) format; many general advertisements,
some of which contrast strikingly with the editorial copy.
   "Helena B. Temple" was the pen-name of Henrietta B. Muller
(d. 1906), sister of Eva McLaren and a prominent feminist. As well
as being in at the start of the Women's Printing Society, she was
a pioneer school board member (for Lambeth), an early tax-resister
(for the vote, in 1884), and later a Theosophist and associate of
Annie Besant.

43. WOMEN'S GAZETTE   1888-1891

   Tl:Women's gazette and weekly news:a journal devoted to the
   social and political position of women, and the official organ
   of the Women's Liberal Federation
   Manchester;London
   Weekly;9 August 1888-7 December 1891
   C BY:item 46
   L:C
   M:Harvester

More Liberal than feminist; factory legislation, unions, Ireland,
etc..

44. WOMAN   1890-1912

   Tl:Woman:for all sorts and conditions of women
   Weekly;3 January 1890-7 September 1912
   L:C
   M:Harvester

At head of title page: "Forward! But not too fast." Started as a

"moderate" feminist paper, in contrast to an "anti-man"
contemporary (presumably item 42), with occasional contributions
from notable feminists, e.g. Millicent Fawcett; but it rapidly
became a fashionable ladies' magazine.

45. WOMEN'S WORLD   ca 1890
Mentioned in item 42 (29 March 1890) in connection with "Mrs
Stopes' meetings". No other trace found.

46. WOMAN'S HERALD   1891-1893
    T1:Woman's herald (late Women's Penny Paper):the only paper
    conducted, written and published by women
    Ed. Helena B. Temple
    T2:Woman's herald:[a liberal paper for women] organ of the
    Women's Liberal Federation
    Ed. Mrs Frank Morrison; then Christina S. Bremner
    T3:Woman's herald:for God and home and every land:a weekly
    record of the progress of the woman's movement
    Ed. Lady Henry Somerset [and Edwin H. Stout]
    Weekly;3 January 1891-28 December 1893
    C:items 42, 43
    C BY:item 60
    L:F, C
    M:UM
At first a straightforward continuation of item 42, until the
editor/proprietor Henrietta Muller (see item 42) went to India.
From 1 May 1892 to 16 February 1893 it became the voice of the
Suffragist Women's Liberal Federation. It also began to develop
links with the temperance movement, which led to its takeover by
Lady Henry (Isobel) Somerset of the BWTA, and it gradual
transformation into the Women's Signal (item 56).

47. CENTRAL AND EAST OF ENGLAND SOCIETY FOR WOMEN'S SUFFRAGE   1891-
    1900
    T1:Central and East of England Society for Women's Suffrage
    occasional paper
    Annual
    M:UM
Slim; basic organisational information.

48. NATIONAL SOCIETY FOR WOMEN'S SUFFRAGE   1891-1900
    T1:National Society for Women's Suffrage occasional paper

Annual
    L:F
    M:IDC
Very similar to item 47.

49. THREEFOLD CORD   1891-1896
    Tl:A threefold cord:a magazine for thoughtful women
    Ed. Emily Janes
    Quarterly
    C BY:item 68
    L:Girton College Library (Blackburn collection), Cambridge
    (incomplete)
    M:Harvester
Early organ of National Union of Women Workers; see item 68.

50. WOMEN WORKERS   1891-1924
    Tl:Women workers:the quarterly magazine of the Birmingham
    Ladies' Union of Workers among Women and Children
    Quarterly
    L:Birmingham Public Library
Not seen. Presumably related to National Union of Women Workers
(see item 68).

51. WOMEN'S TRADE UNION REVIEW   1891-1918
    Tl:Women's trade union review/Women's Trade Union League
    Ed. Gertrude Tuckwell
    Quarterly;June 1891-October 1918 (n.i.c.)
    C:item 24
    L:F, TUC
    M:MF
Continuation of item 24 in much the same style and format; union
news, women at work etc..

52. WOMEN'S SUFFRAGE JOURNAL   1891-1892
    Tl:Women's suffrage journal
    Ed. J. H. Theobald
    Sydney, Australia
    Monthly;June 1891-May 1892
Not found. See Englishwoman's Review, 1900.

53. FEMALE SERVANTS' UNION NEWS   1892
    Tl:Female Servants' Union News

Ed. Mrs M. J. Sales

Monthly?

M:Harvester

One thin issue only, intended for women domestic servants.

54. IRIS 1892

T1:Iris:the organ of the Women's Progressive Society

F.n.k.;April 1892-(n.i.c.)

Not found, even in BM (despite Barrow, 1980). Englishwoman's
Review, 1900, says it "continued a few months only".

55. UNIVERSITY ASSOCIATION OF WOMEN TEACHERS 1892-1895

T1:The journal of the University Association of Women Teachers

Quarterly;irregular;July 1892-November 1895

L:BM;1865 a 9(23)

Thin, dry; useful for lists of members.

56. WINGS 1892-1925

T1:Wings:with which is incorporated the British Women's
Temperance Journal:the official organ of the British Women's
Temperance Association

T2:Wings:with which is incorporated the British Women's
Temperance Journal:the official organ of the Women's Total
Abstinence Union

Monthly;October 1892-December 1925

C:item 35

C BY:item 69

L:BM;PP 1138mb

After the July 1893 split in the BWTA, this became the paper of
the breakaway Women's Total Abstinence Union. The BWTA was briefly
represented by items 59 and 60, before eventually setting up its
own organ (item 69). Differed little in form or content from BWTA
journals, and briefly merged with item 69 before their mutual
demise in 1925.

57. SHAFTS 1892-1900

T1:Shafts:a paper for women and the working classes

T2:Shafts:a monthly magazine of progressive thought

Ed. Margaret Shurmer Sibthorpe

Weekly;monthly;bi-monthly;5 November 1892-April 1900

L:C, F

M:Harvester, UM

16

Lively but slightly odd feminist, "progressive", radical paper, becoming increasingly involved with "higher thought" and a degree of mysticism. Considerable support for anti-vivisection and vegetarian viewpoints. Reported in detail the activities of the Pioneer Club, the Grosvenor Crescent Club, and the Women's Institute (not "jam and Jerusalem", but a more academic and political predecessor). Contributors included E. Wolstenholme Elmy, Dora B. Montefiore and Charlotte Carmichael Stopes. For further information see Brady, 1978.

58. YOUNG WOMAN 1892-1915
    T1:The young woman:a monthly journal and review
    Ed. Frederick A. Atkins
    Monthly;October 1892-August 1915
    L:BM;PP 6004oda, F (to 1900)
    M:Harvester
Not really a feminist paper, but containing a considerable amount of mildly pro-feminist material, including substantial interviews with prominent feminists, e.g. Millicent Fawcett and Josephine Butler. Otherwise aimed slightly down-market to interest reasonably literate (and presumably upwardly-mobile) young women. It was started as a companion to The young man.

59. JOURNAL 1893
    T1:The journal:(official organ pro tem.) of the British Women's Temperance Association
    Ed. ("pro tem.") Mrs Ward Poole, Miss Gorham, Miss Shilston
    Monthly;June-December 1893
    L:C, F
    M:Harvester
A result of the split in the BWTA; created by Lady Henry Somerset, and subsumed into item 60. See also item 56.

60. WOMAN'S SIGNAL 1894-1899
    T1:The woman's signal:with which is incorporated "The Woman's herald"
    T2:The woman's signal:a weekly paper for all women about all their interests, in the home and in the wider world
    T3:The woman's signal:a weekly record and review for ladies
    Ed. Lady Henry Somerset and Annie E. Holdsworth (to 26 September 1895); thereafter Florence Fenwick-Miller
    Weekly;4 January 1894-23 March 1899

```
        C:items 46, 59
        L:C, F
        M:Harvester, UM
```

Although it regularly reported the activities of the BWTA and
WWCTU, it was always more than just a temperance paper, especially
under the editorship of Florence Fenwick-Miller, who also financed
the paper until her patience with BWTA attitudes (and her money)
finally ran out. It gave considerable space to such broader
feminist topics as women's suffrage, women's working conditions
(including protective/restrictive legislation), domestic violence,
education, etc., as well as regular "character sketches" of
prominent women. See also items 62 and 69, and for further
information see VanArsdel, 1979.


```
61. WOMEN'S SUFFRAGE NEWS   1894
        Tl:Women's suffrage news
        Ed. A. B. Louis
        Monthly;January 1894-June 1894
        L:not found
```
Mentioned in Englishwoman's Review, 1900.


```
62. WOMAN'S SIGNAL BUDGET   1894-1895
        Tl:Woman's signal budget:for God and home and every land
        Ed. Lady Henry Somerset
        Monthly;July 1894-August 1895
        L:F
        M:Harvester, UM
```
Short-lived monthly supplement to item 60; temperance, BWTA,
WWCTU, etc..


```
63. WOMAN'S VOICE   1894-1986
        Tl:The woman's voice
        Ed. M. S. Wolstenholme
        Sydney, Australia
        Monthly;1894(?)-1896(?)
        L:not found
```
Mentioned in Englishwoman's Review, 1900.


```
64. WHITE RIBBON   1894-?
        Tl:The white ribbon:organ of the World Women's Christian
        Temperance Union of New Zealand
        Ed. Kate Sheppard
```

Christchurch, New Zealand
Monthly;1894-?
L:not found
Mentioned in Englishwoman's Review, 1900.

65. WOMEN'S NATIONAL LIBERAL ASSOCIATION 1895-1918
    T1:Women's National Liberal Association
    T2:Women's National Liberal Association quarterly review and
    report
    T3:Quarterly review of the Women's National Liberal
    Association
    Quarterly;December 1895-October 1918
    C BY:item 148
    L:BM;PP 3558if (some early issues lacking)
    M:UM
Organ of the party-line Association, as opposed to the overtly
feminist-suffragist Women's Liberal Federation (the two merged
again in 1919).

66. WOMEN'S INDUSTRIAL NEWS 1895-1919
    T1:Women's industrial news:organ of the Women's Industrial
    Council
    Quarterly;October 1895-April 1919
    L:C, F (incomplete)
    M:Harvester
Useful review of issues affecting women involved in industrial
work; a helpful complement to item 51.

67. SISTERS 1895-1898
    T1:Sisters
    T2:Our sisters:a monthly magazine devoted to women of every
    class, clime and creed
    Ed. Mrs Hooper
    Monthly;December 1895-December 1898
Not found. BM holdings destroyed by bombing; no other location
discovered.

68. NATIONAL UNION OF WOMEN WORKERS 1896-1918
    T1:An occasional paper of the National Union of Women Workers
    T2:National Union of Women Workers of Great Britain and
    Ireland:occasional paper
    Irregular (approx. quarterly);issues 1-80

C:item 49

C BY:item 141

L:BM;PP 1103bay [from 1915 only; no location found for earlier
material]

Philanthropic, not industrial, workers, much concerned with
protecting young women against sexual exploitation, and very
prominent in rescue and preventive work, child welfare, etc.. The
organisation soon developed into a "moderate" feminist forum, and
by 1914 was even sponsoring its own Women Police Patrols. In 1919
it became the National Council of Women.

69. WHITE RIBBON 1896-1925

T1:The white ribbon:the official organ of the National British
Women's Temperance Association:for God and home and every land

T2:The white ribbon and Wings

Monthly;November 1896(?)-December 1925

L:C

The organ of the traditional "temperance" women as distinct from
the "total abstainers". Colindale's first issue (for January 1898)
is numbered v.2 n°3, but no trace of earlier issues is apparent.
Briefly merged with item 56 before they both ceased.

70. SCOTTISH WOMEN'S TEMPERANCE NEWS 1897-1972

T1:The Scottish women's temperance news:the organ of the
Scottish Christian Union, British Women's Temperance
Association:for God and home and every land

Monthly;quarterly;January 1897(?)-October/December 1972

L:C

Colindale's holdings begin with January 1899 (v.3 n°1).

71. STORM-BELL 1898-1900

T1:The storm-bell

Ed. "Josephine E. Butler for the Ladies' National Association
for the Abolition of State Regulation of Vice"

London (printed Newcastle)

Monthly;January 1898-July 1900

L:F

M:IDC

Very much Josephine Butler's own little paper, with her views on
prostitution in India, etc..

72. WOMANHOOD   1898-1907
    T1:Womanhood
    Ed. Mrs A. S. Ballin
    Monthly;December 1898-June 1907
    L:BM, F
    M:UM
"Improving" magazine; very little feminism.

73. SCOTTISH WOMEN'S LIBERAL FEDERATION   1899-1900
    T1:Scottish Women's Liberal Federation magazine and county
    reporter
    Glasgow
    Monthly
    L:not found
    M:UM
Not seen.

74. WOMEN'S EMPLOYMENT   1900-1974
    T1:Women's employment:issued by the Central Bureau for the
    Employment of Women
    Last ed. M. Fuge
    Monthly;quarterly;March 1900-November 1974 (n.i.c.)
    L:C (a few 1900 issues only), F (incomplete)
Job advertisements and general information about white collar
employment opportunities for women. No apparent connection with
the Women's Employment Federation.

75. WOMEN'S FARM AND GARDEN ASSOCIATION   1900-1976
    T1:Women's Farm and Garden Association quarterly leaflet
    T2:Women's Farm and Garden Association monthly circular
    T3:Women's Farm and Garden Association quarterly leaflet
    T4:Women's Farm and Garden Association newsletter
    Quarterly;monthly;irregular;March 1900-March 1976 (n.i.c.)
    L:BM;PP 2244c(1) (for T1);PP 2295db (for T2);PP 2244c(2) (for
    T3);WP 15307 (for T4)
Concerned almost entirely with women farmers and market gardeners.

76. WOMEN'S LABOUR NEWS   1900-1904
    T1:Women's labour news
    Ed. Esther Roper and Eva Gore-Booth

Manchester and Salford
Not found. Only mention occurs in Roper, 1929.

77. IMPERIAL COLONIST 1902-1927
    T1:The imperial colonist:the official organ of the British
    Women's Emigration Association and the South African Expansion
    Committee
    T2:The imperial colonist:the official organ of the Society for
    the Oversea Settlement of British Women
    Monthly;January 1902-March 1927
    C BY:Oversea settler (not listed)
    L:F
    M:IDC
General emigration information; no wider feminist interests.

78. LIBERAL WOMAN 1902-1915
    T1:Liberal woman:a monthly record of the Women's Liberal
    League of N.S.W. [sic]:founder, Mrs Molyneux Parkes
    Sydney, Australia
    Monthly;October 1902-December 1915
    C BY:item 130
    L:F
Mainly organisational news.

79. WOMEN'S SUFFRAGE RECORD 1903-1906
    T1:Women's suffrage record/National Union of Women's Suffrage
    Societies
    Ed. Edith Palliser
    Monthly;June 1903-November 1906
    L:C, F
    M:BL
Very thin and short on information.

80. NURSING TIMES 1905-c.
    T1:Nursing times:official journal of the Royal College of
    Nurses
    Weekly;16 March 1905-c.
    L:C
Organisational information and professional advice; no perceptible
feminism.

81. NURSING MIRROR   1905-c.

    T1:Nursing mirror and midwives' journal

    Weekly;1 April 1905-c.

    L:C

Similar to above, but less official; more midwifery.

82. ASSOCIATION NOTES   1906-1920

    T1:Association notes/Association of Post Office Women Clerks

    T2:Association notes/Federation of Civil Service Women Clerks

    T3:Association notes/Federation of Women Civil Servants

    Irregular;annual;quarterly;December 1906-October/December 1920

    "For private circulation only"

    C BY:item 156

    L:F

Campaigning for equal treatment, especially equal pay, for women
clerks.

83. JUS SUFFRAGII   1906-1929

    T1:Internat. [sic] Woman Suffrage Alliance:bulletin or monthly
    correspondence

    T2:Jus suffragii:international woman suffrage news/
    International Woman Suffrage Association

    Rotterdam;then London

    Eds. included Martina G. Kramers, Mary Sheepshanks, Margery
    Corbett Ashby

    Quarterly;monthly;September 1906-December 1929

    C BY:item 174

    L:F

    M:IDC

Published in English, with numerous articles in French. Contained
detailed reports of suffrage and general feminist activity in a
large number of countries. Very internationalist/"progressive" in
outlook; reflects feminist peace efforts in World War 1. (For
further information see Oldfield, 1984). The Latin title means
"the right to vote".

84. WORKING GENTLEWOMAN'S JOURNAL   1906-1910

    T1:Working gentlewoman's journal: issues by the Working
    Gentlewoman's Guild

    Monthly;March 1906-December 1910 (n.i.c.)

L:BM;1103 bae

M:Harvester

Articles on various form of genteel employment e.g. teaching,
secretarial work, bee-keeping; also emigration and general
information on education.

85. WOMEN'S TRIBUNE   1906

T1:Women's tribune/Women's Franchise Declaration Committee

Weekly;18 May-10 August 1906

C BY:item 86

L:C, F (incomplete)

M:Harvester

Rather unco-ordinated general support of women's suffrage and
feminism.

86. WOMEN AND PROGRESS   1906-1907

T1:Women and progress

Weekly;2 November 1906-14 June 1907

C:item 85

L:C, F (incomplete)

M:Harvester

Continues item 85 under a different title.

87. WOMEN'S FRANCHISE   1907-1911

T1:Women's franchise/Women's Franchise Office

T2:Women's franchise/Woman Citizen Publishing Company

Prop. John E. Francis

Weekly;27 June 1907-27 July 1911

L:C, F

M:Harvester

A substantial paper representing all major tendencies within the
suffrage movement, it featured contributions from societies
(especially WSPU, WFL, NUWSS) and from individuals (e.g.
Pankhursts, Charlotte Despard, Millicent Fawcett). Initially it
had close organisational and financial links with the NUWSS, but by
1909 the latter were becoming dissatisfied with the support it was
giving to their militant rivals (particularly the WFL). Since in
any case they wanted to concentrate their resources on their own
paper Common cause (item 90), the NUWSS withdrew their financial
support, with the following complicated consequences.
   Women's franchise effectively ceased publication of new
material with the issue of 16 September 1909. Thereafter, each new

weekly issue had a text identical with this one, differing only in date and issue number, until 11 November 1909, when some new material was introduced on p.1 only. The content of this issue was then repeated weekly for the remainder of 1909. However, the first issue of 1910 was completely new in content – except for p.1, which was identical to that which had been published since 11 November 1909! This new issue was then repeated weekly until Women's franchise was discontinued on 27 July 1911. At this point, the title was changed to Everywoman, but the content remained identical until Everywoman ceased in 1913.

A further complication was occasioned by the existence of the Woman citizen from 1908 onwards. This was not in fact a separate publication, but exactly duplicated the content, layout, etc. of the current issue of Women's franchise or Everywoman, until the latter ceased. This procedure was probably followed in order to keep the titles from lapsing, in case anything could be done with them; it is unlikely that either Woman citizen or Everywoman was ever published in anything but a very technical sense.

88. WOMEN'S SUFFRAGE   1907
    T1:Women's suffrage:the official organ of the National Union
    of Women's Suffrage Societies
    Monthly;July–September 1907
    L:C
    M:Harvester
Not a "genuine" periodical, but reprints of NUWSS campaign
leaflets at monthly intervals.

89. VOTES FOR WOMEN   1907–1918
    T1:Votes for women:official organ of the [National] Women's
    Social and Political Union
    T2:Votes for women
    T3:Votes for women:official organ of the United Suffragists
    Ed. and prop. Emmeline and F. W. Pethick Lawrence
    Monthly with weekly supplements;weekly;monthly;October 1907–
    February 1918
    L:C, F
    M:LC, DA
The pioneer of popular journalistic styles in the suffrage press;
it started as a relatively sober-looking magazine, but soon
introduced newspaper format (though not dimensions), lead cartoons,
banner headlines, "actuality" photographs, "punchy" style, etc.

Considerable detail of all sorts of militant suffrage activities, local branches, individual suffragettes, etc.. Very well indexed by annual volume.

In October 1912 the Pethick Lawrences were expelled from the WSPU by Emmeline and Christabel Pankhurst, and took <u>Votes for Women</u> with them (the new WSPU organ was item 111 q.v.). The paper spent 14 months as an independent militant suffrage journal, and in January 1914 became the organ of the United Suffragists, a regrouping of dissident and disillusioned ex-WSPU suffragettes. The paper maintained an ambivalent attitude toward the war, although both the Pethick Lawrences were prominent in the peace movement (both were members of the Union of Democratic Control, and Emmeline was one of the founders of the Women's International League). It kept up a steady campaign for the vote, and ceased when victory in this campaign was assured.

90. WOMAN WORKER 1907-1921
    T1:The woman worker:official organ of the National Federation
    of Women Workers
    T2:The woman worker:a journal for women trade unionists:the
    official organ of the National Federation of Women Workers
    Ed. Mary MacArthur
    Monthly;weekly;monthly;September 1907-26 January 1910;January
    1916-July 1921
    L:C, F
    M:BL
Vigorous socialist feminism (though with its feminism definitely subordinated to socialist and syndicalist priorities). It campaigned for better working conditions for women, for the suffrage (both women's and adult), for removal of sex barriers (though not in the field of protective/restrictive legislation), etc.. Contributors included Mary MacDonald and husband, Ethel Snowden and husband, etc.. Briefly merged with item 88 in 1910; was revived in 1916 as a result of the special conditions of women's war work. Very much "our Mary" MacArthur's paper, and died with her and the NFWW.

91. WOMAN 1908-1932
    T1:The woman:official organ of the Australian Women's National
    League
    Sydney, Australia

Monthly;March 1908-October 1932 (n.i.c.)

L:F (incomplete)

Explicitly anti-socialist, imperialist, for home and family.

92. WOMEN FOLK 1908-1910

T1:Women folk

Ed. Winifred Blatchford;pub. Utopia Press

Weekly;20 December 1908-29 June 1910

L:C

M:Harvester

Thin; much more socialist than feminist (contributors included Robert Blatchford and L. A. Borsman). Briefly "incorporated" item 90.

93. ANTI-SUFFRAGE REVIEW 1908-1918

T1:The anti-suffrage review

Pub. Women's National Anti-Suffrage League to December 1909, thereafter National League for Opposing Woman Suffrage

Monthly;December 1908-March 1918

L:C, F (incomplete)

M:RP to 1912

Solid journal; much detail of events, membership, etc., as well as anti-suffrage argument and polemic. Contributors included Mrs Humphry Ward, Violet Markham, Earl of Cromer, etc.. For further information about the anti-suffrage organisation see Harrison, 1978.

94. COMMON CAUSE 1909-1920

T1:The common cause:the organ of the women's movement for reform

T2:The common cause:organ of the National Union of Women's Suffrage Societies

T3:Women's suffrage:the common cause of humanity

T4:The common cause of humanity:organ of the National Union of Women's Suffrage Societies

T5:The common cause

Eds. included H. M. Swanwick, Clementina Black, A. Maude Royden

Weekly;15 April 1909-30 January 1920

C BY:151

L:C, F (incomplete)

27

M:F

Whatever it was called at any given time, this was always the
official organ of the NUWSS. It covered a wide range of feminist
topics as well as suffrage; in early years especially it
frequently carried discussion of the specifically sexual
oppression of women, though its main content tended to be
constitutional non-militant (even at times anti-militant)
suffragist. Sober in appearance, but often very well written, it
reflected in its early years the personal style of Helena
Swanwick, who was already a regular contributor to the Manchester
Guardian. Its attitude to the war was at first ambivalent, then
moderately patriotic, being very strong on "women's service", i.e.
women doing "men's" jobs to help the war effort. It followed
carefully all the lobbying and negotiation over the vote right up
to the Royal Assent in March 1918. Considerable local federation
and branch information; fairly well indexed by annual volume. For
further information see Swanwick, 1935, Hume, 1982.

95. ENGLISHWOMAN 1909-1921
    Tl:The Englishwoman
    Ed. Elisina Grant Richards to January 1910; thereafter Maude
    Meredith (described as "assistant editor")
    Monthly;February 1909-January 1921
    L:BM, F
Effectively a NUWSS attempt to provide a woman-oriented equivalent
of such "mainstream" literary-intellectual magazines as the
Nineteenth century, Contemporary review etc.. It acted as a forum
for serious feminist discussion at greater length and higher
intellectual level than was possible in the suffrage campaign
papers. Many distinguished contributors (Millicent Fawcett, Mary
Lowndes, John Galsworthy, Bernard Shaw etc.); it consisted
entirely of long articles and reviews (the latter are particularly
interesting).

96. WOMEN'S FREEDOM LEAGUE TEMPORARY NEWS SHEET 1909
    Tl:Women's Freedom League temporary news sheet
    Weekly;16 September-21 October 1909
    C BY:item 99
    L:F
    M:IDC
Thin bulletin printed by J. E. Francis in the same format as item
84. The Women's Freedom League was the group of independent-minded

suffragettes, including Charlotte Despard, Teresa Billington-Greig, Edith How-Martyn, Nina Boyle, etc., who broke away from the Pankhurst-dominated WSPU in late 1907; their more representative paper is item 99.

97. MEN'S LEAGUE FOR WOMEN'S SUFFRAGE 1909-1914
    Tl:Men's League for Women's Suffrage monthly paper
    Monthly;October 1909-July 1914 (n.i.c.)
    L:F
Slim, mainly propagandist.

98. SUFFRAGIST 1909
    Tl:The suffragist/Suffragists' Vigilance League
    One issue only (October 1909)
    L:C
    M:Harvester
One-off publication consisting mainly of humorous suffrage propaganda, with strong pro-militant bias (both WFL and WSPU). Edited by anonymous man; it included many cartoons by Osmond Garrick. The Suffragists' Vigilance League is not otherwise known.

99. VOTE 1909-1933
    Tl:The vote:organ of the Women's Freedom League
    Ed. Charlotte French Despard (at first)
    Weekly;28 October 1909-10 November 1933
    C:item 96
    C BY:item 181
    L:C, F (incomplete)
    M:IDC, BL (to 1914)
Least attractive of the major suffrage journals of the early 20th century in appearance, but quite substantial and interesting; despite the title, it was always concerned with feminist issues other than the suffrage, e.g. sexual oppression, restrictions on women's employment (particularly the marriage bar in the 1920s), prostitution (especially the provisions of DORA), women police, etc.. Although orginally a very militant group, by about 1912 the WFL had moved to a more constitutionalist position, and in the 1920s often appeared to be the epitome of restricted "achievementist" "bourgeois" feminism; however, this was more the result of its tendency to ignore potentially divisive issues, e.g. birth control, abortion, etc.. In fact, it covered a wide range of feminist issues, and campaigned successfully not only for equal

franchise (won in 1928) but for "ladies only" compartments on trains. In its latter years, the <u>Vote</u> was heavily subsidised by Dr Elizabeth Knight (of the "Knight's Castile" family), and had to cease abruptly when she died intestate in a road accident in 1933. Indexing erratic and variable in quality. For further information, see Linklater, 1979.

100. ONLY WAY   1909-1910
    T1:The only way:Edinburgh University Women's Suffrage Society magazine
    Annual?;(n.i.c.)
    L:F, National Library of Scotland (one issue each)
Small paper of local interest

101. WOMEN'S FREEDOM LEAGUE OCCASIONAL PAPERS   1909
    T1:Women's Freedom League occasional papers
    Ed. Teresa Billington-Greig
    Irregular;only n°3 ("The hour and the woman") seen, no date, but internal evidence suggests ca 1909
    L:F
Collection of polemical articles by Marion Holmes, Ford Madox Hueffer, Margaret Wynn Nevison, et al.

102. CONSERVATIVE AND UNIONIST WOMEN'S FRANCHISE REVIEW   1909-1916
    T1:The Conservative and Unionist Women's Franchise review
    Quarterly;monthly;November 1909-April/June 1916
    L:C, F
    M:Harvester, IDC
Mainly organisational; some longer articles.

103. WOMAN JOURNALIST   1910-c.
    T1:Society of Women Journalists:bureau circular
    T2:The woman journalist:with which is incorporated the bureau circular, the bi-monthly organ of the Society of Women Journalists
    Irregular;bi-monthly;May 1910-c.
    L:BM;PP 5264mc (to 1925), F (a few recent issues)
    M:Harvester
Slim, organisational, little feminist interest.

104. LEAGUE LEAFLET   1911-1913
    T1:The League leaflet:being a paper to interest and to help

members of the Women's Labour League and other friends of the
Labour Party/National Women's Labour League
Ed. Margaret MacDonald
Monthly;January 1911-April 1913
C BY:item 118
L:C
M:BL, Harvester

Slim, but vigorous and wide-ranging; more socialist than feminist,
but usually ready to put a feminist viewpoint even when it
conflicted with the official Labour line. Contributors included
Katharine Bruce Glasier and Margaret Bondfield.

105. LINK 1911-1913
    T1:The link:organ of the Women's Socialist Movement
    Ed. Norman Young
    Weekly;September 1911-February 1913
    L:C

A socialist publication presumably aimed at women, though with no
perceptible feminist content, and mainly written by men.
Contributors included Margaretta Hicks and George Lansbury.

106. WOMAN VOTER 1911-1918
    T1:The woman voter:the [weekly] letter of the Women's
    Political Association
    Ed. Vida Goldstein
    Melbourne, Australia
    Weekly;fortnightly;8 September 1911-18 December 1918 (n.i.c.)
    L:F (incomplete)

Strongly socialist feminist, internationalist, pacifist; reported
activities of the Women's Peace Army. Wide coverage of feminist
issues.

107. FREEWOMAN 1911-1912
    T1:The freewoman:a weekly feminist review
    T2:The freewoman:a weekly humanist review
    Ed. Dora Marsden, with Mary Gawthorpe to 7 March 1912
    Weekly;23 November 1911-10 October 1912
    C BY:item 119
    L:C, F
    M:BL

Sexual reform ("free love") feminism with strong literary and
avant-garde inclination; some anti-spinster material, but

generally sympathetic to "Uranians" i.e. homosexuals, both female
and male. Many pieces by men. Contributors included Rebecca West.
Mary Gawthorpe gave up her part in it for reasons of health. It was
disapproved of by many feminists, including Millicent Fawcett, who
tore the first issue into little pieces (Strachey, 1931).
Circulation less than 200 (see Lidderdale, 1970).

108. CHURCH LEAGUE FOR WOMEN'S SUFFRAGE 1912-1917
    T1:The Church League for Women's Suffrage:monthly paper
    Monthly;January 1912-December 1917
    C BY:item 137
    L:C, F
    M:Harvester
Church of England suffrage organisation numbering among its
activists Agnes Maude Royden and the Rt Rev. William Temple, later
Archbishop of Canterbury.

109. ENTERPRISE CLUB MAGAZINE 1912-1913
    T1:Enterprise Club Magazine/Enterprise Club Ltd.
    Monthly;February 1912-January 1913
    L:BM;PP 1103 bam(1)
    M:Harvester
For women clerks; thin, with mainly organisational news.

110. BUSINESS GIRL 1912
    T1:Business girl:with which is incorporated "The shorthand
    typist":the official organ of the Institution of Women
    Shorthand-typists
    Ed. and pub. Helen Houston
    Monthly;February-March 1912
    L:C
    M:Harvester
Contributors included Ruth Phillips, Alice Kershaw and Charlotte
Despard.

111. IRISH CITIZEN 1912-1920
    T1:The Irish citizen:For men and women equally the rights of
    citizenship:for men and women equally the duties of
    citizenship/Irish Women's Franchise League
    Eds. include James Cousins, Francis Sheehy Skeffington and
    Hannah Sheehy Skeffington
    Weekly;monthly;25 May 1912-July/August 1920 (n.i.c.)
    L:C

M:IM

A strongly pro-women's suffrage paper, reporting comprehensively
on feminist organisations and activities in Ireland and Britain;
contributors included Margaret E. Cousins, Charlotte Despard,
Emmeline Pethick Lawrence, Lawrence Housman (occasional pieces in
Irish languages in early issues). At first, it claimed to "stand
neutral as regards Home Rule", and distanced itself considerably
not only from the Irish Nationalist Party (not noted for its
support of women's causes), but from the women's nationalist
league Cumann na mBan, as being effectively the subordinate
women's affiliate of a male organisation. From August 1914 it took
a definitely pacifist position, with prominent support of the
Union of Democratic Control and the Women's International League;
it also moved closer to a "Home Rule" position. This latter
tendency was sharply accelerated after Easter 1916, when Francis
Sheehy Skeffington was summarily executed by the British army. By
1917 it had become an active supporter of Sinn Fein, and in its
later years chronicled the activities of nationalist women.
Essential reading for students of British as well as Irish
feminism. For further information see Levenson, 1983, 1985 and
Ownes, 1984.

112. EYE-OPENER 1912
     Tl:The eye-opener/Frank Witty
     Weekly;1 June-3 August 1912
     C BY:item 115
     L:F
     M:IDC
Close connections with the Men's Society for Women's Rights;
concerned principally with prostitution and "white slavery", but
has many articles on specifically sexual oppression, and campaigns
strongly for suffrage.

113. WOMEN'S OUTLOOK 1912-1921
     Tl:Woman's outlook:organ of the Women's Enfranchisement
     Association of the Union of South Africa
     T2:Woman's outlook:suffrage organ of the women of South
     Africa
     Grahamstown;then Port Elizabeth, South Africa
     Monthly;September 1912-December 1921
     C BY:item 159
     L:F

Thin; almost entirely suffrage.

114. SUFFRAGETTE 1912-1915
     T1:The suffragette:official organ of the Women's Social and
     Political Union
     Ed. Christabel Pankhurst
     Weekly;16 October 1912-7 August 1914;9 April-8 October 1915
     C:item 89
     C BY:item 128
     L:C, F
     M:BL
Very much Christabel's own paper; at first, edited by her from
exile in Paris as the voice of the extreme militant wing of the
suffrage movement (arson, etc.). Very vivid, even racy in
appearance, with some outstanding graphic work;it was occasionally
liable to official raiding, censorship and suppression, and in
general had the air of a barely-tolerated paper on the border of
legality. It was notable, especially in 1913, for its stance on
prostitution, venereal disease and the dangers of marriage ("Votes
for women and purity for men").
     After an issue on 7 August 1914 denouncing war as the
ultimate expression of male violence, it ceased publication, only
to resume in 1915 as a super-patriotic pro-war journal, with
little feminism remaining.

115. AWAKENER 1912-1914
     T1:The awakener
     T2:The awakener:W. T. Stead's memorial
     Ed. Albert William Gray Jamrach to July 1914
     Weekly;16 November 1912-3 October 1914
     C:item 112
     L:C, F (incomplete)
     M:IDC
A soldier version of item 112, with very similar concerns:
prostitution, "white slavery", suffrage, etc.. Definite links with
the Men's Society for Women's Rights. According to item 119,
Jamrach resigned because many of the readership felt that he was
too closely identified with the WSPU's particular brand of
militancy. Rosa Frances Swiney (of the NUWSS) and her League of
Isis are increasingly in evidence after his departure. The paper
seems to have ceased through lack of funds.

34

116. FREE CHURCH SUFFRAGE TIMES   1913-1915
     Tl:Free Church Suffrage Times:organ of the Free Church League
     for Women's Suffrage
     Monthly;April 1913-December 1915
     C BY:item 129
     L:C, F
     M:Harvester
Thin, evangelical, internationalist, fairly pacifist. Contributors
included A. Maude Royden, Philip Snowden and H. M. Brailsford.

117. HUMANITY   1913-1914
     Tl:Humanity:devoted to the emancipation of sweated female
     workers/British Federation for the Emancipation of Sweated
     Women
     Monthly;May 1913-August 1914 (n.i.c.)
     L:BM;PP 1103bae
Mainly philanthropic;dealt with the evils of sweating,
prostitution, etc., but included some general feminism and support
for suffrage.

118. LABOUR WOMAN   1913-1971
     Tl:Labour woman/National Women's Labour League
     Eds. included Marion Phillips, Betty Lockwood
     Monthly;May 1913-September 1971
     C:item 104
     C BY:Labour weekly (not listed)
     L:C
     M:Harvester
At first simply a continuation of item 104, but soon became more
substantial, with news and general items of interest to Labour
Party women, including articles on socialism, recipes, patterns,
children's page, etc.. Contained reports of the National
Conference of Labour Women, and occasionally gave space to
feminist viewpoints at variance with the N.E.C. line (e.g. on
birth control), but did this more rarely from the late 1920s
onward, as the Women's Labour League was increasingly pressured
into conforming. Carried some articles in Welsh in the 1920s. It
finally ceased because a separate women's paper was felt to be
unnecessary. It remains a very useful source, especially for the
inter-war period.

119. NEW FREEWOMAN   1913

   T1:The new freewoman:an individualist review
   Ed. Dora Marsden
   C:item 107
   C BY:Egoist (not listed)
   L:C, F
   M:BL

By this time, far more literary/progressive than feminist;
financed by Harriet Shaw Weaver, with occasional contributions by
Stella Browne, Rebecca West et al.. The Egoist was an extremely
influential avant-garde literary magazine (Joyce, Pound, Lawrence
etc.). See Lidderdale, 1970.

120. FRIEND OF WOMEN'S SUFFRAGE   1913-1914

   T1:The friend of women's suffrage:issued by the National
   Union of Women's Suffrage Societies
   Quarterly?;July 1913-July 1914
   L:BM;PP 3611 mhc(1)
   M:Harvester

Extremely thin; entirely suffrage rhetoric. Only last two issues
found.

121. ALTRUIST   1913-1915

   T1:Men's Society for Women's Rights:monthly paper
   T2:The altruist/Men's Society for Women's Rights
   Ed. Albert W. Gray Jamrach
   Monthly;November 1913-April 1915 (n.i.c.)
   L:C, F (both incomplete)

Similar to item 115, but much thinner; mainly concerned with
prostitution.

122. WOMEN'S CHARTER REVIEW   1913

   T1:Women's charter review
   Ed. Lady Laura McLaren
   L:F

Apparently a one-off publication in support of Lady McLaren's
campaign for a women's charter.

123. MONTHLY NEWS OF THE CONSERVATIVE AND UNIONIST WOMEN'S
   FRANCHISE ASSOCIATION   1914-1924
   T1:Monthly news of the Conservative and Unionist Women's
   Franchise Association

T2:Monthly news of the Conservative Women's Reform
Association
Monthly;March 1914-December 1924 (n.i.c.)
L:C, F (incomplete)
M.Harvester
A thin monthly supplement to item 102; organisational news.

124. WOMAN'S DREADNOUGHT   1914-1924
T1:The woman's dreadnought/East London Federation of
Suffragettes
T2:The workers' dreadnought/Workers' Suffrage Federation
T3:The workers' dreadnought/Workers' Socialist Federation
T4:The workers' dreadnought:an organ of the Communist Party
of Great Britain
Ed. Estelle Sylvia Pankhurst
Weekly;8 March 1914-14 July 1924
L:C, F
M:DA, WMP, BL
Sylvia Pankhurst's own left-socialist paper, with much East End
information, and an increasingly noticeable move from women's
suffrage to adult suffrage. Militantly anti-war; broad coverage of
feminist issues, e.g. the campaign against section 40 D of the
Defence of the Realm Act. Sylvia and the Dreadnought were only
members of the CPGB for a few months before being expelled for
leftism and individualism.

125. LIBERAL WOMEN'S REVIEW   1914
T1:The Liberal women's review:published by the Liberal
Women's Suffrage Union
Ed. Mary Somerville
Monthly?;June(?)-July 1914 (n.i.c.)
L:F
July 1914 only issue found. It represents a group of influential
Liberal women (Eva McLaren, Lady Aberconway et al) protesting
against the Liberal government's attitude to women's suffrage.

126. CATHOLIC SUFFRAGIST   1915-1918
T1:The Catholic suffragist:organ of the Catholic Women's
Suffrage Society
Monthly;January 1915-January 1918
C BY:item 138
L:BM, F

M:IDC

Self-explanatory; but see item 138 for later developments.

127. WOMAN'S OPINION   1915-1916
     T1:Woman's opinion:the new army of international peace
     T2:Woman's opinion:the official organ of the "Citiznes of the
     world" movement
     Weekly;monthly;14 May 1915-February 1916
     L:BM;PP 1126aba
     M:Harvester

A strange mixture: pro-feminism, anti-sweating, anti-taxation,
anti-Kaiser, with a collection of odd "general-knowledge" items.
It carried advertisements for a large number of esoteric and
occult works, many of them by "Princess Karadja". Contributions by
Edith Porch (Mrs Fred Maturin). Not even remote connections with
other peace movements.

128. BRITANNIA   1915-1918
     T1:Britannia:official organ of the Women's Social and
     Political Union
     T2:Britannia:official organ of the Women's Party
     Ed. Christabel Pankhurst, Emmeline Pankhurst, Flora Drummond,
     Annie Kenney
     Weekly;9 October 1915-20 December 1918
     C:item 114
     L:C, F
     M:BL, LC

Continued the WSPU's pro-war, pro-Lloyd George line; denounced
shirkers, conscientious objectors, pacifists, "pro-Germans",
Asquith, Bolsheviks, etc.. Favoured using women's labour to free
men for military service, break unpatriotic strikes, etc.. Some
suffrage campaigning continued. It ceased altogether with the
Women's Party shortly after the 1918 "coupon" election.

129. COMING DAY   1916-1920
     T1:The coming day/Free Church League for Women's Suffrage
     Monthly;January 1916-June 1920
     C:item 116
     L:C, F (incomplete)
     M:Harvester

Straightforward continuation of its predecessor: Christian
feminism, internationalism, Maude Royden, etc.

130. WOMAN'S VOICE   1916-1918
    T1:Woman's voice:a monthly record of women's work/Women's
    Liberal League of New South Wales
    Sydney, Australia
    Monthly;January 1916-June 1918 (n.i.c.)
    C:item 78
    L:F (incomplete)
Much as its predecessor.

131. SUFFRAGETTE NEWS SHEET   1916
    T1:Suffragette news sheet:produced by the Committee of
    Suffragettes of the Women's Social and Political Union
    Monthly;February-December 1916 (n.i.c.)
    L:C
Short-lived but interesting paper of one of the groups which broke
away from the official WSPU during the War; feminist,
"progressive", pro-Irish. See also item 133.

132. WOMEN'S INTERNATIONAL LEAGUE   1916-1952
    T1:Women's International League monthly news-sheet
    T2:Women's International League (British Section of the
    Women's International League for Peace and Freedom) monthly
    news-sheet
    Monthly;April 1916-July/August 1952
    C BY:item 217
    L:BM;PP 3611mhd
The main voice of feminist pacifism in Britain. Strong support for
League of Nations and United Nations Organisation, together with
general feminist information and comment. Very independent;
followed nobody's line except its own.

133. INDEPENDENT SUFFRAGETTE   1916-1918
    T1:The independent suffragette:published by the Independent
    Women's Social and Political Union
    Monthly;August(?) 1916-July 1918 (n.i.c.)
    L:C (2 issues);F (3 issues);no others found
    M:Harvester
Another and longer-lasting WSPU breakaway (as compared with item
131); more narrowly concerned with the vote. Contributors included
Charlotte Marsh and Dorothy E. Evans.

134. URANIA   1916-1940
     T1:Urania:not published or offered for sale. 'There are no
     "men" or "women" in Urania. "All'eison hos angeloi"
     Bi-monthly;irregular;December 1916-May/August 1940 (n.i.c.)
     L:F (from 1924)
A strange sort of mystical androgyny (the Greek motto means: "but
they are as angels"), with extensive (and often obscure)
information about Japan. Eva Gore-Booth appears to have been
editor until her death.

135. DILUTION OF LABOUR BULLETIN   1916-1918
     T1:Dilution of labour bulletin:a monthly publication
     primarily for officers working in connection with the D.A.
     Section (Dilution) of the Labour Supply Department/Ministry
     of Munitions
     Monthly;October 1916-October 1918
     L:BM, F
     M:Harvester
Reported on role of women as replacements for men in munitions
work.

136. GFS MAGAZINE   1917-1951
     T1:GFS magazine:the magazine of the Girls' Friendly Society
     Monthly;July 1917-May 1951
     C:items 23, 34
Self-explanatory.

137. CHURCH MILITANT   1918-1928
     T1:The Church militant/League of the Church Militant:working
     primarily for the admission of women to holy orders
     Monthly;January 1918-October 1928 (n.i.c.)
     C:item 108
     L:C, F
     M:Harvester
Continues the Anglican feminist tendency, with emphasis changed
from the vote to ordination. Maude Royden prominent.

138. CATHOLIC CITIZEN   1918-c.
     T1:The Catholic citizen:organ of the Catholic Women's
     Suffrage Society
     T2:The Catholic citizen:organ of St Joans's Social and
     Political Alliance

T3:The Catholic citizen:organ of St Joan's [International]
Alliance
Monthly;quarterly;irregular;February 1918-c.
C:item 126
L:BM, F
M:IDC
Concerned with a wide range of feminist issues, especially equal
pay, education and prostitution; has sometimes taken positions at
variance with those of the hierarchy (e.g. over the ordination of
women), but in its earlier years at least tended to follow the
Curial line, e.g. on birth control. The name change resulting in
T2 was due to a Papal prohibition of the use of the name "Catholic"
by non-ecclesiastical groups.

139. DAWN   1918-1972
Tl:The Dawn:a monthly journal containing news of progressive
movements affecting social welfare in the Australian
Commonwealth and other countries./Women's Service Guilds of
Western Australia
T2:The Dawn:a monthly journal for the service of Australian
Women Voters
T3:The Dawn news-sheet
T4:The Dawn:an Australian women's index-digest:published by
the Australian Federation of Women Voters
Perth;thereafter Sydney, Australia
Monthly;July 1918-April 1972
L:F
Feminist and internationalist, with special emphasis on the
Commonwealth; also much general social reform. Printed to 1949,
thereafter mimeographed. See also item 227.

140. STRI-DHARMA   1919-1936
Tl:Stri-dharma:official organ of the Women's Indian
Association
Eds. include D. Jinjarajadasa, Malati Patwardhan, Margaret E.
Cousins, S. Muthulakshmi Reddi
Bombay, India
Monthly;January 1919-August 1936 (n.i.c.)
L:F
The Sanskrit title means approximately "justice for women".
Nationalist-feminist, and very pro-Congress; its Hindu sympathies
were very apparent, although it showed tolerance to other

viewpoints (including Muslim). Some regular contributions in Tamil, Telegu and Hindi.

141. NATIONAL COUNCIL OF WOMEN 1919-1922
    Tl:National Council of Women of Great Britain and Ireland:
    occasional paper
    Irregular;n°s 81-112
    C:item 68
    C BY: item 161
    L:BM, F
Moderate feminism and social reform in the style of its
predecessor.

142. WOMAN'S CHARTER 1919
One issue only in C (2 April); feminist-looking headlines and
sub-heads have no relation to the content, which is exclusively
concerned with dairy farming and animal husbandry!

143. WOMAN TEACHER 1919-1961
    Tl:The Woman teacher:the organ of the National Federation
    [Union] of Women Teachers
    Eds. include Emily Phipps, Edith E. Crosby, Ethel Stead,
    Florence E. Key, A. Muriel Pierotti
    Weekly;fortnightly;monthly;16 September 1919-April 1961
    L:C, F
    M:Harvester
Autonomous journal of women teachers campaigning against
professional restrictions (e.g. the marriage bar) and for equal
pay. Strong links with the Women's Freedom League and St Joan's
Alliance. Ceased when equal pay in teaching was achieved.

144. WOMAN ENGINEER 1919-c.
    Tl:The woman engineer:the organ of the Women's Engineering
    Society
    Quarterly;September 1919-c.
    L:BM, F (incomplete)
Information on women in all areas of technology, together with
purely organisational news. Strongly feminist; it continues to
campaign vigorously for equal employment and educational
opportunities.

145. WOMAN'S OUTLOOK   1919-1967
    T1:Woman's outlook:a popular magazine
    T2:Woman's outlook/Women's Co-operative Guild
    T3:Woman's outlook/Co-operative Women's Guild
    Eds. include Mary Peirce (i.e. Mary Stott)
    Weekly;fortnightly;monthly
    L:BM;PP 6004oq (from 1941 only)
    M:Research Publications
The Guild's general interest magazine, combining home hints,
stories and recipes with socialist-feminist political articles. It
does not contain conference reports of the Guild; these are to be
found in Co-operative news (not listed; L:C).

146. HOME AND COUNTRY   1919-c.
    T1:Home and country/National Federation of Women's Institutes
    Monthly
    L:F (incomplete)
Women's Institute news and general articles, e.g. child care,
cooking, gardening, rural life, etc..

147. WOMAN CLERK   1919-1931
    T1:The woman clerk:organ of the Association of Women Clerks
    and Secretaries
    Monthly;quarterly;(1)December 1919-October 1921;(2)September
    1925-Spring 1931 (n.i.c.)
    L:(1)C, (2)BM;PP 1103baw
    M:Harvester
Organisational news; equal pay and opportunities in the lower
grades of the civil service. See also item 150.

148. WOMEN'S LIBERAL MAGAZINE   1920
    T1:The women's Liberal magazine:organ of the Women's National
    Liberal Federation
    Ed. Lucy Masterman
    Monthly;January-December 1920
    C;item 65?
    C BY:item 155
    L:BM;PP 3558fa
    M:Harvester
Organisational news, together with some general articles.

43

149. NEW CITIZEN 1920

    Tl:The new citizen:the organ of the National Women Citizens'
    Association
    Weekly?;20 January 1920 (n.i.c.)
    L:BM;PP 3611mk

One issue only found. Very slim; concerned mainly with new fields
opened to women by the passing of the Sexual Disqualifications
(Removal) Act 1919, e.g. as Justices of the Peace.

150. TAXETTE 1920-1923

    Tl:Taxette:the organ of the Association of Temporary Women
    Tax Clerks
    Eds. include D. Rogozin, Rose J. Florence, Dorothy C. Kelly
    Monthly;February 1920-June 1923
    L:C
    M:Harvester

Expansion of a half-page in the early issues of item 147.
Concerned with grading, equal pay etc. in the civil service.

151. WOMAN'S LEADER 1920-1932

    Tl:The woman's leader and common cause/National Union of
    Societies for Equal Citizenship
    T2:The woman's leader/National Union of Townswomen's Guilds
    Weekly;monthly;6 February 1920-December 1932
    C:item 94
    C BY:item 179
    L:C, F
    M:Research Publications

An external appearance which was sober to the point of greyness
camouflaged what was probably the most substantial and vigorous
feminist periodical of the 1920s, campaigning for equal franchise,
abolition of the marriage bar, equal knowledge of birth control,
equal pay, and many other feminist issues. It also provided a
forum for feminists of disparate tendencies. Its own line tended
to be "liberal" feminist, although it tended to find itself on the
same side as at least the women of the Labour Party (of which it
could be highly critical). Regular contributors included Mary
Stocks, Eva Hubback and Eleanor Rathbone.

    The National Union of Societies for Equal Citizenship was the
successor fo the NUWSS, campaigning mainly for equal franchise.
After this was achieved, the Union began to question its role, and
eventually handed over its "educational" function (including

<u>Woman's leader</u>) to the relatively new National Union of
Townswomen's Guilds. The paper then underwent a drastic change:
articles on the economic crisis gave way to the care of household
pets, and the like.

152. TIME AND TIDE   1920-c.

    T1:Time and tide:an independent non-party weekly review

    T2:T & T:time and tide

    T3:Time and tide:John O'London's

    T4:Time and tide:the British news magazine

    T5:Time and tide business guide

    T6:Time and tide:a quarterly review

    Weekly;monthly;annual;14 May 1920-c.

    L:C

    M:BL, DA

"Time and tide wait for no man", and Margaret Haig, Lady Rhondda,
started this review of politics, literature and the arts in
vigorous feminist style; for a period it even carried reports of
the Six Point Group, a new feminist organisation founded by Lady
Rhondda. Between the wars there hardly seems to have been a
prominent woman who did not write something for <u>Time and tide</u>;
regular contributors included Vera Brittain, Crystal Eastman,
Cecily Hamilton, Winifred Holtby, Naomi Mitchison, Gwendolen
Raverat, Elizabeth Robins, Christopher St. John, Helena Swanwick,
Rebecca West, Virginia Woolf and many others. In the 1920s its
general standpoint was liberal feminist, with a marked
internationalist-pacifist tendency; however, in the 1930s the
feminism gradually faded away till it was restricted mainly to
Lady Rhondda's own "Notes on the way" (Cecily Hamilton even
contributed a regular review column entitled "men and books").
After World War Two it was a respectable but fairly unremarkable
literary-political review of steadily declining fortunes and
reputation. In 1963 it merged with <u>John O'London's weekly</u>, another
failing review. By the late 1960s it appears to have ceased as a
general interest magazine, the title only being used for a
business directory. In 1984 it was revived as a right-wing
political quarterly (no feminist connection). For the first decade,
see Spender, 1984.

153. WOMAN'S TIMES   1920-1922

    T1:The woman's times

    Monthly;January 1920-October 1922

L:C

A very thin attempt at a <u>Times</u> supplement for women. Not even faintly feminist.

154. HOME AND POLITICS   1920-1930
     Tl:Home and politics/Women's Unionist Association
     Monthly;September 1920-February 1930
     C BY:<u>The popular view</u> (not listed)
     L:C
     M:Harvester

Very much a Conservative Party women's paper; from 1925 it was included in local Conservative women's papers (e.g. item 156). extremely anti-Labour (MacDonald, Snowden etc. are explicitly equated with Bolsheviks) and anti-Co-operative. Not feminists, except when claiming noted feminists (e.g. Mrs Pankhurst) for Conservatism. Very self-congratulatory about the Conservative government's equal franchise measure in 1928, though <u>Home and politics</u> had not noticeably campaigned for it. Some details of its history, circulation, etc. in the August 1927 issue.

155. FEDERATION NEWS   1921-1924
     Tl:Federation news/Women's National Liberal Federation
     Ed. Grace Newbould
     Monthly;January 1921-March 1924
     C:item 148
     C BY:item 164
     L:BM;PP 3558ifa
     M:Harvester

At first, just organisational news; but gradually more general articles were introduced.

156. OPPORTUNITY   1921-1940
     Tl:Opportunity:the organ of the Federation of Women Civil
     Servants
     T2:Opportunity:the organ of the National Association of Women
     Civil Servants
     Quarterly;January 1921-July 1940
     C:item 82
     L:F

Concerned mainly with equal pay and Whitley Council.

157. WOMEN'S LOCAL GOVERNMENT NEWS   1921-1925
     T1:Women's local government news:monthly organ of the Women's
     Local Government Society
     Monthly;January 1921-April 1925 (n.i.c.)
     L:F
Thin; mainly concerned with the representation of women in local
government, both in elected posts and as officials.

158. CONSERVATIVE WOMAN   1921-1929
     T1:The Conservative woman/Leeds Women's Conservative and
     Unionist Publications Ltd
     Ed. Blanche L. Leigh
     Monthly;March 1921-May 1929 (n.i.c.)
     L:BM;PP 3558ab
     M:Harvester
Local organisational news. From May 1925 includes item 154.

159. FLASHLIGHT   1922-1930
     T1:The flashlight:the quarterly organ of the Woman's
     Enfranchisement Association of the Union of South Africa
     Port Elizabeth, South Africa
     Monthly;January 1922-July 1930
     C:item 113
     L:F (incomplete)
Single-issue women's suffrage paper; ceased on the achievement of
the suffrage.

160. BIRTH CONTROL NEWS   1922-1946
     T1:Birth control news:the statesman's newspaper/Society for
     Constructive Birth Control
     Ed. Marie Carmichael Stopes
     Monthly;quarterly;monthly;May 1922-December 1946
     L:C, F (incomplete)
     M:DA
Thin and propagandist, but nevertheless the authentic voice of
Marie Stopes; hence, essential reading.

161. N.C.W. NEWS   1923-1930
     T1:N.C.W. news/National Council of Women of Great Britain and
     Northern Ireland
     Monthly (except August);January 1923-December 1930
     C:item 141

        C BY:item 179
        L:BM, F
Organisational news along the lines of its predecessor, but more
frequent and more regular. At this period, the N.C.W. was almost
acting as an umbrella for the varying tendencies of the feminist
movement, and was involved in a number of controversial campaigns
(e.g. birth control).

162. CHURCH MILITANT SUPPLEMENT 1924-1926
        T1:The Church militant supplement
        Monthly;January 1924-December 1926
        C BY:item 169
        L:C, F
Really sermons by Maude Royden, issued in conjunction with item
137.

163. FAMILY ENDOWMENT COUNCIL 1924-1937
        T1:Family Endowment Council:monthly notes
        T2:Family Endowment Society:monthly notes
        T3:Monthly notes
        T4:Family Endowment Chronicles
        Monthly;quarterly;April 1924-February 1937 (n.i.c.)
        L:BM, F
Organisational paper of the campaign for family allowances paid
to the mother; Eleanor Rathbone prominent.

164. LIBERAL WOMAN'S NEWS 1924-1936
        T1:Liberal woman's news/Women's National Liberal Federation
        Ed. Grace Newbould
        Monthly;April 1924-January 1936
        C:item 153
        L:BM, F
        M:Harvester
Liberal Party and WNLF news, together with general interest
articles, e.g. on the prison system, on monetary reform, etc.. Its
cessation seems to have had much to do with the declining fortunes
of the Liberal Party in the 1930s.

165. WOMAN FREEMASON 1925-1975
        T1:The ray/The Honourable Fraternity of Ancient Freemasons
        T2:The woman Freemason:the only masonic fraternity organised
        entirely by women for women

Irregular;six-monthly;February 1925-May 1975 (n.i.c.)

    L:BM;PP 1055fb

News of lodges. The Fraternity is a highly unorthodox group of women Freemasons.

166. WOMAN'S VIEW 1925-1929

    T1:Woman's view

    T2:Women's view

    T3:Woman's view

    Irregular;April 1925-January 1929 (n.i.c.)

    L:BM;PP 1139ffd, F (incomplete)

Produced by the Women's Committee of the True Temperance Association; really a series of brief temperance tracts.

167. SEED 1925-1926

    T1:The seed

    Watford

    Monthly?;August 1925(?)-April 1926(?) (n.i.c.)

    L:Bodleian (John Johnson Collection);only April 1926 seen

A communist women's paper, apparently produced by a Watford local Women's Committee of the CPGB.

168. WOMAN WORKER 1926-1927

    T1:The woman worker/Communist Party of Great Britain

    Monthly;March 1926-January 1927

    C BY:item 170

    L:C

    M:Harvester

Very party-line; devoted some space to criticism of the Women's Co-operative Guild.

169. GUILDHOUSE FELLOWSHIP 1927-1955

    T1:The Guildhouse monthly

    T2:The Guildhouse Fellowship

    Ed. A. Maude Royden

    Monthly;January 1927-October 1955

    C:item 162

    L:F

Maude Royden's personal brand of Christian feminism.

170. WORKING WOMAN 1927-1929

    T1:The working woman/Communist Party of Great Britain

Monthly;February 1927-March 1929 (n.i.c.)

C:item 168

L:C

M:Harvester

Much as its predecessor.

171. HACKNEY WOMAN WORKER 1927

T1:The Hackney woman worker

Weekly;26 April-1 November 1927 (n.i.c.)

L:Bodleian (John Johnson Collection) (incomplete)

Officially produced by the Women's Section of the Hackney Trades
Council; in fact a Communist paper.

172. WOMAN OF TODAY AND TOMORROW 1929

T1:Woman of today and tomorrow/National Union of Conservative
and Constitutional Associations

One issue only

L:BM;PP 6004os

One-off Conservative women's paper.

173. OPEN DOOR 1929-1939

T1:Open door:organ of the Open Door International:for the
economic emancipation of the woman worker

Irregular (24 issues);September 1929-November 1939

L:BM, F

Very slim paper of the campaign against restrictive/"protective"
legislation, e.g. women's right to work in mines. Genuinely
international; contributors included Winifred Holtby, Dorothy E.
Evans, Franciska Plaminkova, etc..

174. INTERNATIONAL WOMEN'S NEWS 1930-c.

T1:International Women's news/International Woman Suffrage
Alliance

T2:International women's news:realist, independent,
democratic

T3:International women's news/International Alliance of Women

Quarterly;January 1930-c.

C:item 83

L:C, F

M:IDC, UM

Continues international information on the women's movement;
Margery Corbett Ashby prominent until late 1970s. Some

contributions in French.

During World War Two, because of the impossibility of getting
contributions from occupied Europe, the paper was taken over for
the duration by the Women's Publicity and Planning Association,
who kept it going as a mainly British feminist journal; regular
contributors included Dorothy E. Evans, Stevie Smith, Inez Holden,
Patricia Gardner, Elaine Burton, etc..

175. SOROPTIMIST 1930-c.
    T1:The British Soroptimist:the magazine of the Soroptimist
    Clubs of Great Britain
    T2:Soroptimist:the magazine of the Soroptimist International
    Monthly;January 1930-c.
    L:BM;PP 1103bbd, F (incomplete)
A Rotarian-type women's organisation; philanthropic and social
rather than feminist.

176. NATIONAL COUNCIL OF WOMEN IN INDIA 1930-1941
    T1:Bulletin of the National Council of Women in India
    Eds. Leelabai Phadke, Kamala Chatterjee
    Bombay, India
    Bi-monthly;June 1930-January 1941 (n.i.c.)
    L:F
Cautious general feminism; European contributors predominated, but
some Hindi articles appeared in later issues.

177. COMING MINISTRY 1930-1939
    T1:The coming ministry:the organ of the Society for the
    Ministry of Women (Interdenominational)
    Quarterly;Christmas 1930-January 1939 (n.i.c.)
    L:F
Campaigning for women's ordination; Maude Royden prominent.

178. WIDENING HORIZONS 1930-c.
    T1:Widening horizons/International Federation of Business
    and Professional Women
    Quarterly;Spring 1930(?)-c.
    L:F (incomplete)
Thin, organisational.

179. WOMEN IN COUNCIL 1931-1972
    T1:Women in council:"N.C.W. news"

T2:Women in council/National Council of Women of Great
Britain and Northern Ireland
Monthly;quarterly;January 1931-Summer 1972
C:item 161
C BY:item 298
L:F
Useful for 1930s, but gradually gets thinner.

180. TOWNSWOMAN 1933-c.
T1:The townswoman/National Union of Townswomen's Guilds
Monthly;April 1933-c.
C:item 151
L:C, F
The urban equivalent of the Women's Institutes; household hints,
activities of the N.U.T.C., etc. - little or no feminism.

181. WOMEN'S FREEDOM LEAGUE BULLETIN 1934-1961
T1:Women's bulletin
T2:Women's Freedom League bulletin
Weekly;irregular
C:item 99
L:C, F
M:IDC
Rather shabbily mimeographed, but the only non-specialised fully
feminist periodical to continue through the lean decades. It
provided wide (though often skimpy) coverage of feminist issues -
except where too potentially diverse for the Women's Freedom
League (e.g. abortion). It is a most useful reference source for
British feminism throughout all but its last few years.

182. BULLETIN OF THE INDIAN WOMEN'S MOVEMENT 1934-1951
T1:Bulletin of the Indian Women's Movement
Eds. Grace Lankester, Maud Dickinson
Irregular (55 issues)
L:F
Mimeographed information about feminism in India, aimed mainly at
a British feminist audience, and sponsored by the British
Commonwealth League, Women's International League, Women's Freedom
League, Six Point Group and St Joan's Alliance.

183. COUNCIL OF WOMEN CIVIL SERVANTS 1934-1956
T1:Quarterly bulletin of the Council of Women Civil Servants

T2:Bulletin of the Council of Women Civil Servants
Quarterly;irregular;July 1934-November 1956 (n.i.c.)
"Strictly confidential to members and associate members of
the Council"
L:F

Mainly equal pay and opportunities; for higher grades of women
civil servants.

184. N.C.W. NEWS   1936-c.
T1:N.C.W. news/National Council of Women of South Africa
Cape Town, South Africa
Monthly;January 1936-c.
L:F (incomplete)

Status of women (mainly white), organisational news, etc..
Originally "non-political", but has found itself drawn
increasingly into opposition to the Nationalist government and
concern with black and coloured women.

185. WOMAN TODAY   1936-1940
T1:Woman today/British section of the Women's World Committee
Against War and Fascism
T2:Woman today/Women's Committee for Peace and Democracy
Ed. Charlotte Haldane
Weekly;monthly;12 September 1936-February 1940
L:C

Began as a general illustrated magazine; "popular front" articles
on Spain, Ethiopia, the means test and pictures of Charlotte
Despard mingled with stories by Ethel Mannin and Naomi Mitchison,
and articles on make-up, knitting, shopping and babies. Fairly
soon, however, the format and illustrations were much reduced,
together with the "general" element; it ended as a small
grey-looking left magazine.

186. FANFARE   1936-1947
T1:Fanfare/Women's Gas Council
Quarterly;Spring 1936-Winter 1947
C BY:item 203
L:BM;PP 6004obi

News of the Women's Gas Council (president: Dame Vera
Laughton-Matthews), together with cooking hints, general interest
articles, stories, etc.

187. INDUSTRIAL NEWSLETTER FOR WOMEN   1938-1962
     Tl:Industrial newsletter for women/Trades Union Congress
     Monthly;irregular;January 1938-January 1962 (n.i.c.)
     L:TUC, F
     M:Harvester
Thin, mimeographed bulletin of trade union news concerning women.

188. SPINSTER   1938-1941
     Tl:The spinster:official organ of the National Spinsters'
     Pensions Association
     Shipley, Yorks.
     Monthly;February 1938-January 1941 (n.i.c.)
     L:BM;PP 1103bd
Campaigned for pensions for unmarried working women at age 55;
also recipes romantic stories, knitting patterns, astrology, etc..
Florence White prominent.

189. WOMAN'S NATIONAL NEWSPAPER   1938
     Tl:The woman's national newspaper:first independent newspaper
     in the world owned and controlled entirely by women and
     supported by women/Women's League of Unity
     Weekly;September-November 1938
     C BY:item 190
     L:C
General interest paper with a feminist slant; contributions by
prominent feminists (e.g. Flora Drummond), articles on the
international situation (e.g. Palestine from the Arab viewpoint),
stories, bridge, Women's League of Health and Beauty . . . . All
records of the Women's [National] League of Unity seem to have
vanished, but it appears to have had the active support of a
number of active feminists, e.g. Emmeline Pethick Lawrence, Edith
Summerskill.

190. WOMAN'S DAILY NEWSPAPER   1938
     Tl:Woman's daily newspaper/Women's National League of Unity
     Daily?;only issue 1 (7 November 1938) found
     C:item 189
     C BY: item 191
     L:C
Same style as item 189. There is nothing to indicate whether or
not it really was daily.

191. WOMAN'S NEWSPAPER   1939
    Tl:Woman's newspaper:incorporating the first journal of
    woman's national service/Women's League of Unity
    Weekly;June-November 1939 (n.i.c.)
    C:item 190
    L:C
Even more of a mixture than its predecessors: WVS, Women's League
of Health and Beauty, ATS, bridge and radio columns, Agatha
Christie serial, Storm Jameson on Europe, Edith Summerskill on
milk for children, Emmeline Pethick Lawrence, etc.. The first
issue of the war combines belligerent pictures of young ARP women
with a near-pacifist editorial.

192. WIFE AND CITIZEN   1940-1952
    Tl:Wife and citizen:published by the Married Women's
    Association to advocate the economic and social emancipation
    of all women
    Ed. Juanita Frances
    Monthly;January 1940(?)-February/March 1952 (n.i.c.)
    L:BM;PP 1103bg, F (both incomplete)
Earliest issue found is January 1945. The Married Women's
Association (first president: Edith Summerskill) was formed in
1938 to campaign for equal financial and legal rights for married
women, equal rights in the marital home, family allowances, equal
taxation for wives, etc.. See also item 195.

193. LAND GIRL   1940-1947
    Tl:The land girl
    Ed. Margaret A. Pyke
    C BY:item 201
    L:F
For members of the Women's Land Army; information articles on
agriculture together with letters, local news, etc..

194. WOMEN AT WORK   1940-1951
    Tl:Women at work:quarterly bulletin of the British Federation
    of Business and Professional Women
    Ed. Isabel Curry
    Quarterly;November 1940-Winter 1951
    C BY:item 218
    L:BM; PP 1103bcg

Reports of Woman Power, Women's Engineering Society, Women's Gas Council, etc.; some general feminism. Contributors included Caroline Haslett, Vera Brittain, Ruth Tomlinson, etc..

195. MARRIED WOMEN'S ASSOCIATION   1941-1942
     Tl:Married Women's Association (Housewives' Trade Union):
     Hampstead Group
     Monthly?;1941(?)-1942(?)
     L:F (2 issues)
Thin, mimeographed. Connected with item 192?

196. AUSTRALIAN WOMEN'S DIGEST   1944-1948
     Tl:Australian women's digest
     Ed. Vivienne Newson
     Sydney, Australia
     Bi-monthly;August 1944-May 1948 (n.i.c.)
     L:F
Small-format general women's magazine (stories, etc.), with some not very obtrusive feminism.

197. WOMEN IN KENYA   1944-1957
     Tl:Women in Kenya:the journal of the East Africa Women's
     League
     Nairobi, Kenya
     Monthly;January 1944-December 1957 (n.i.c.)
     L:F (incomplete)
Organisational news, general interest articles. No perceptible feminism.

198. WOMAN TODAY   1944-1959
     Tl:Woman today/Tamara Rust
     Quarterly;bi-monthly;monthly;August 1944-January 1959
     L:BM;PP 3558iho
Small-format, lively Communist magazine, with the party line relatively unobtrusive (articles on Russian youth, etc.). Nor is feminism heavily emphasised, apart from occasional articles on such women as the Pankhursts and Charlotte Despard. Otherwise, very similar to the general women's magazines of the time: household hints, stories, advice page, etc..

199. WOMEN FOR WESTMINSTER   1945-1949
     Tl:Women for Westminster:newsletter

Eds. included Teresa Billington-Greig, Alice Hemming

Irregular;quarterly;1945(?)-Spring 1949 (n.i.c.)

L:F (incomplete)

Earliest issue seen is n°4 (May 1946). Slim printed (later mimeographed) bulletin concerned with women's representation in parliament, and with equal citizenship. Contributors included Margery Corbett Ashby and Edith Summerskill.

200. ROSHNI   1946-c.

Tl:Roshni:journal of the All-India Women's Conference

Eds. Lakshmi N. Menon, Avabai B. Wadia, Tapati Mookerji

Bombay, India;Delhi, India

Monthly;quarterly;January 1946-c.

L:F

Separate Hindi and English language editions; concerned with status of women particularly in rural society, maternal and child welfare, etc.. The Hindi title means "light".

201. LAND ARMY NEWS   1947-1950

Tl:Land Army news/Women's Land Army

Monthly;June 1947-November 1950

C:item 193

L:F

A much more official publication than its predecessor.

202. LANKA MAHILA SAMITI   1947

Tl:Lanka Mahila Samiti magazine

Colombo, Sri Lanka

Monthly?:July 1947-(?) (only n°1 seen)

L:F

The magazine of the Association of Women's Institutes in Ceylon.

203. COMMENTARY   1948-1966

Tl:Commentary:the magazine of the Women's Gas Council [Federation]

Quarterly;Spring 1946-Winter 1966

C:item 185

C BY:item 241

L:BM;PP 6004obi

Much the same as its predecessor.

204. SIX POINT GROUP   1948-1980
    Tl:Six Point Group
    T2:Six Point Group Newsletter
    Eds. Stella Newsome, Hazel Hunkins Hallinan
    Irregular;May 1948-Spring 1980
    L:BM (incomplete), F
Thin mimeographed newsletter; organisational news and matters of
general feminist concern.

205. WOMEN'S EMPLOYMENT FEDERATION   1948-1970
    Tl:Women's Employment Federation bulletin
    3 issues per year;October 1948-Autumn 1970
    L:F (incomplete)
Slim, mimeographed bulletin of careers news for women.

206. WOMEN'S REVIEW   1948
    Tl:Women's review
    Ed. M. A. Hunter-Henderson
    Quarterly;(n°2 only seen)
    L:F (incomplete)
Feminist articles by various hands, including Teresa
Billington-Greig.

207. MEN'S REVIEW   1948
    Tl:Men's review:quarterly of the "Anti-Women" Society for
    men's rights
    Ed. Andrew Risbridger
    Quarterly;1948(?)
    L:BM;PP 1103db
Two issues only found, of one printed leaflet each (undated).
Anti-alimony, anti-Married Women's Association, anti-feminist
generally.

208. WOMAN COUNCILLOR AND CITIZEN   1949-1951
    Tl:Woman councillor and citizen/National Women Citizen's
    Association
    Bi-monthly;January/February(?) 1949-November/December 1951
    (n.i.c.)
    L:F
Slim printed paper mainly concerned with women's civic
responsibility; some mild feminism. Contributors include Vera
Douie, Constance Rover.

209. DOROTHY EVANS SERIES   1949

    Tl:Dorothy Evans series:monthly papers

    Monthly;April-July 1949 (n.i.c.)

    L:F

Instructional leaflets on parliamentary procedure, public
speaking, etc., issued in memory of Dorothy E. Evans, British
feminist who died in 1944.

210. RAILWAY WOMEN'S ANNUAL   1949

    Tl:Railway women's annual

    Ed. Thomas Ashcroft

    C BY:Railwaymen's year book (not listed)

    L:Bodleian

One issue only;information on women working in British Railways
and London Transport, plus some household hints, etc..

211. WOMEN'S COUNCIL   1949-1979

    Tl:The Women's Council

    Twice yearly?(June 1979 is issue 59);1949(?)-June 1979
    (n.i.c.)

    L:F (two issues only)

Apparently an international and Commonwealth group, liaising with
women's organisations. No connection with the National Council of
Women.

212. REPORT TO WOMEN   1950-1952

    Tl:Report to women:a review of the economic situation
    prepared by the Economic Information Unit of H.M. Treasury

    Monthly;June 1950-January 1952 (n.i.c.)

    L:BM, F

Slim bulletin containing mainly information on prices, household
goods, etc..

213. ST JOAN'S, AUSTRALIA   1950-1954

    Tl:St Joan's, Australia:magazine of the Australian section of
    St Joan's Social and Political Alliance

    Eds. included Jean Daly, Anna Brennan

    Sydney, Australia

    Quarterly;September 1950-December 1954 (n.i.c.)

    L:F

Slim, mimeographed newsletter containing mainly organisational
reports, and campaigning, among other things, for an equal moral

standard and against the Federal divorce bill.

214. SPEAKING OF WOMEN   1951-1958
    Tl:Speaking of women:international news dedicated to women of
    intelligence and vision
    Ed. Edith Hooper May
    Irregular (27 issues)
    Motto:"The bird of the spirit of humanity cannot fly on only
    one wing (Vivekananda)"
    C BY:item 228
    L:BM;PP 1126aha, F (incomplete)
Internationalist feminism with a slight "mystical" tendency;
included some anti-vivisection material. Mainly fairly substantial
articles, together with some reports of women's achievements. See
also Hodge, 1984.

215. CALLING ALL WOMEN   1951-1977
    Tl:Calling all women:newsletter of the Suffragette Fellowship
    Annual;irregular
    L:BM, F
"Survivors' club" newsletter; mainly information about
ex-suffragettes. The last issue contains a report of the
demolition of the "suffragette wing" of Holloway Prison, in which
the Suffragette Fellowship organiser, Enid Goulden-Bach, was
invited to participate.

216. WOMAN'S ANGLE   1952-1963
    Tl:Woman's angle newsletter:featuring items of interest and
    information for all members of the Women's and Girls'
    Sections of the A.E.U.
    T2:Woman's angle
    Monthly;August 1952-September 1963
    C BY:The way:for women and youth (not listed)
    L:BM;PP 7611ig
Printed magazine of the Amalgamated Union of Engineering Workers
for and by women in the engineering trades; fairly strong "Labour"
feminism, articles, letters, organisational news, etc., plus a
little fashion and household hints. Later issues were increasingly
dominated by the union hierarchy. Its successor was much more of a
general interest paper, with much more exhortation from the top,
and articles on sport, entertainment, fashion "and other items of
interest to women and young people".

217. PEACE AND FREEDOM   1952-c.
    T1:Peace and freedom/Women's International League for Peace
    and Freedom
    Bi-monthly;September/October 1952-c.
    C:item 132
    L:BM;PP 3611mhd, F (incomplete)
Organisational information; news of peace movements, CND, etc..

218. BRITISH FEDERATION OF BUSINESS AND PROFESSIONAL WOMEN   1952-
    1967
    T1:British Federation of Business and Professional Women:
    newsletter
    Quarterly;irregular;October 1952-Summer 1967 (n.i.c.)
    C:item 194
    L:BM;PP 1103, F (incomplete)
Mimeographed, thin organisational bulletin with occasional
contributions of general feminist interest.

219. EAST AFRICA WOMEN'S LEAGUE   1953-1956
    T1:East Africa Women's League:newsletter
    T2:East Africa Women's League:news bulletin
    Nairobi, Kenya?
    Monthly;irregular;January 1953-June 1956 (n.i.c.)
    L:F
The format of the newsletter was literally that of a letter, i.e.
printed on an aerogramme, which was then presumably mailed to
subscribers. Mainly concerned with European women facing Mau Mau
and related events.

220. UNITED ASSOCIATIONS OF WOMEN   1953-1973
    T1:United Associations of Women news sheet
    Eds. Vivienne Newson, E. Sims
    Sydney, Australia
    10 issues a year;November(?) 1953-July 1973 (n.i.c.)
    L:F
Thin, mimeographed organisational bulletin with some general
feminism.

221. WOMEN CLEANERS' JOURNAL   1953-1958
    T1:Women cleaners' journal:the Civil Service Union
    Publication for Non-industrial Women Cleaners in Government
    Service

Bi-monthly;October/December 1953-March 1958
    L:TUC
Concerned with pay and conditions.

222. INTERNATIONAL FEDERATION OF UNIVERSITY WOMEN   1953-c.
    T1:International Federation of University Women:newsletter
    Quarterly;October 1953-c.
    L:F
Self-explanatory.

223. AFRICAN WOMEN   1954-1963
    T1:African women:issues by the Department of Education in
    Tropical Areas, University of London Institute of Education
    Twice yearly;December 1954-June 1963
    C BY:item 236
    L:F
Informative articles and reports (mainly unsigned) on the
education and general situation of women in African countries.

224. SOCIETY FOR THE MINISTRY OF WOMEN IN THE CHURCH   1954-c.
    T1:S.E.M.C. newsletter
    T2:Society for the Ministry of Women in the Church:newsletter
    Irregular (59 issues by September 1984)
    L:F
Begins mimeographed, but later issues offset. News of (mainly
Anglican) campaigns for the ordination of women. S.E.M.C. stood
for: The Society for the Equal Ministry of Men and Women in the
Church.

225. BLACK SASH   1956-c.
    T1:The black sash:die swart serp
    T2:Sash
    Cape Town, South Africa
    Quarterly;January 1956-c.
    L:F (from 1961)
Independent organisation of (mainly) white women campaigning
against apartheid; articles and news of the South African
situation. Occasional articles in Afrikaans in earlier issues. The
organisation was originally called the Women's Defence of the
Constitution League; the black sash is a sign of mourning for the
original constitution of the Union of South Africa. For
information on the origins of the movement, see Rogers, 1956.

226. WOMEN ON THE MARCH   1957-c.
     Tl:Women on the march:issued by the Women's Department of
     All-India Congress Committee
     New Delhi, India
     Monthly;January 1957-c.
     L:F (incomplete)
General political news and articles from Congress Party viewpoint,
with some mild feminism; strongly pro-Indira Gandhi.

227. EQUALITY   1957-1977
     Tl:Equality:for equal status, opportunity and reward between
     men and women/New South Wales League of Women Voters
     Sydney, Australia
     Monthly;bi-monthly;August 1957-December 1977
     L:F (incomplete)
Thin, mimeographed, strongly feminist.

228. WOMEN SPEAKING   1958-1982
     Tl:Women speaking
     Eds. Edith Hooper May, C. Esther Hodge
     Quarterly;October 1958-October/December 1982
     C:item 214
     L:BM; 5109a, F (incomplete), Flic (incomplete)
Articles on a wide range of feminist issues, from a variety of
contributors (e.g. Vera Brittain, Sophie H. Drinker, Roxane
Arnold, Vera Douie, Sybil Cookson, Hazel Hunkins Hallinan, Sheila
Rowbotham). Topics covered included work, religion, education,
peace, development, etc.. A strangely neglected magazine (see
Hodge, 1984).

229. BRITISH FEDERATION OF UNIVERSITY WOMEN   1959-c.
     Tl:British Federation of University Women:newsletter
     Annual;twice yearly;January 1959-c.
     L:F
Self-explanatory.

230. CRUSE   1961-c.
     Tl:Cruse Club chronicle
     T2:Cruse chronicle:monthly newsletter of the national
     organisation for the widowed and their children
     Monthly;February 1961-c.
     L:BM, F

For widows (and widowers, to a lesser extent); not perceptibly
feminist.

231. PRESSWOMAN 1961-1962
    Tl:Presswoman/Women's Press Club of London Ltd.
    Monthly;December 1961(?)-February 1962 (n.i.c.)
    L:BM;PP 7617co
Chatty, social: wine and cheese, bridge, antiques, etc..

232. ALL PAKISTAN WOMEN'S ASSOCIATION 1961-1968
    Tl:All Pakistan Women's Association newsletter
    Karachi, Pakistan
    Quarterly;November(?) 1961-October 1968 (n.i.c.)
    L:F
Semi-official governmental body; organisational news, family law,
women's rights in a Muslim context.

233. CALL TO WOMEN 1962-c.
    Tl:Call to women:Liaison Committee for Women's Peace Groups
    Monthly;quarterly;September 1962-c.
    L:BM, F, Flic (incomplete)
At first printed, later photoset from typescript; peace movements,
CND, etc..

234. COMMONWEALTH COUNTRIES LEAGUE 1963-c.
    Tl:British Commonwealth League newsletter
    T2:Commonwealth Countries League newsletter
    Quarterly;April 1963-c.
    L:F
Mimeographed, with printed cover. General news of women in the
Commonwealth; contributors have included Margery Corbett-Ashby and
Alice Hemming.

235. B.C. VOICE 1963-c.
    Tl:B.C. voice/British Columbia Voice of Women
    Ed. Deeno Birmingham
    Nanaimo, British Columbia, Canada
    F.n.k.;1963(?)-c.
    L:not found
Not seen. Appears in Ulrich, 1982.

236. WOMEN TODAY   1963-1965
      T1:Women today:a journal for women in changing societies
      Twice yearly;December 1963-December 1965 (n.i.c.)
      C:item 222
      L:F
As item 222, but included developing countries outside Africa.

237. ARENA THREE   1964-1973
      T1:Arena Three
      Pub. Esme Langley & Company Ltd, BCM/Seahorse
      1969 editorial team included Esme Langley, Lorna Gulston and
      Emma Stone
      Monthly;irregular;January 1964-1973
      C BY:items 293, 315
      L:Flic (incomplete)
Printed magazine in variable format. Was among the first in Europe
to have been "written by and for homosexual women". After the
split from Arena Three of the future editors of Sappho (item 293),
the magazine was produced in rotation by different groups
throughout the country. It contributed to the establishing of
women's social groups and to the founding of the Minorities
Research Trust. Attempted to look at the national and
international scene. Fiction, poetry, book reviews.

238. NATIONAL NEWSLETTER   1965-c.
      T1:Newsletter:A meeting point for the lively minded woman
      T2:National Newsletter:A meeting point for the lively minded
      woman
      Various eds., including Lesley Moreland (1970), Jeannine
      Bolingstroke (1974), Hazel Bell (1976), Sue Jones
      Pub. National Housewives Register National Group (Stourbridge,
      Worcestershire)
      Potters Bar, Hatfield, etc. Herts;Plymouth
      Twice yearly
      L:F, Flic (both incomplete)
Internal newsletter. Most members are married, tied to the house
by young children and have followed some kind of career before
marriage (see October 1970 issue). The Housewives Register is
active in some 30 countries. Its declared aim is to give women an
opportunity of regaining their self-confidence and identity. The

newsletter reports the activities of N.H.R. local groups across
the United Kingdom. Contents are not restricted to N.H.R. affairs
and domestic topics but have a broader scope. Book reviews.
Moderate feminism. Issue n°36, 1984, claims a circulation of
28,500 copies. See also item 519.

239. ALRA NEWSLETTER 1965-1974
     Tl:ALRA newsletter
     Ed. and pub. ALRA
     Occasional;1965(?)-1974(?)
     C BY:item 502
     L:F (incomplete)
Organisational newsletter of the Abortion Law Reform Association
founded in 1936 by a group of radical women. Was the major
pressure group behind the 1967 Abortion Act.

240. STANDING CONFERENCES OF WOMEN'S ORGANISATIONS 1966-1980
     Tl:News Letter of the Standing Conferences of Women's
     Organisations
     T2:Newsletter of Women's Forum and the Standing Conferences
     of Women's Organisations
     Ed. Helen Wittick
     Crawley, West Sussex
     Quarterly?;1966(?)-Autumn 1980
     L:F (incomplete)
Thin. Organisational news. This was a co-ordinating committee of
women's voluntary organisations largely concerned with social
welfare.

241. SCOPE 1967-1971
     Tl:Scope:magazine of the Women's Gas Federation and Young
     Homemakers
     Ed. Barbara Sim
     Quarterly;Spring 1967-Winter 1971 (n.i.c.)
     C:item 203
     L:F, Flic (both incomplete)
Straight continuation of its predecessors. News of the Federation,
features, plus fashion, cooking, shopping, book reviews, etc.. No
perceptible feminism.

242. WOMEN IN THE WORK FORCE 1967-1970
     Tl:Women in the work force

Ed. Women's Bureau of the Department of Labour and National
Service
Melbourne, Victoria, Australia
Irregular (9 issues);July 1967-October 1970 (n.i.c.)
L:F (incomplete)
Not a genuine newsletter. Research findings, articles, statistical
data dealing with various aspects of women's employment. Series
designed for "those involved in personnel management, employer and
employee organisations, . . .education and training officers . . .
research workers . . .". Moderate feminism.

243. JEWISH WOMAN'S REVIEW 1967-1978
T1:The Jewish woman's review
Pub. editorial board of the Federation of Women Zionists
Monthly;bi-monthly;February 1967(?)-January 1978 (n.i.c.)
L:F (incomplete)
Organisational news and general articles. No obvious feminism.
See also item 364.

244. SHREW 1968-1978
T1:Harpies Bizarre
T2:Bird
T3:Shrew
Ed. various collectives
Pub. Women's Liberation Workshop
Monthly;irregular;1968-Summer 1978
L:F, Flic (both incomplete)
The first magazine to come out of the Women's Liberation Movement
in Britain. Variable format including tabloid newspaper and
printed A4. Circulation under 3,000 copies. "Designed to break
down the isolation between women by discussing the ideas and aims
of the Women's Liberation Movement". Originally produced in
rotation by existing groups within the London Women's Liberation
Workshop (the Children's Books Group, the Tufnell Park Group, the
Cleaners' Collective, the Notting Hill Group, the Belsize Lane
Group to name but a few out of some forty groups at one time). To
some extent, Shrew reflected their preoccupations. Due to changes
in the structure of the Movement, the Workshop ceased to represent
the federation of women's groups in London and Shrew ceased being
the workshop paper. From 1973 onwards, occasional thematic issues
only: autumn 1974 - Marriage Shrew; autumn 1976 - Shrew; spring
1977 - Goddess Shrew; summer 1978 - Shrew:Feminism and Non-violence.

245. FAWCETT SOCIETY NEWS ITEMS   1969-c.
     Tl:Fawcett Society News Items
     Ed. Nina Popplewell, Catherine Denis, Pauline Catterall
     Pub. Fawcett Society
     Monthly;1969-c.
     L:F (incomplete)
Society news, courses, book lists, short articles.

246. NEW FEMINIST   1969-1973
     Tl:The new feminist
     Ed. Joan Johnson
     Editorial board in 1970:Maryon Kantaroff, Bonnie Kreps, Joan
     Lawler, Julia Masters
     Toronto, Ontario, Canada
     Monthly;1969-1973(?)
     L:F, Flic (both one issue only v.1, n°5, March 1970)
A4 duplicated publication including calendar of events
of interest to women in the Toronto area but also film and
book reviews, essays, articles and reports. "The total
society is based on discrimination of sex roles, and the
total society must be changed . . . We are totally, radically,
opposed to a society in which sexuality is destiny . . . We
are radical feminists" (March 1970). The board refuses to
associate with any other left or radical movement. Latest
mention seen occurs in item 294 (v.2, February 1973).

247. PEDESTAL   1969-1974
     Tl:The Pedestal:a Women's Liberation Newspaper
     Ed. Vancouver Women's Caucus.
     Vancouver, British Columbia, Canada
     Monthly;1969-February 1974
     C BY:item 353
     L:Flic (1 issue only)
A tabloid publication.

248. SOCIALIST WOMAN   1969-1972
     Tl:Socialist Woman
     Ed. Nottingham Socialist Women's Committee including
     A. Black, A. Torode, A. Gorton, J. O'Brien
     Nottingham (from May/June 1970 printed in London)

Bi-monthly;February 1969-1972 (n.i.c.)

　　　L:F, Flic (both incomplete)

The editorial board claimed to be independent, non-partisan and
willing to print material from all socialist parties and groups
and not only from the International Marxist Group. It denied any
connection with item 270. Its motto: "United we stand, divided we
fall". Thin printed publication with trade union and women's
liberation groups news. Letters, cartoons, photos.

249. WOMEN'S LIBERATION WORKSHOP NEWSLETTER 1969-1976

　　　T1:Women's Liberation Workshop Newsletter

　　　T2:Women's Liberation Workshop Newsheet

　　　T3:Women's Liberation Workshop Newsletter:W.I.N.S.

　　　Ed. London Women's Liberation Workshop

　　　Weekly

　　　C BY:item 493

　　　L:F, Flic (both incomplete)

Originally a very thin publication put together by the London
Women's Liberation Workshop which acted as a co-ordinator for
London Women's Liberation groups. When due to the growth of the
Movement, the Workshop was no longer representative of all women's
groups, it dissolved. A collective operating from A Woman's Place
went on publishing the newsletter. See item 492 for details on
contents and policy.

250. WOMEN'S LIBERATION 1970-1975

　　　T1:Women's liberation

　　　T2:Women's liberation:journal of the Women's Liberation Front

　　　F.n.k.;1970-1975(?)

　　　L:F, Flic (both 2 issues only)

Originally published by the Women's Equal Rights Campaign and the
Women's Liberation Front. Then became the journal of the Women's
Liberation Front. Parallels women's liberation with people's
liberation struggles in Vietnam.

251. WOMEN'S BULLETIN 1970

　　　T1:Women's bulletin

　　　Ed. and pub. International Socialist Women

　　　Monthly?

　　　C BY:item 267

　　　L:Flic (n°4 June 1970 only)

Self-explanatory. See items 267, 290, 488.

252. ENOUGH   1970-1973

> T1:Enough (or not enough?)
>
> T2:Enough:journal of the Bristol Women's Liberation group
>
> Editorial board included:Marilyn Porter, Sarah Braun, Monica
> Sjoo, Pat Van Twest, Beverly Skinner, Ellen Mallos, Janet
> Parham, et al
>
> Bristol
>
> Irregular;February 1970-1973
>
> L:F, Flic (both incomplete)
>
> M:Harvester

Interesting publication printed in variable format including A3
and A4. Contents were not restricted to matters of local interest
but covered a wide range of feminist issues: abortion, education,
etc.. In an issue focusing on "the father-centred family: refuge
or prison?" the editorial group - Ellen Mallos, Janet Parham, Pat
Van Twest and Monica Sjoo - stated "We are not anti-men! . . . But
we are aware of how men and women alike are trapped by the
conventional view of women (and hence the family) held in our
society." Enough also conveyed women's feelings and experiences
through interviews, poetry, fiction and cartoons. See Lipshitz,
1977, pp.19-20. Not to be confused with item 354.

253. WOMEN'S STRUGGLE   1970-1977

> T1:Women's struggle:Bulletin of the Women's National
> Co-ordinating Committee
>
> T2:Women's struggle:Journal of the Women's National
> Co-Ordinating Committee
>
> Ed. Maysel Bar
>
> Hemel Hempstead, Hertfordshire
>
> Quarterly;September 1970-1977(?)
>
> L:F, Flic (both incomplete)
>
> M:Harvester

A4 duplicated journal of about 30 pages. Latest issue seen: V.3,
n°3, 1973, yet Lipshitz, 1977 (p.25) and Noyce, 1979 (p. 332)
mention it as continuing. The Women's National Co-ordinating
Committee was set up at the Ruskin Conference in Oxford on 27
February-1 March 1970. The women who attended the conference
represented a wide variety of views and opinions on women's
oppression and the women's movement. They tried to resolve the
problem of the conflict between the need for unity in action and
the divergence of opinion about the organisation and the aims of
the women's movement. A resolution passed at the end of the

conference established the Committee, it was "to coordinate
actions, ideas and news from all the women's groups". The third
Term of Reference adopted at Sheffield on 27 June 1970 stated its
task was: "to disseminate information to promote better
understanding of the viewpoints of various groups and their
activities and facilitate towards unity and broadening of the
women's liberation struggle". The W.N.C.C. was the first central
structure of the British Women's Liberation Movement. It
functioned as a federation but had no decision-making power. Each
affiliated group sent two voting delegates who composed the
Committee. The latter was to try and draw the diverse groups into
common action but could not dictate anything to them. All groups
could submit contributions to be printed unaltered in the journal.
Interesting reports on the early discussions on the aims of the
WLM were published. The Committee failed to fulfil its function of
co-ordinator. It was taken over by the Union of Women's
Liberation. Gradually groups ceased affiliating and the Committee
was dissolved. Issue n°2 was produced by the Women's Liberation
Front. Not to be confused with item 365.

254. CONTINUUM 1970-1977
    Tl:Continuum:trends, patterns, issues in the continuing
    education of women
    Pub. Department of Adult Education, Ontario Institute for
    Studies in Education (O.I.S.E.);from 1973, Canadian
    Association For Adult Education
    Toronto, Ontario, Canada
    Monthly;October 1970-1977(?)
    L:F (incomplete)
A4 research journal. Newspaper clippings and information focusing
on opportunities for the continuing education of women. Latest
mention found occurs in item 294 (v.6, n°1, February 1977).

255. ANVIL 1970
    Tl:Anvil
    Ed. and pub. Wivenhoe Women's Liberation Group
    Wivenhoe, Essex (printed Colchester)
    F.n.k.;ca 1970
    L:F, Flic (both issue 2 only, undated)
The group wanted "more women to see that they have much more
potential than society allows them to realise . . . In
relationships with men, it is all too often important that we

71

smile invitingly without really meaning it, and give in in
arguments, just for the sake of calming him down . . . Many of us
know that to act like this is humiliating and dishonest". Issue 2
had 16 pages. Though local, the publication carried general
features on women and advertising, equal pay, working in a small
factory, birth control, etc..

256. BULLETIN OF THE WIS WOMEN'S CAUCUS 1970
      Tl:Bulletin of the WIS Women's Caucus
      Pub. Women International Socialists
      Monthly?;1970(?)-?
      L:Flic
Only one issue seen May 1970. See also item 290.

257. BUSINESS AND PROFESSIONAL WOMAN 1970-c.
      Tl:Business and professional woman
      Ed. and pub. (1)National Federation of Business and
      Professional Women's Clubs of Great Britain and Northern
      Ireland;(2)United Kingdom Federation of Business and
      Professional Women (from Spring 1977)
      L:F (incomplete)
Self-explanatory. No organisational links with items 194 and 218.

258. MOTHERS IN ACTION NEWSLETTER 1970-1971
      Tl:Mothers in action newsletter
      F.n.k.;1970(?)-1971(?)
      C BY:item 306?
      L:not found
Not seen. Mentioned in Noyce, 1979, p.193, as a possible
predecessor to item 306.

259. THIS PAPER IS FOR WOMEN 1970-?
      Tl:This paper is for women
      F.n.k.;1970(?)-?
      L:not found
Not seen. Listed in Noyce, 1979, p.302. A4 newsletter documenting
"the sexist nature of the British Broadcasting Corporation.
Connected with Urinal?" (Not listed: Underground paper in the BBC,
see Noyce, 1979, p. 306.)

260. WOMEN UNITE 1970-1976
      Tl:Women unite

Ed. and pub. Oxford Women's Action Group including Sian
Doddderidge and Hilary Wainwright
Oxford
Irregular;1970(?)-1976(?)
C BY:item 535?
L:Flic (1 undated issue;1970?)
Local paper. Circulation: 1,000 (Noyce, 1979, p.332)

261. WOMEN'S LIBERATION INFORMATION SERVICE NEWSLETTER 1970-1971
Tl:Women's Liberation Information Service Newsletter
Leamington, Warwickshire
Monthly?;1970(?)-1971(?)
L:F (1 issue only;n°11, 20 September 1971)
Two page A4 newsletter.

262. WOMEN'S NATIONAL CANCER CONTROL CAMPAIGN NEWSLETTER 1970-?
Tl:Women's National Cancer Control Campaign Newsletter
Monthly;March 1970(?)-?
L:F (1 issue only)
The campaign was founded by Mrs Joyce Butler M.P.. March 1970
issue was a well produced 16 page newsletter carrying campaign
news, articles on health education and fatherless families.
Contributors included men. In spite of the feminist symbols on the
cover, only moderate feminism.

263. CLEANERS' VOICE 1971
Tl:The cleaners' voice
Ed. and pub. Cleaners' Action Group
L:Flic (1 undated issue only)
A two page newsletter devoted to the women night cleaners' strike
and claiming a circulation of 2,000 copies.

264. ME JANE 1971-c.
Tl:Me Jane
Syndney, New South Wales, Australia
Monthly;irregular;1971-c.
L:Flic (2 issues only)
Radical feminist newspaper. News, features plus book, film and
play reviews.

265. OBAA SIMA 1971-c.
Tl:Obaa Sima:ideal woman

Ed. Kate Abbam
Accra, Ghana
Bi-monthly
L:not found
Not seen. Listed in Gallagher, 1981 (p.180) and in Ulrich, 1982.
"The magazine for the woman who looks ahead. Text in English.
Circulation: 10,000 copies". Item 294 (v.7, n°4, 1978, p.62),
describes it as "a general women's bi-monthly with a pronounced
feminist stance on some issues".

266. WOMEN'S LIBERATION UNION NEWSLETTER 1971-1973
    T1:Union of Women For Liberation
    T2:Women's Liberation Union Newsletter
    Bi-monthly?;1971-April/May 1973 (n.i.c.)
    L:Flic (v.3,n°2, April/May 1973)
    M:Harvester
Published by a Maoist group based in Hertfordshire, all the
newsletters end with "Women,unite to fight for your own
liberation! Women, unite to fight with all other workers and
oppressed people for an end to domestic slavery and an end to all
exploitation of man by man". The group took on capitalists,
imperialists, Trotskyists, Revisionists and the Women's Liberation
Movement. "They asserted that no other group values Marxism or had
the correct line on it and thus on the way to struggle for
discussion of ways to achieve women's liberation", see Lipshitz,
1977, pp.24-5. See also item 253.

267. WOMEN'S NEWSLETTER 1971
    T1:Women's Newsletter:An International Socialist pamphlet
    Irregular
    C:item 251
    C BY:item 290
    L:F (n°3, April 1971 only), Flic (issues 4 to 6, 1971 only)
A4 newsletter "started by women who are also active in the WLM.
Our aims are to co-ordinate activities and to maintain discussion
on the theoretical aspects of Women's Liberation both within I.S.
and within the various WL groups that we belong to" (n°3).
Contributors included Margaret Renn.

268. WOMEN'S VOICE 1971-?
    T1:Women's voice
    Coventry, Warwickshire

74

F.n.k.;1971-?

    L:F, Flic (both 1 issue only)

"A magazine solely produced by women for women". It was the organ
of the "Women's Total Freedom Movement", originally called "The
Committee for Civil Rights for Women and Children of Broken
Families", and working in the interest of the divorced, single and
widows. The group changed its name when it decided to broaden its
scope and fight against the whole range of injustices and
prejudices towards all women in society and to dedicate itself to
"the equality of women of the working class throughout the world".
"There is no party in or out of power that represents women or
intends to make any sweeping changes to rectify women's double
task, slavery." Condemning both the Labour and Conservative
parties, the group only believes in the power of a National
Women's Movement. Not to be confused with items 250 and 488.

269. WOMEN'S NEWSPAPER 1971

    T1:Women's newspaper

    3 issues only;6 March/28 March/3 June 1971

    L:F, Flic

Produced by a women's collective distributed through women's
groups, the contents of this short-lived eight page tabloid were
broad and interesting. National and international news, articles
dealing with lesbians, Black women, "Women on the Buses", etc.,
plus reviews.

270. SOCIALIST WOMAN 1971-1978

    T1:Socialist Woman:National paper of the Socialist Woman
    Groups

    T2:Socialist Woman:A Journal of the International Marxist
    Group

    Editorial board included Margaret Coulson, Linda Fryd,
    Joanna Griffiths, Leonora Lloyd, Pat Masters, Linda Smith,
    Felicity Trodd, Judith White, Carl Gardiner, Geoff Sheridan,
    et al

    4 to 6 issues per year;March/April 1971-Spring 1978 (n.i.c.)

    L:F, Flic, BM;P 703/213 (all incomplete)

    M:Bell & Howard, Wooster, Ohio

Printed in variable format and originally put together by women
from Oxford, Manchester, Lancaster, Glasgow and London. The paper
was set up following the emergence of Socialist Woman Groups in
many parts of the country. It presented itself as the continuation

of item 248 but the editorial group of the latter denied any
connection. Though aimed at women active both in the Women's
Liberation Movement and in the Left, it was more socialist than
feminist. "Women's liberation is a political question. Our
oppression in rooted in the economic, social and political system,
and until the system is overthrown, our liberation is impossible"
(March/April 1971, p.2). Originally aligned but independent from
the International Marxist Group, it was taken over by the IMG.
There were then some men on the editorial board. The paper carried
information on the activities and policies of the Women's
Liberation Movement, articles on women's issues such as sexism, a
women's right to control their own body. Yet it mainly expanded on
the campaign for equal pay and equal work against low pay, the
Working Women's Charter, social and industrial struggles e.g. the
night cleaners' strike and on the anti-working class policies of
government - public spending cuts and its consequences e.g.
closures of hospitals, etc.. It also campaigned against racism and
national chauvinism and publicised people's liberation struggles
in Vietnam, Ireland etc.. It also included news, letters and book
reviews.

271. WOMEN NOW   1971-1975
     Tl:Women now
     Ed. and pub. Nottingham Women's Liberation Group
     Nottingham
     Irregular;March/April 1971-September 1975 (n.i.c.)
     L:F, Flic, BM;P 523/194 (all incomplete)
National A4 journal. "We want our journal to survive because we
try to make it speak to all women, not just to women in the
movement. The majority of women misunderstand our aims, which are
so often misrepresented" (v.1, n°6, 1974, p.(2)). Not to be
confused with item 405 and with Women Now, USA (not listed).

272. SCARLET WOMAN 1971
     Tl:Scarlet woman
     Pub. York University
     York
     One issue only;Spring Term 1971
     L:F
A4 newsletter of the York Women's Liberation Group. The single
issue found included features of local interest such as one about
York Mothers' Alone group but also gave coverage to British and

International matters: one article was devoted to the Women Night
Cleaners' strike, another to the Women's Liberation Movement in
France. Not to be confused with items 426 and 451.

273. WOMEN ARE PEOPLE 1971-?
    Tl:Women are people
    Cambridge
    Quarterly;April 1971-?
    L:Flic (n°1 only issue found)
Duplicated local newsletter of some twenty pages written by
members of the organisation Women Are People, for people in and
around Cambridge. Women Are People was a Cambridge Women's
Liberation group. Its members aimed "to improve the status of
women in . . . society and to break down the traditional notions
regarding male and female 'roles'". They believed that "women's
liberation primarily involves changes in every one's personal
attitudes towards the sexes" and that "women's liberation is
men's liberation too". Many of their members were men. They said
the magazine would contain organisational news, a summary of
events on a local, national and international level, legal and
financial articles but with an emphasis on local matter. No trace
of later issues.

274. WOMEN'S NATIONAL COMMISSION 1971-c.
    Tl:Women's National Commission:quarterly bulletin
    Ed. Dr Grace Thornton
    Pub. Women's National Commission, Government Office
    Quarterly;twice yearly;April 1971(?)-c.
    L:F, Flic (both incomplete)
Free, official bulletin mainly reporting on the work of the
Commission, an umbrella group of some 50 member organisations
advising the government on issues concerning women. See also item
443.

275. NEWS AND VIEWS OF THE JOSEPHINE BUTLER SOCIETY 1971-c.
    Tl:Josephine Butler Society newsletter
    T2:News and views of the Josephine Butler Society
    Pub. Josephine Butler Society, formerly the Association for
    Moral and Social Hygiene
    Hatfield, Hertfordshire
    Annual;irregular;October(?) 1971-October 1973 (n.i.c.);August
    1977-c.

```
C:item 13
L:F
```

The Josephine Butler Society "works for the removal of sex discrimination from the laws relating to prostitution and the enforcement of the laws designed to prevent its exploitation". Its A4 internal newsletter mainly contains organisational news. Due to the Society's extreme financial distress, its publication was interrupted for several years. It was relaunched in August 1977 with Margaret Schwarz as editor.

276. WOMEN TOGETHER 1971-?
```
Tl:Women together
Belfast
Monthly?;December 1971-?
L:BM;P 803/373 (incomplete)
```
News sheet of Belfast Women's Liberation Group. Not to be confused with items 393 and 342.

277. LESBIANS COME TOGETHER ca 1971
```
Tl:Lesbians come together
Only one issue found
L:F
```
A4 printed paper produced by gay women after the split from the male-dominated publication of the Gay Liberation Front Come Together. Seems to have been a one-off publication.

278. MISPRINT 1971-1974
```
Tl:Misprint
Pub. Working Women's Charter Campaign
Monthly?;1971(?)-1974 (n.i.c.)
L:not found
```
Not seen. Item 297 (n°28, October 1974, p.32) mentions issue 27. No other trace found. Not to be confused with item 565. See also item 453.

279. MAJORITY REPORT 1971-1976
```
Tl:Majority report
Jamaica
Monthly
L:not found
```
Not seen. The list of holdings of Bath Feminist Archive mentions one issue: v.6, n°9, September 4-17, 1976.

280. N.O.W.   1971-1975
    Tl:N.O.W.
    Pub. Nigerian Organisation of Women
    Nigeria
    Quarterly;1971(?)-1975(?)
    L:F (October 1975, series 4, n°4 only)
Thin publication printing organisational news and features
highlighting the problems Nigerian students face abroad.

281. BROADSHEET 1972-c.
    Tl:Broadsheet:the magazine for women who are learning to be
    liberated
    T2:Broadsheet:Mews Zealand's feminist magazine
    Ed. Sandra Coney
    Auckland, New Zealand
    10 issues per year
    L:F, Flic (both incomplete)
Substantial, lively, printed magazine. "Broadsheet is a radical
feminist magazine which consciously strives to be anti-racist and
to incorporate the views of indigenous women. The main focus is
on New Zealand women and events, with some coverage of Pacific
concerns and issues facing women and feminists everywhere".
Contents include lists of feminist contacts, letters, news,
non-academic in-depth articles as well as fiction, poetry, book
reviews.

282. LIBERATION 1972-c.
    Tl:Liberation
    Pub. Adelaide Women's Liberation Movement
    Adelaide, South Australia
    Quarterly
    L:not found
Not seen. Mentioned in Ulrich's, 1982. Book reviews. Circulation:
300 copies.

283. OXFORD STRUMPET 1972-?
    Tl:Oxford strumpet
    Oxford
    Weekly
    L:F (1 issue only n°35, December 1972)
The only issue seen was a twelve page printed local newsletter
produced by women within the Women's Liberation Movement. It

contained not only listings of interest to local women but also features of more general feminism.

284. RED RAG 1972-1980
    Tl:Red Rag
    Irregular;1972-n°13, August 1980
    L:F, Flic
    M:Harvester

A4 printed journal produced by "a Marxist collective in the Women's Liberation Movement" (n°2, p.1). The collective composed of revolutionary and Marxist feminists included among others: Sally Alexander, Bea Campbell, Val Charlton, Sue Cowley, Rosalind Delmar, Alison Fell, Mandy Merck, Sue O'Sullivan, Ruth Petrie, Jean Radford, Sheila Rowbotham, Michelene Wandor, Elizabeth Wilson. In issue 2, Red Rag was described as "a journal that challenges whatever and whoever demeans women, and stands in the way of their struggle". The collective was "committed to the destruction of capitalism, and the struggle of the working class for liberation from a dehumanizing and divisive society" (n°2). It aimed "to help build an alliance between women liberators and the working class movement" (n°1). It is said that the Women's Movement has not been concerned enough with women's relationships to the trade unions and the working class movement. "The organised labour movement - that is the trade unions, the co-ops and the left political parties - is the decisive force in this country for social progress and for socialism. Its wholehearted and active support is essential for the success of the women's liberation movement" (n°1). Yet though the labour movement has accepted the principles of women's rights, it has not done much for women. "Women's liberation will only be achieved by a movement autonomous from the male-dominated unions and left political parties. What is important is not to reject the unions, but to inject into them persistent and comprehensive demands for change" (n°2). Red Rag discussed the political practices of left groups and their strategies within the Women's Liberation Movement. It published well documented debates on feminist theory and politics. Issue 2 reproduced a summary of Selma James's pamphlet "Women, the Unions and Work" which advocated "wages for housework". It also printed several articles opposing the demand. Red Rag consisted of fairly long articles, letters, poems, reviews, photographs and drawings. With issue 11, Autumn 1976, the collective "decided to take Red Rag into a single-and-related format" to explore Marxist feminism

in depth, by concentrating each issue on a theme. Some of the
issues tackled were the nature of the current women's movement,
sexuality and women and work. Circulation varied from 3-4,000
copies per issue.

285. REFRACTORY GIRL 1972-c.
     Tl:Refractory girl:A women's studies journal
     T2:Refractory girl:A journal of radical feminist thought
     T3:Refractory girl:A feminist journal
     Ed. and pub. Refractory Girl Collective
     Sydney, New South Wales, Australia
     Quarterly
     L:F (1 issue only), Flic (incomplete)
Substantial journal claiming a circulation of over 5,000 copies
(n°6, Autumn 1974). Some issues were commissioned: issue 6 was
produced by the Liberaction group. Refractory Girl carries both
debates and issues raised by the women's movement and scholarly
work. It focuses on sex roles and the different ways in which
patriarchy flourishes everywhere. It gives strong coverage of
women's history and women's writings. Most issues include a
resource guide, poetry and reviews.

286. WAGES FOR HOUSEWORK 1972-c.
     Tl:Wages for housework:international campaign bulletin
     T2:Wages for housework:international campaign journal
     Ed. Wilmette Brown
     Bristol (UK) and Brighton (Massachusetts, USA)
     Quarterly?
     L:F (1 issue only)
Thin printed tabloid. Free. Focuses on the campaign both in the
United States and in the United Kingdom. Contributions by
Housewives in Dialogue (England) and Women in Dialogue (USA) and
Wilmette Brown, Linda Butcher, Suzie Fleming, Solveig Francis,
Ruth Hall, Selma James, Judit Kertez, Nina Lopez-Jones (English
Collective of Prostitutes), Jo Pacino and Rona Rothman. See also
items 494 and 355.

287. WOMAN 1972-1980
     Tl:Woman
     Ed. and pub. The Dunedin Collective
     Dunedin, New Zealand
     Fortnightly;1972-1980 (n.i.c.)

L:F (incomplete)

A4 newsletter of about 10 pages. Women's Liberation news, poems.

288. WOMEN'S ELECTORAL LOBBY NEWSLETTER   1972-c.
     Tl:Women's Electoral Lobby newsletter
     Melbourne, Victoria;Sydney, New South Wales, Australia
     Monthly;bi-monthly;1972-c.
     L:Flic (incomplete)

Self-explanatory.

289. WOMEN'S STUDIES   1972-c.
     Tl:Women's studies:An interdisciplinary journal
     Ed. Wendy Martin
     Pub. Gordon and Breach Science Publishers Ltd
     London and New York
     3 issues per year
     L:F, Flic (both incomplete)

Substantial wide ranging academic journal mainly aimed at
scholars. Carries research and theoretical articles, poetry, book
reviews. Publishes special thematic issues.

290. WOMEN'S VOICE   1972-1976
     Tl:Woman's voice
     T2:Women's voice
     Ed. and pub. International Socialist Women
     London;Harlow (Essex)
     Bi-monthly;monthly (35 issues);1972-November/December 1976)
     C:item 267
     C BY:item 488
     L:F, Flic (both incomplete)
     M:Harvester

Printed A4 publication up to issue 10, then newspaper format.
Aimed at working class women "who want to read something that
tries to deal with their real life". Much more Trotskyite than
feminist, the group advocates revolution as the only solution to
overthrow the capitalist and imperialist system deeming reformism
as dangerous. Only socialism can bring about women's liberation.
Women must join trade unions and socialism must be their first
struggle. Women's oppression is part of general oppression, the
group is opposed to an autonomous women's movement. The newspaper
contents focus on class struggle, workers' solidarity, women's
struggles in industry, unemployment, class and sex discrimination

in education and health.

291. COVENTRY CISTERS 1972-?
    Tl:Coventry cisters
    Pub. Coventry International Socialists
    Stoke, Coventry
    Only one issue found;n°l January 1972-?
    L:Flic
A four page publication printed in small format.

292. LIBERTARIAN WOMEN'S NETWORK NEWSHEET 1972-1975
    Tl:Libertarian Women's Network newsheet
    London;Leeds;Oxford;etc.
    Monthly;every six weeks;March 1972-July 1973 (n.i.c.);August
    1975-?
    C BY:item 527?
    L:Flic, F, BM;P 525/118 (all incomplete)
Each issue of this duplicated A4 newsletter was produced by a
different group around the country. Ros Nathan of Leeds
co-ordinated many of the early issues. Predecessor to item 527 -
set up in Dundee? Or was the newsheet revived in August 1975 after
a temporary hiatus?

293. SAPPHO 1972-1981
    Tl:Sappho
    T2:Sappho:Lesbian feminist voice
    Eds. Jackie Forster and Sappho Collective
    Pub. Sappho Publications Ltd
    Monthly;April 1972-v.8,n°9, November 1981
    C:item 237
    L:F (incomplete)
    M:Harvester
Sappho, named after the Greek poet, grew our of item 237, and was
one of the earlier lesbian magazines printed in Europe. It was put
together on a voluntary basis, by the coordinating editor Jackie
Forster and a changing editorial board, many of whom initially
came from the collective of item 237. Produced in A3, then A4
format it never printed more than 1,100 copies (item 297, n°116,
March 1982, p.31). Publication was interrupted because women
ceased reading Sappho and subscriptions shrivelled creating
financial difficulties. Sappho "was no longer, the
only-one-a-month contact with other lesbians" (item 834,n°17, June

1984, pp.30-1). A second reason was that after ten years Jackie
Forster wished to retire and found no successor. When Sappho
started, it was very difficult for lesbians to "come out" to their
family and friends. Sappho aimed "to disperse the isolation of gay
ghettos" (v.2,n°1, April 1973) "and to reach out to others by the
written word in an attempt to bring (lesbians) closer together
through love and understanding in a sometimes hostile world" (v.8,
n°9, 1981); it hoped to help women who felt unable to declare
themselves lesbian. Subscribers received an ads sheet for
penfriends, contacts, accommodation, etc.. Sappho was also
designed "to support all minority groups regardless of politics,
colour or creed who work to counteract oppression" (v.2,n°1, April
1973). It accepted "articles, stories, poems etc. of
non-pornographic content from all those with an intelligent
interest and empathy for homophiles" (ibid.). Contents were aimed
at intellectual middle-class lesbians. They included short
features, news of groups and contact addresses, letters, poems,
fiction, book, film and theatre reviews and a horoscope. Features
focused on the advantages of lesbian relationships, on the
difficulties of finding partners. They reflected the campaigns and
debates Sappho had initiated. Sappho not only organised some of
the first women's discos but also helped start several groups,
among them Action for Lesbian Parents and the Gay Teachers Group.
It pioneered Artificial Insemination by Donor by making
arrangements for lesbians wanting to conceive through AID.

294. CANADIAN NEWSLETTER OF RESEARCH ON WOMEN   1972-1978
     Tl:The Canadian newsletter of research on women:recherches
     sur la femme - bulletin d'information Canadien
     Pub. Department of Sociology, O.I.S.E.
     Editorial Board
     Toronto, Ontario, Canada
     Quarterly;May 1972-1978
     C BY:item 613
     L:F (incomplete)
Solid interdisciplinary research journal. No in-depth features but
abstracts, book reviews, bibliographies and updated lists of
periodicals. Text in English and French.

295. CHILDREN'S BOOKS NEWSLETTER   1972-1974
     Tl:Non-sexist children's books newsletter
     T2:Children's books newsletter

Ed. and pub. Women's Liberation Literature Collective
including Astra Blaug, Camilla Nightingale, Lee Sanders, Sue
Turner
Leeds
Irregular (8 issues);14 May 1972-October 1974 (n.i.c.)
L:F, Flic (both incomplete)
Thin newsletter, the first issue had four pages, the last one seen
eight. Duplicated A4, then foolscap. "The newsletters consist of
reviews of children's books - fiction and non-fiction (including
careers books and sex education books) sent in by people all over
the country. We do not edit any contributions, nor do we stipulate
which books can or can't be reviewed" (Sue Turner in Shrew,
Children's Books issue v.5,n°4, 1974). The collective listed not
only hopeful books but also the ones to be avoided. The reviewers
concentrated on looking for the non sexist/racist/classist
qualities of the content. A few articles on the various issues
raised by children's literature were published. The collective
also aimed "to produce literature and non-fiction for children
which challenges, or at least questions, the stereotyped
male-female roles . . ." (Sue Turner in Noyce, 1979). Not to be
confused with Children's Rights/Kids (November 1971-September
1972), Children's Rights Workshop Newsletter (December 1974-
1978(?)) and Children's Books Bulletin (1979(?)-c.), not listed,
see Noyce, 1979.

296. FOWNES STREET JOURNAL 1972-1973
     T1:Fownes Street journal:women's liberation journal
     Dublin
     Monthly;May 1972-December 1973 (n.i.c.)
     L:Flic (1 issue only found)
Self-explanatory. The undated issue seen was a well produced
twelve page journal. Printed quarto. The Feminist Archive's list
of holdings mentions issue v.2,n°3, December 1973 but this has not
been seen.

297. SPARE RIB 1972-c.
     T1:Spare rib:The new women's magazine
     T2:Spare rib:A news magazine
     T3:Spare rib:A women's magazine
     T4:Spare rib:A women's news magazine
     T5:Spare rib
     T6:Spare rib:A women's liberation magazine

Monthly;July 1972-c.

L:F, Flic, BM;P 523/344

M:Harvester

Spare Rib was started by women who worked in the underground press
as an alternative both to the traditional women's magazine and to
the underground press. It was first produced by a hierarchic
group with two editors Marsha Rowe (from OZ) and Rosie Boycott
(from Frendz). The founding editors stated: "there is the most
urgent need for a magazine that will reach ALL women - that is,
women who are frustrated by the limitations of existing magazines.
Commercial journalese gives unrealistic solutions to problems,
thus increasing loneliness and isolation". Spare Rib was launched
to "put women's liberation on the news stands". After several
economic crises it is now financially viable and is among the
oldest publications of the Movement. Its main assets of success
were its regularity of publication and its professional look. It is
the only women's liberation magazine distributed through
newsagents nationally. Averaging 27,000 copies per issue in 1983,
its circulation is the largest of all. It is also available on
tape. Over the years, Spare Rib altered its style and format, it
also grew from 48 to 56 pages. Articles from men are no longer
accepted. Well known women such as Fay Weldon and Germaine Greer,
ceased writing for Spare Rib. By issue 18, 1973 the magazine was
put together by a collective. Nowadays all the original members
have left. By 1984 over 100 women had worked on the collective.
To name but a few: Rose Ades, Eileen Fairweather, Alison Fell,
Laura Mulvey, Jill Nicholls, Ruthie Petrie, Rosie Parker, Michele
Roberts, Sheila Rowbotham, Amanda Sebestyen, Michele Wandor, Ruth
Wallsgrove. Most of the magazine is written by women outside the
collective. Spare Rib carries many articles of the personal
experience type. For the first two or three years it incorporated
elements to be found in traditional women's magazines such as
recipes, household hints, the agony column, beauty, fashion and a
do-it-yourself section called "Spare Parts". Contents now include
features, poetry, fiction and reviews plus regulars: newshorts,
letters, a shortlist of things to do, see and read and classified
ads. They have always been very broad and eclectic. The areas most
consistently covered have been: health, education, sexuality,
work, the arts. Topics have reflected the development of ideas in
the Women's Liberation Movement. Over the last years Spare Rib has
broadened its coverage of nuclear power, militarism, violence
against women. It has also tried to give wider space to all

oppressed minorities: disabled women, old women and more particularly lesbians and black women. However, it still mainly caters for white middle class women. In its early years, <u>Spare Rib</u> described itself as socialist, nowadays it disclaims any label. Most articles are written from a socialist feminist viewpoint though some radical feminist elements are at times included. However, the magazine being on public sale, the collective has always been reluctant to air debates internal to the Movement. <u>Spare Rib</u> is a very useful resource material for up-to-date information on campaigns, conferences and groups. It is a notice board for feminist communication. Easy to read, more attractive than the other publications of the movement and available regularly on a national scale, it has played an important role in introducing women to feminism. See Fell, 1979; Rowe, 1982; Hemmings, 1982.

298. WOMEN'S COUNCIL 1972-c.
    T1:Council:newsletter of the National Council of Women of Great Britain
    T2:Women's Council:newsletter of the National Council of Women of Great Britain
    Monthly;bi-monthly;irregular (59 issues);September 1972-c.
    C:item 179
    L:F (incomplete)
Organisational news.

299. WOMEN'S ABORTION AND CONTRACEPTION CAMPAIGN NEWSLETTER 1972-1975
    T1:Women's Abortion and Contraception Campaign newsletter
    Various locations
    Bi-monthly?;Autumn 1972-v.4,n°1, Spring 1975 (n.i.c.)
    C BY:item 408?
    L:F, Flic (both incomplete)
A single campaign periodical published in rotation by local groups. Much useful campaign information and exhortation. Reports on groups' activities in the United Kingdom and abroad, articles on abortion and contraception as a right for all women but also material on sterilisation, the I.U.D. and the Church. Not to be confused with item 239, this campaign was started by women involved in the Women's Liberation Movement. Predecessor to item 408?

300. BRISTOL WACC NEWSLETTER 1972-1974
     Tl:Bristol Women's Abortion and Contraception Campaign
     newsletter
     Ed. and pub. Bristol WACC
     F.n.k.;Autumn 1972(?)-June 1974 (n.i.c.)
     L:Flic (2 issues only)
Self-explanatory. See also item 299.

301. EUROPEAN NEWS-SHEET 1972-1974
     Tl:European News-Sheet
     Pub. Women's Group on Public Welfare, National Council of
     Women Committee;thereafter Women's European Committee, NCW
     Irregular (5 issues);October 1972-January/March 1974 (n.i.c.)
     L:F (incomplete)
Covers "meetings, visits and reports of interest to women in
Europe".

302. WOMEN'S LIBERATION REVIEW 1972-1974
     Tl:Women's Liberation Review
     Ed. and pub. Women's Literature Collective including Astra
     Blaug, Lee Sanders Comer, Jenny Stern
     Annual;October 1972-1974 (n.i.c.)
     L:F, Flic, BM;P 521/1616 (all incomplete)
Substantial well produced A5 printed publication. The Women's
Liberation Literature Collective came into being at the National
Women's Liberation Conference in Manchester in March 1972, as a
result of a workshop discussion on Women and Literature. The
material of the first issue mainly came from members of the
collective. The 64 pages of the second issue had material from
other contributors (Angela Hamblin, Chandra Masoliver, Lilian
Mohin, Angela Phillips, to name a few). Poems, photographs,
graphics and also articles from women belonging to writers'
workshops sparked off by the National Conference were brought
together. "We want our writing to be saying our lives and thoughts,
not to be a specialized craft . . . We would like our work here to
encourage other women to write, make journals, set up workshops,
talk about writing, or join in or contribute to the making of the
next Review" (n°2, p.2). Numbers 1 and 2 were the only issues
found. Noyce, 1979, mentions a review of number 3. No trace of
later issues.

303. BIRMINGHAM WOMEN'S LIBERATION NEWSLETTER 1972-c.

    Tl:B'Ham women's liberation news/views

    T2:Birmingham women's liberation newsletter

    T3:Brum women's liberation newsletter

    T4:Birmingam Women's Liberation Newsletter

    Birmingham

    Monthly;bi-monthly;October 1972(?)-Summer 1975;?-1978;

    approximately monthly;January/February 1980-c.

    L:F, Flic (both incomplete)

Local A4 duplicated newsletter for women only produced by an open
collective. Its publication was interrupted several times. Revived
in January 1980 "as an internal newspaper temporarily", the new
editorial collective thought the newsletter should be "an organ
for all women in Birmingham, not just those within the movement".
Its 30 pages or so carry one fairly long feature, plus short
articles, reports on local groups, letters, reviews and a diary
of events. Not to be confused with item 406.

304. WOMEN'S REPORT 1972-1979

    Tl:Women's report

    Wealdstone, Harrow, Middlesex

    Bi-monthly;November 1972-June 1979 (v.7,n°4)

    L:F, Flic, BM;P 525/140

    M:Harvester

National A4 printed magazine averaging twenty pages. Started with
a gift of £200 from the Fawcett Society, it was originally
produced by an editorial collective and published jointly by
Women's Lobby and the Fawcett Society. The magazine soon became
financially self-supporting and its format evolved. At first only
disseminating news, it started commenting on it and printing one
or two feature articles, together with book and film reviews. It
remained a feminist news magazine essentially and advertised
itself as "a factual, non-party political bulletin", aimed at all
women, not focusing on information of interest to women in the
liberation movement only. The group collected and reproduced news
from a variety of sources including national newspapers, the
alternative press, feminist periodicals, press releases from
government and other bodies, readers' letters, etc.. It gathered
into a single publication, information on what was happening to,
for or against women worldwide, news and events not covered in the

national press, and commented on events which, although reported, were of particular relevance to women or were misrepresented. The news items were divided into broad categories such as "Home", "Legal", "Work", "Education", "Image", "Mind and Body". Women's Report included a solid international news section not to be found elsewhere. Its circulation varied from about 1,300 copies in Autumn 1973 (see Noyce, 1979) to anything from 2-3,000 copies (see v.7,n°4, June 1979, p.2). Packed with information, it remains a valuable resource and reference material.

305. WOMEN'S WAY 1972-1973
    Tl:Women's way:feminist news and comment
    Ed. and pub. Women's Liberation Workshop
    Only two issues found;n°1, 4 November 1972;n°2, December
    1972/January 1973
    L:F (1 issue only), Flic (2 issues)
Very thin A4 publication. See also item 249.

306. MOTHERS IN ACTION 1972-1974
    Tl:Mothers in Action
    Ed. and pub. Mothers in Action
    Monthly;December 1972(?)-December 1974 (n.i.c.)
    C:item 258?
    L:F, Flic (both incomplete)
A4 bulletin mainly carrying news and information aimed at members of the Mothers in Action group. See also item 321.

307. EDINBURGH WOMEN'S LIBERATION NEWSLETTER 1972-c.
    Tl:Edinburgh Women's Liberation Newsletter
    Edinburgh
    Monthly;bi-monthly;1972(?)-c.
    L:Flic (a few issues only)
Local women only newsletter produced by an open collective of women. Earliest dated issue found was January 1974 but Isis (n°16, 1980, p.38) says the newsletter has been in existence for eight or nine years. "Aimed at women both inside and outside the Women's Liberation Movement" (ibid.). News, reports, features, poems.

308. LIBERACTION 1972-1977
    Tl:Liberaction
    Ed. and pub. Hobart Women's Action Group
    Hobart, Tasmania, Australia

        Monthly;1972(?)-1977
        L:not found
Not seen. Item 285 (n°6, Autumn 1974, p.4) quotes issue 26, June
1974. Also mentioned in item 285 (v.3,n°1, February 1977, p.5).

309. PENT UP 1972
        Tl:Pent Up
        Southampton
        F.n.k.;1972(?)
        C BY:item 326
        L:Flic (1 undated issue)
Newsletter produced by Southampton Women's Liberation Group.

310. WOMEN'S PAPER 1972-?
        Tl:Women's Paper
        Only one undated issue found;1972(?)-?
        L:Flic
Newspaper. See Noyce, 1979.

311. BRANCHING OUT 1973-1977
        Tl:Branching out:Canadian magazine for women
        Various eds. including Susan McMaster, Sharon Batt
        Pub. New Women's Magazine Society
        Edmonton, Alberta, Canada
        Bi-monthly;1973-1977(?)
        L:not found
        M:MML
Not seen. Seems to have been an intermediate publication between
the traditional women's magazines and the more radical feminist
periodicals. Ulrich's, 1982 gives a circulation of 4,000. See
item 294 (February 1974 and October 1977) and item 312 (June
1974, p.7).

312. CLEARING HOUSE FOR FEMINIST MEDIA 1973-1974
        Tl:Clearing house for feminist media
        Eds. Lorna Marsden, Linda Fisher and Clearing House for
        Feminist Media
        Ancaster, Ontario, Canada
        Quarterly;1973-v.2,n°4, October 1974 (n.i.c.)
        L:F (2 issues only)
"Clearing House for Feminist Media is a national organization
whose aim is to facilitate access to information necessary for

91

feminists learning about and entering the media field" (October 1974, p.1). Their publication is very thin. Each year an issue is devoted to a listing of feminists in media and feminist media in Canada. Latest trace found occurs in item 294 (v.4,n°2, May 1975).

313. EMERGENCY LIBRARIAN 1973-1978
     T1:Emergency librarian
     Winnipeg, Mannitoba;Toronto, Ontario, Canada
     Bi-monthly;1973-1978(?)
     L:F (1 issue only:v.2,n°2, December 1974)
Earliest mention found (v.1,n°5, June 1974) occurs in item 312 (October 1974). Latest one in item 294 (v.7,n°4, 1978, p.50). Articles on the status of librarians, reviews of recent publications and periodicals, bibliographies.

314. FORWARD 1973-?
     T1:Forward
     Ed. and pub. Nurses' Action Group
     L:not found
Not seen. Listed in Noyce, 1979 (p.104). Printed foolscap, then A4 newsletter produced by "a London-based group fighting for improved conditions of work for nurses".

315. GAY GIRL 1973-?
     T1:Gay Girl
     C:item 237
     L:not found
Not seen. Listed in Noyce, 1979 (p.113). "This magazine continued its predecessor's function as a forum for lesbians".

316. LESBIAN-FEMINIST CIRCLE 1973-c.(?)
     T1:Circle
     T2:Lesbian-feminist Circle
     Ed. and pub. Circle Collective
     Wellington, New Zealand
     Quarterly;1973-c.(?)
     L:not found
Not seen. Listed in Ulrich's, 1982. Circulation: 250 copies.

317. MAYUR 1973-?
     T1:Mayur
     Ed. J. D. Singh

Pub. Women's India Association of the United Kingdom
    L:F (November 1973 only)
A4 printed magazine produced by the Association founded in 1960
with a view to "bringing together Indian Women in Britain and
forming a link between British and Indian Women". Contributors
included men. May have been a one-off issue.

318. PRIORITIES 1973-c.
    T1:Priorities:A feminist socialist perspective
    T2:Priorities:A feminist socialist analysis
    Pub. Standing Committee on Women's Rights of the B.C. New
    Democratic Party
    Vancouver, British Columbia, Canada
    Monthly;bi-monthly
    L:Flic (a few issues only)
Forty-page magazine. "Its intent is to provide a means of
communication and discussion for NDP women in order to further
the interests of the women's movement and of democratic socialism"
(v.3,n°9, September 1975).

319. OTHER WOMAN 1973-1977
    T1:The other woman:Canadian feminist
    Ed. The Other Woman Collective
    Toronto, Ontario, Canada
    Bi-monthly
    L:F, Flic (both incomplete)
Illustrated twenty page tabloid newspaper from the Canadian
Women's Liberation Movement. Circulation: 2,000 copies (see
Ulrich's, 1982). Substantial and broad contents including
addresses of organisations and other newsletters, local, national
and international news, feature articles and book reviews. The
collective announced the cessation of publication with vol.v,n°1.

320. SLAG 1973-?
    T1:Slag
    Ed. and pub. Sexual Liberation Action group
    Belfast, Northern Ireland
    L:not found
Not seen. Listed in Noyce, 1979, p.276.

321. TARGET 1973-1975
    T1:Target:bulletin

Ed. and pub. Mothers in Action
Monthly;1973-September 1975 (n.i.c.)
L:F, Flic (both incomplete)
Very slim bulletin campaigning for better living standards for
one-parent families. See also items 258 and 306.

322. FEMINIST COMMUNICATIONS COLLECTIVE 1973-?
T1:Feminist Communications Collective
Montreal, Quebec, Canada
Monthly?;January(?) 1973-?
L:not found
Not seen. Mentioned in item 294 (v.3, 1974 and v.4, 1975).

323. BRIGHTON AND HOVE WOMEN'S LIBERATION NEWSLETTER 1973-c.
T1:A Woman's place? Brighton and Hove Women's Paper
T2:Brighton and Hove Women's Liberation Newsletter
Brighton
Bi-monthly;fortnightly;monthly;March 1973-c.
L:F (1 issue only);Flic (incomplete)
Thin local A4 newsletter produced by the Brighton Women's Centre
and available to women only. See Noyce, 1979, p.18.

324. LINK 1973-c.
T1:Link
Editorial board including in 1982:Shelley Adams, Mary Davis,
Sarah Gasquoine, Linda Smith, Margaret Bowden, Jean French,
Jane Mace, Elizabeth Wilson
Quarterly;Spring 1973-c.
L:F (incomplete)
This twenty page printed A4 magazine redesigned in December 1981,
is a professional-looking publication. Distributed on a national
level, it has a circulation of 2,200 copies according to Ulrich's,
1982. "Link is a magazine of women's liberation produced by the
Communist Party . . . Only a change in the system - only
Socialism - can provide for women's equality and freedom. The
Communist Party . . . is the only political party with a planned
programme of how this change can be achieved" (n°1, Spring 1973,
p.2). Link is mainly aimed at Communist women, "it is the only
women's journal which attempts to link the women's movement and
the labour movement" (n°39, Winter 1982/83, p.2). It discusses
"issues and campaigns of the Labour movement as well as issues
and campaigns of special concern to women as women" (n°1, ibid.).

It has devoted articles to trade unions, pay, employment, social
services and peace and has dealt with abortion, nursery, child
care, sex discrimination, etc.. It also aims to provide "a forum
on ideological questions" (n°l, ibid.). Along with discussion
articles, it carries letters, book and film reviews, a calendar of
events, photos, and cartoons. Not to be confused with items 39 and
103.

325. STATUS OF WOMEN NEWS 1973-c.
     Tl:Status of women news
     Eds. have included Moira Armour and Catherine Devlin
     Pub. National Action Committee on the Status of Women
     Toronto, Ontario, Canada
     4 or 5 issues per year;Summer 1973-c.
     L:Flic (2 issues only)
Not seen. Listed in items 294 and 612. National, bilingual
publication. Described as "A political magazine for women with
articles, news stories, book reviews and coverage of controversial
and political issues" in item 294 (v.7,n°4, 1978, p.53). See also
item 769.

326. THE OTHER HALF LIVES 1973-?
     Tl:The other half lives
     Eds. J. Clark and E. Crowley
     Pub. Southampton Women's Liberation Group
     Southampton
     Quarterly;July 1973-?
     C:item 309
     L:not found
Not seen. Mentioned in Noyce, 1979, p.216. No other trace found.

327. WOMEN'S LIBERATION NEWS 1973-1977
     Tl:News from Women's Liberation
     T2:Women's Liberation News
     Monthly (approximately);July 1973-February 1977
     L:F, Flic (both incomplete)
Thin duplicated newsletter produced by an editorial collective.
Circulation: 200 copies (see Noyce, 1979, p.203). Originally
though focusing on international news, it carried some national
news too. When item 409 started, national coverage was mainly left
to it. No long articles. Item 297 (n°59, June 1977, p.25)
announced its cessation due to lack of woman power and money.

328. MEN AGAINST SEXISM   1973-1974
    T1:Brothers (n°1)
    Ed. and pub. Birmingham Men's Liberation Group including Roy
    Coyle and others
    T2:Men against sexism (n°2)
    Ed. and pub. South London Men Against Sexism group including
    Marshall Harris, Dan Muir and others
    T3:Brothers against sexism (n°3)
    Ed. and pub. South London Men Against Sexism group
    T4:Men against sexism (n°s 4 and 5)
    Issue 4:ed. and pub. Nottingham Men Against Sexism group
    Issue 5:ed. and pub. Stoke Newington (London) Men Against
    Sexism group
    Various locations
    Irregular;August 1973-1974
    L:F, Flic (both incomplete)
Duplicated A4 newsletter that evolved out of a number of "Men
Against Sexism" national conferences. The Birmingham group was
delegated by the first conference held in London in June 1973.
The group thought their twenty six page issue was "the first
national men's liberation newsletter". The newsletter consisted of
reports on the national conferences, accounts of the groups'
activities, discussion articles on pornography, violence against
women, etc.. Not to be confused with Brother, USA (not listed).

329. MANCHESTER WOMEN'S LIBERATION GROUP NEWSLETTER   1973-1975
    T1:Manchester Women's Liberation Group Newsletter
    Manchester
    Monthly?;August 1973(?)-1975(?)
    C BY:item 438?
    L:F (August 1973 only)
Slim duplicated newsletter of interest to local women. No long
articles. Mainly carried news of groups and contact lists.

330. FREE WOMEN   1973-?
    T1:Free women
    Prestwich
    F.n.k.;September 1973(?)-?
    L:not found
Not seen. The only mention occurs in item 323 (August 1973, p.2).
"New journal to be published by the women who produced the
'Feminist issue of Socialist Women'. First issue due

out in September".

331. WOMEN AND EDUCATION 1973-c.
     Tl:Women and Education Newsletter (n°s 1-7, 1973-1975)
     T2:Women and Education (n°8, 1976)
     Ed. and pub. Manchester Women and Education Newsletter group
     including among others Flick Harris, Jill Walker, Jill
     Norris, Judy Samuel and Joy Rose
     Manchester
     3 per year approximately (25 issues by 1983);October 1973-c.
     L:Flic (incomplete), F (a few issues missing)
     M:Harvester
Duplicated to number 5, it is now a well produced printed
magazine, distributed on a national level and especially aimed at
feminist women involved in education whether as students, teachers
or parents. The Manchester Women and Education Group began at the
Women in Education workshop at the Bristol Women's Liberation
Conference in July 1973. Flick Harris and Jill Walker volunteered
to produce a national newsletter which would help to break the
isolation of women in education and to coordinate campaigns around
equal education, one of the first four demands of the Women's
Liberation Movement. "Education is important because it is one of
the main methods by which women are socialised into being
second-class citizens" (n°2, editorial). Since 1973, the group
involved in production has varied in size and composition:
teachers, students, women belonging or not to Women's Liberation
groups. It has included men (see n°2, editorial). The newsletter
never had a formal alignment or political affiliation. It has only
carried material reviewing the educational system with the view of
fighting sexism. "Our brief for the newsletter is to publish
anything to do with sexism and education together-including
attitudes and institutionalised aspects of discrimination. A
further important task is to publicise positive ways in which the
experience of women is dealt with at all levels of education,
such as Women's Studies courses and curricular and organisational
changes . . . We regard the newsletter as a forum . . . We limit
ourselves to sexism and education (although this is not all we
consider important in education) in order to be effective" (n°3,
editorial). At first, the newsletter mainly carried news items and
details of events. It has grown and has between 20 and 28 pages.
Its circulation has risen from 600 copies in 1975 (item 297,n°32)
to a thousand copies. The magazine has included letters, newspaper

cuttings, statistics, booklists, contact addresses, book reviews,
cartoons. The articles have covered the whole age-range in
education from pre-school to college of education and polytechnic,
analysed reading schemes, exam results, etc. or reported
individual experiences. After ten years, "the existence of sexism
in education has generally been accepted, though of course pockets
of resistance remain . . . We have established the general nature
of the situation; our object must now be to change it" (n°24,
editorial p.3). The group tries to publish articles on strategies
for change, on new projects.

332. WOMEN AT WORK   1973-1977
    T1:Women at work
    Pub. Women's Bureau, Canada Department of Labour
    Ottawa, Ontario, Canada
    Bi-monthly;October 1973-1977
    C BY:item 593
    L:not found
Not seen. Listed in item 294 (v.3,n°2, May 1974, p.15). Free
newsletter published in English and French. "Discusses government
and lay participation in a wide variety of activities related to
improving the status of women". Not to be confused with item 477.

333. LEEDS WOMEN'S LIBERATION NEWSLETTER   1973-c.
    T1:Women's Liberation Newsletter - Leeds
    T2:Leeds Women's Liberation Newsletter
    Leeds
    Monthly;irregular;bi-monthly;November 1973(?)-c.
    L:F, Flic (both incomplete)
Duplicated and rather shabbily produced A4 newsletter. Locally
based and for women only. It evolved from a 6 page publication to
a twenty-six page one. In their own words, "as well as the
oppression shared by all women in this male world, (the editorial
collective) recognise the additional oppressions suffered by women
of colour, women of many cultures, working class women, fat women,
lesbians, mothers, disabled women, young women, old women, women
who have been put in prisons or mental institutes" (issue December
1983/January 1984). They "oppose the forces of capitalism,
imperialism, and patriarchy that are responsible for all
oppressions" (February(?) 1983, p.1). The newsletter includes news
of concern to local women but also national ones. Together with
letters, a calendar of events, contact lists, short stories,

poetry, it carries a few articles. December 1983/January 1984
issue featured marriage, women hating films in the USA, Jewish
women and Leeds lesbian mothers' group.

334. BOADICEA   1973-?
     Tl:Boadicea:Colchester Women's Liberation Magazine
     F.n.k.;1973(?)-?
     L:Flic (1 undated issue)
Local newsletter produced by Colchester and Essex University
Women's Liberation groups. Bath Feminist Archive holdings dated
1973.

335. BRIXTON WOMEN'S CENTRE NEWS-SHEET   ca 1973-?
     L:not found
Not seen. Newsletter for black women listed in Noyce, 1979, p.40.
Item 831 (n°14, March 1984, p.21) says the first black women's
group was formed in Brixton in 1973. An article in item 786 (1978)
made us think the centre existed in 1973.

336. IFL NEWSLETTER   1973-1975
     Tl:IFL Newsletter
     Pub. International Feminist League of Hong Kong
     Hong Kong
     Monthly;1973(?)-v.3,n°11, November 1975 (n.i.c.)
     L:F (a few 1975 issues only)
Newsletter about twelve pages long carrying a calendar of events,
short articles, letters and book reviews. Topics covered ranged
from UNO activities to violence against women.

337. LILITH   ca 1973
     Tl:Lilith
     Pub. The Women's Press
     Dublin
     Bi-monthly
     L:not found
Not seen. Mentioned in item 297 (n°19, January 1974, p.28),
"published to rebuild our lost heritage". No other trace found.
Not to be confused with item 824.

338. LIVING AS WOMEN   ca 1973
     Tl:Living as women:Notting Hill women's paper
     Only one issue found

L:Flic

The issue seen was an A5 printed periodical ten pages long. "This news sheet is about the needs of women in this area, and about what we can do to get these needs met. Women Can get organised to get the things they need". Topics covered were nurseries, Social Security rights. The date given here is from Noyce, 1979.

339. NIRJHAR 1973-?

   Tl:Nirjhar
   Pub. Bangladesh Women's Association in Great Britain
   F.n.k.;1973(?)-?
   L:F (issue v.1,n°1 only)

Printed A4 publication. Bilingual English and Bengali. The title means "The Fountain". The 52 page issue seen had a feature entitled "why I am a Commonwealth feminist". News of interest to Bangladeshi women in the United Kingdom and in Bangladesh.

340. SCOTTISH WOMEN'S LIBERATION NEWSLETTER 1973-1974

   Tl:Scottish Women's Liberation Newsletter
   Ed. and pub. Edinburgh Women's Liberation Group
   Edinburgh
   Irregular;1973(?)-n°5, 1974 (n.i.c.)
   C BY:item 427?
   L:F, Flic (both incomplete)

Self-explanatory. Earliest issue seen: n°3, 1973. Not to be confused with item 499.

341. VASHTI'S VOICE 1973-1977

   Tl:Vashti's voice
   Melbourne, Victoria, Australia
   F.n.k.;1973(?)-1977 (n.i.c.)
   L:Flic (issue n°4, 4 July 1973 only)

Printed magazine produced by a collective "dedicated to reflecting the diverse views of women in the feminist movement". Issue 3 was published in March 1973. Latest mention found occurs in item 394 (v.3,n°1, February 1977, p.5). See also item 429.

342. WOMEN COME TOGETHER 1973-1975

   Tl:Women come together
   Ed. and Pub. Swansea Women's Liberation Group
   Swansea, Wales
   Irregular;1973-1974 (n.i.c.)

```
     L:F, Flic (both incomplete)
Free paper. Information on local issues but also some general
articles. Not to be confused with items 276 and 392.


343. WRAG NEWSLETTER   ca 1973
     Tl:WRAG Newsletter
     Brighton
     L:Flic (issue n°1 only, undated)
Local newsletter produced by the Women's Centre.


344. ASPEN   1974-c.
     Tl:Aspen:A newsletter by and for Northern women
     Prince George, British Columbia, Canada
     Quarterly
     L:not found
Not seen. Latest mention found occurs in item 612 (v.10,n°4,
December 1981/January 1982, p.39). Thematic newspaper produced
by the Women's Equal Rights Association (WERA) of Prince George
and associated women's groups.


345. CAULDRON   1974-c.?
     Tl:Cauldron:A feminist journal
     Sydney, New South Wales, Australia
     Quarterly
     L:not found
Not seen. Listed in Ulrich's, 1982.


346. IWY NEWSLETTER - AFI BULLETIN   1974-1976
     Tl:International Women's Year newsletter - Bulletin de
     l'Annee Internationale de la Femme
     Ed. and pub. International Women's Year Secretariat, Privy
     Council Office/Secretariat de l'Annee Internationale de la
     Femme, Bureau du Conseil Prive
     Ottawa, Ontario, Canada
     Monthly;bi-monthly
     C BY:item 481
     L:F, Flic (both incomplete)
Bilingual A4 printed newsletter about 10 pages long. Last mention
found occurs in item 294 (v.5, October 1976). See also item 394.


347. WOMEN IN CANADIAN SOCIOLOGY BULLETIN   1974-1978
     Tl:Women in Canadian Sociology - Femmes et Sociologie
```

Canadienne, Bulletin

Pub. Department of Sociology, York University, Downsview,

Ontario, Canada

L:not found

Not seen. Bilingual publication first listed in item 294(v.3,n°2,

May 1974); end of publication announced in ibid. (v.7,n°4, October

1978).

348. YORK WOMEN'S ACTION GROUP NEWSLETTER   1974-?

Tl:York Women's Action Group newsletter

York

Twice-monthly

C BY:item 815?

L:Flic (2 issues)

Very thin A4 duplicated newsletter of interest to local feminists.

349. GHANAIAN WOMAN   1974-c.

Tl:The Ghanaian woman:The magazine of the Ghana Assembly of

Women

Accra, Ghana

Quarterly;January 1974-c.

L:F (a few issues only)

Not new a revival of the same name published by the erstwhile

"Federation of Ghana Women", now the "Ghana Assembly of Women".

The Association founded in August 1969 is "a voluntary women's

body which serves as a central women's organisation in Ghana".

Short articles, organisational news.

350. REDSTOCKING   1974-?

Tl:Redstocking:Cambridge Anti-Discrimination Against Women

Group

Cambridge

Monthly?;January 1974(?)-?

L:F (January 1974 only)

Thin local newsletter produced by a collective including Jill

Nicholls.

351. HULL WOMAN   1974-?

Tl:Hull woman

Eds. Claire Bertschinger et al

Hull

Monthly;March 1974-?

C BY:item 629?

L:F (issue n°1 only)

Local duplicated A4 newsletter. The only issue seen was ten pages
long and featured Hull Women's Aid, anorexia. Book reviews.

352. NEMESIS 1974-?

Tl:Nemesis:The monthly newsletter of Women's Aid

Ed. for number 1 John Ashby

Monthly;March 1974-?

C BY:item 538?

L:F, Flic (both issue n°1 only)

Only one issue seen. Thin A4 printed newsletter produced by
Women's Aid organisation. Contributions from Erin Pizzey who set
up the first refuge for battered women and their children in
Chiswick in 1972 and later founded and chaired Women's Aid.
Contents included organisational news as well as stories of women
who seeked help. The emphasis was on the male dominated social
structures and on the problem of violence in society. But Erin
Pizzey stated in number 1 "Nemesis . . . will not be anti-male
(one Editor is a man . . .). While Nemesis will reflect and
publicize the work and attitudes of WA, all final decisions will
be that of the Editor, who will not be beholden to any
committees." No trace of later issues, maybe a one-off.

353. WOMEN CANADA 1974-?

Tl:Women Canada

Vancouver, British Columbia, Canada

Monthly;March 1974-?

C:item 247

L:not found

Not seen. Only mention found occurs in item 294 (v.4,n°2, February
1975, p.46). "Vancouver Women's Liberation newspaper."

354. BRISTOL WOMEN'S LIBERATION NEWSLETTER 1974-c.

Tl:Bristol Women's Liberation Newsletter

Ed. Bristol Women's Liberation Group including among others
Fiona Campbell

Bristol

Monthly;March 1974(?)-c.

L:F (1 issue only), Flic (incomplete)

Local duplicated A4 newsletter available to women only. Bath
Feminist Archive holding dated March 1974 was the earliest issue

found. At first a rather thin publication between six and ten pages long it has expanded to some twenty pages long. It lists activities and relevant events within the Women's Liberation Movement in Bristol. It has regularly published news on WACC, NAC, Wages for Housework local groups and other campaigns such as the sanitary protection one. It includes many short notices and reports but no genuine features. Not to be confused with item 252. See also item 363.

355. POWER OF WOMEN   1974-1976
    T1:Journal of the Power of Women Collective
    T2:Power of women:magazine of the International Wages for Housework Campaign
    Ed. Power of Women Collective including Deirdre Parrinder, Suzie Fleming and others
    Irregular;March/April 1974-1976(?)
    L:F (n°s 1 to 5), Flic (incomplete)
Printed A4 journal of the London Wages for Housework Committee. National and international news and articles. The group's stand and tactics have often been criticised by other feminists. Latest issue seen:n°5, 1976, latest mention found in item 294 (v.7,n°4, 1978, p.4).

356. FRIENDS OF HAGAR NEWSLETTER   1974-1978
    T1:Friends of Hagar newsletter
    Toronto, Ontario, Canada
    Quarterly;Spring 1974-1978?
    L:not found
Not seen. Latest mention found in item 294 (v.7,n°4, 1978, p.50). "A medium for the sharing of experiences and ideas about women's spiritual quest. An ecumenical network, not affiliated to any particular denomination."

357. MEN'S NEWSHEET   1974
    T1:Men's newsheet
    Monthly;bi-monthly;April 1974-n°5, October 1974
    L:not found
Not seen. Described in Noyce, 1979 as an A4 duplicated news-sheet for the men's movement (including men against sexism) produced by Gordon Mackerron and others on the Stoke Newington men's groups.

358. VIVA MAGAZINE   1974-c.

    Tl:Viva magazine
    Pub. Trend Publishers
    Nairobi, Kenya
    Monthly;May(?) 1974-c.
    L:F (2 issues only)

Glossy magazine printed in English. A mixture of section to be
found in traditional women's magazines e.g. fashion, beauty and of
rather feminist reports on women's issues in Kenya e.g. women's
legal rights, education, work.

359. NEWSLETTER OF THE WOMEN'S PLACE   1974-?

    Tl:Newsletter of the Women's Place, Toronto
    Toronto, Ontario, Canada
    F.n.k.;June 1974(?)-?
    L;not found

Not seen. Earliest mentions found occur in items 312 (October
1974, p.10) and item 294 (v.3, 1974).

360. COUNTRY WOMEN   1974-1981

    Tl:Country women
    T2:The Country woman (n°10)
    T3:Country women
    Various locations:Cumbria;Lancashire;Cornwall;Devon;etc.
    Irregular (11 issues by 1981);July 1974-1981 (n.i.c.)
    L:F (2 issues only), Flic (incomplete)

This duplicated occasional A4 newsletter for feminists living in
rural areas, evolved out of the workshop on country women at the
Edinburgh National Women's Liberation Conference. It was set up to
try to break down the isolation of rural life, build up links
among women and a network of support. Each slim issue is produced
by a small group of women from different areas with coordination
from Laurieston Hall Commune in Scotland. Contents include
information on the national organisation "Country Women", letters,
dates of relevant events, contact addresses. The feature articles
provide practical information related to country living:
gardening, livestock, wildlife . . . ., accounts of personal
experiences and a few more general articles on sex roles and
women's liberation. Latest trace found occurs in item 297 (N°104,
March 1981, p.35). Not to be confused with The Country Woman

(not listed).

361. WITCH AND CAMELEON   1974-1978
     T1:The Witch and the Cameleon
     Ed. Amanda Sankier
     Hamilton, Ontario, Canada
     4 to 6 issues per year;irregular;August 1974-1978?
     L:not found
Not seen. Listed in item 294 (v.4, 1975 to v.7, 1978). Articles,
science fiction, poems, book reviews.

362. HUMBER COLLEGE CENTRE FOR WOMEN   1974-1975
     T1:Humber College Centre for Women:news magazine
     Pub. Centre for Women, Humber College of Applied Arts and
     Technology, Centre for Continuous Learning
     Rexdale, Ontario, Canada
     Irregular;September 1974-1975 (n.i.c.)
     L:not found
Not seen. Latest mention found occurs in item 294 (v.4,n°2,
February 1975, p.46).

363. MOVE   1974-1980
     T1:Bristol Gay Women's Group newsletter
     T2:Move:A publication of the Gay Women's Group-Women's
     Liberation Bristol
     Founding ed. Billie Dee
     Pub. the Other Image (INK)
     Bristol
     Monthly to issue 37, June 1978;the irregular September
     1974-n°42, July 1980
     L:F, Flic (both a few issues only)
     M:Harvester
Duplicated lesbian feminist newsletter produced from Bristol
Women's Centre by the Bristol Gay Women's Group. The first issue
was unnamed and contained an appeal for a name. The size of Move
varied from an A5 to an A4 format, the number of pages grew from
24 to 36 pages. Though there was an editor, editorial decisions
were taken by an open collective with no chairperson. It had a
circulation of 150 to 200 copies per issue. Publication was
interrupted due to lack of material, money and woman power. Some
of Move's aims were as follows: "to relieve the isolation of Gay
Women; to offer information to Gay Women and to the general public

through the media and a regular newsletter; to raise the
consciousness of women and to join the fight to remove the social
oppression of all women everywhere". Its motto was "United we
stand, divided we fall". Move published occasional contributions
from men and was criticized for it. The collective stated in issue
16, "Move is female orientated . . . but . . .the voice of the
lesbian should be heard by the male". The newsletter was aimed not
only at the converted, that is "the feminist brothers" and
"women's liberationists", but also at the vast gay male and female
world and at women who do not go to Women's Liberation Movement
conferences or meetings. The group rejected any separatism and so
it refused to produce a women-only newsletter internal to the
Movement. Move attempted not to exclude lesbian sisters who were
not yet feminist. It carried "straight gay" together with
"feminist gay" material. In the collective's own words, Move also
existed to publish articles from women alienated from the
Women's Liberation Movement. Even though at times, the newsletter
was shabbily produced, it remained attractive because it was
accessible and non-patronising. It was first informational and
carried news from the Women's Liberation Movement as well as from
the Gay Movement locally and nationally, groups and services
lists and a diary of events. Articles discussed wide-ranging
issues and were written in an informal style. Many contributions
came from the West, the South-West, and Wales. Contributors have
included among others: Renee Bailey, Chad Berwick, Sue Cowan,
Jean Cox, Billie Dee, Jackie Forster, Anne Gunn, Lynette Michel,
Marlene Packwood and Monica Sjoo. Contents also included letters,
poems, stories, horoscopes, crosswords and cartoons. Not to be
confused with item 354.

364. F W Z REVIEW   1974-c.
     Tl:F W Z Review
     Ed. Federation of Women Zionists (British WIZO)
     Monthly;quarterly;September 1974(?)-c.
     C:item 243
     L:F (incomplete)
Organisational news. No perceptible feminism.

365. WOMEN'S STRUGGLE NOTES   1974-1977
     Tl:Women's Struggle Notes
     London, Sheffield
     Bi-monthly;September/October 1974-1977

L:F, Flic (both incomplete)

A4 national newsletter aimed at working class women. It was
produced alternately in the North and the South of England by an
open group of socialist women. Some members in the editorial
collective were in Big Flame, a mixed national revolutionary
socialist organisation formed in Liverpool in 1970, which "fights
against sexism" and "supports the independent organisation of
women". The collective stated: "we think that only the united
strength of all the working class people will ever change society
for the better. But within this, we women have to fight for
equality, for our liberation". The newsletter focused on the
struggles of working class women in claimants' unions and in the
place of work (factories, hospitals, offices, etc.) widely
reporting on women's strikes. It campaigned for sexual freedom
and women's rights to control their bodies. It fought against
cut-backs in health care, education, etc. and advocated improved
social services such as childcare facilities and housing.
Articles emphasized what women were doing to bring about change.
Some information was first hand, some taken from newspapers. Not
to be confused with item 253.

366. NATIONAL LESBIAN NEWSLETTER 1974-1975
     Tl:National Lesbian Newsletter
     Nottingham
     2 issues only;December 1974-November 1975
     L:Flic
Short-lived A4 duplicated newsletter for women only. It aimed to
be "a forum for discussion between lesbian groups and individuals"
at a time when no national coherent lesbian movement existed (see
item 410,n°30). Issue 1 was produced by the Harrow Gay Women's
Group, issue 2 by the Nottingham one. Contributors included Maggie
Seelers. Mainly listings and short articles.

367. ABERDEEN WOMEN'S LIBERATION NEWSLETTER 1974-1977
     Tl:Aberdeen Women's Liberation Newsletter
     Aberdeen
     Monthly?;1974(?)-1977(?)
     L:Flic (1 issue only:20 May 1974)
Self-explanatory. Latest trace found occurs in item 297 (n°63,
October 1977, p.34).

368. ABORTION LAW REFORM ACTION GROUP 1974-1976
     Tl:Abortion Law Reform Action Group:newsletter
     Ed. and pub. Abortion Law Reform Association - A Women's
     Right to Choose Campaign
     Irregular;1974(?)-March 1976 (n.i.c.)
     L:F (n°7, 1975 and March 1976 only)
Self-explanatory.

369. BUSINESS AND PROFESSIONAL WOMAN 1974-c.
     Tl:The Business and Professional Woman
     Ed. and pub. Canadian Federation of Business and Professional
     Women's Clubs
     Ottawa, Don Mills, Ontario, Canada
     5 issues per year;1974(?)-c.
     L:not found
Not seen. Earliest mention found in item 294 (v.3,n°1, February
1974), latest one in item 612 (v.10,n°4, December 1981/January
1982, p.39). See also item 193.

370. C.A.C.S.W. BULLETIN 1974-c.
     Tl:ACSW bulletin:Advisory Council on the Status of Women
     bulletin
     T2:CACSW bulletin:Canadian Advisory Council on the Status of
     Women bulletin
     Ottawa, Ontario, Canada
     F.n.k.;1974-c.
     L:not found
Not seen. Earliest mention occurs in item 294 (v.3,n°2, May 1974,
p.13), latest one in item 612 (v.10,n°4, December 1981/January
1982, p.33). Free. Published in English and French.

371. INTERACTION 1974-1978
     Tl:Interaction
     Ed. and pub. Office of Equal opportunities for Women, of the
     Public Services Commission
     Ottawa, Ontario, Canada
     F.n.k.;1974(?)-1978(?)
     L:not found
Not seen. Mentioned in item 294 (v.3, May 1974, to v.7, October
1978). Bilingual. "Reports on happenings within the Public Service

Commission, at federal level, and contains general information relating to women in the labour force."

372. K-W WOMAN'S PLACE NEWSLETTER 1974-?
    Tl:K-W Woman's Place Newsletter
    Waterloo, Ontario, Canada
    F.n.k.;1974(?)-?
    L:not found
Not seen. Listed in item 294 (v.3, 1974).

373. NORWICH WOMEN'S CENTRE NEWSLETTER 1974-?
    Tl:Norwich Women's Centre Newsletter
    Norwich
    F.n.k.;1974(?)-?
    L:Flic (n°4 only, undated)
The issue seen was sixteen pages long. Reports on the activities of the centre and of the local Women's Liberation Movement. See also item 374 and 530.

374. NORWICH WOMEN'S MOVEMENT NEWSLETTER 1974-?
    Tl:Norwich Women's Movement newsletter
    Norwich
    F.n.k.;1974(?)-?
    L:F, Flic (both one issue only)
"It is the first newsletter to be produced jointly by the following women's groups in Norwich: Norwich Nursery Campaign, National Abortion Campaign, Norwich Women's Liberation, U.E.A. Women's Liberation, Leeway Norwich Women's Refuge." A one-off publication? See also items 373 and 531.

375. ON OUR WAY 1974-1975
    Tl:On our way:A women's newspaper
    Edmonton, Alberta, Canada
    F.n.k.;1974(?)-1975(?)
    L:not found
Not seen. Mentioned in item 294 (v.3, 1974 and v.4, 1975).

376. OPTIONS FOR WOMEN 1974-1975
    Tl:Options for women
    Edmonton, Alberta, Canada
    F.n.k.;1974(?)-1975(?)
    L:not found

Not seen. Local newsletter listed in item 294 (v.3,n°2, May 1974 and v.4,n°2, May 1975). See also item 428.

377. PLUS 1974-?
     Tl:Plus magazine
     T2:Plus
     Pub. a collective of women of Ottawa-Hull
     Ottawa, Ontario, Canada
     Quarterly;1974(?)-?
     L:not found
Not seen. Listed in item 294 (v.3,n°2, May 1974). Bilingual.

378. SASKATOON WOMEN'S LIBERATION NEWSLETTER 1974-1975
     Tl:Saskatoon Women's Liberation Newsletter
     Saskatoon, Saskatchewan, Canada
     Monthly;1974(?)-1975(?)
     C BY:item 587?
     L:not found
Not seen. Listed in item 294 (v.3, 1974 and v.4, 1975).

379. SCOTTISH MINORITIES GROUP NEWSLETTER 1974-?
     Tl:Scottish Minorities Group (Edinburgh All-Women Branch)
     Newsletter
     Edinburgh
     Monthly?;1974(?)-?
     L:not found
     M:Harvester
"Newsletter of the branch for 'gay women connected with SMG
Edinburgh', the first issue of which, as far as they knew, was the
'first time a newsletter for gay women has been issued in
Scotland'", see Noyce, 1979 p.268. Started in late 1974 or in
January 1975.

380. WAGRAG 1974-1977
     Tl:WAGRAG
     Ed. Women's Action Group (WAG)
     Pub. Richmond Community Centre
     Bi-monthly;1974(?)-n°25, September/October 1977 (n.i.c.)
     L:Flic (2 issues only)
A4 duplicated local newsletter.

381. WOMEN IN ACTION NEWSLETTER 1974-1975
     Tl:Women in Action Newsletter
     Glasgow
     F.n.k.;August/September 1974(?)-1975?
     L:F, Flic (both incomplete)
Very slim A4 newsletter.

382. ASIAN WOMAN 1975-c.
     Tl:Asian Women's Institute Newsletter
     T2:Asian Woman:Official publication of the Asian Women's
     Institute
     Ed. Dr Eva Shipstone until September 1981, then Mrs Santosh
     Singha
     Pub. Asian Women's Institute International Office
     Lucknow, India
     Monthly;quarterly;1975-c.
     L:F, Flic
Newsletter reporting the activities of the nine Asian Women's
Institute centres of Women's Studies on university campuses in
Lebanon, Pakistan, India, Japan, Korea. Much space devoted to
features on education, the United Nations Organization and the
peace movement. Plus general news about women around the world,
book reviews, etc..

383. BRITISH PREGNANCY ADVISORY SERVICE NEWSLETTER 1975-c.
     Tl:British Pregnancy Advisory Service Newsletter
     Ed. and pub. British Pregnancy Advisory Service (B.P.A.S.)
     Solihull, West Midlands;East Twickenham, Middlesex
     Bi-monthly;1975-c.
     L:Flic (incomplete)
The British Pregnancy Advisory Service provides counselling,
support and termination of pregnancy. The collective publishes an
A4 newsletter some 40 pages long, carrying organisational news,
plus features about counselling, women's health, sexuality,
contraception, pregnancy, infertility, etc. and book reviews.

384. CALGARY WOMEN'S NEWSPAPER 1975-c.
     Tl:Calgary Women's Newspaper
     Ed. Karen Lodl
     Pub. Calgary Status of Women Action Committee
     Calgary, Alberta, Canada
     Eleven issues a year;monthly;1975-c.

L:not found

Not seen. Listed in Ulrich's, 1982 and in item 612 (v.10,n°4,
December 1981/January 1982).

385. COMMUNIQU'ELLES   1975-c.
        T1:Bulletin, Women's Information and Referral Centre
        T2:Communiqu'elles
        Ed. Jacquie Manthorne
        Pub. Editions Communiqu'elles, Women's Information and
        Referral Centre
        Montreal, Quebec, Canada
        Monthly;1975-c.
        L:F, Flic (both incomplete)
Local bulletin mainly carrying news and listings of interest to
women in the Montreal area. French and English editions.
Circulation of 7,500 copies (see item 612, v.10,n°4, December
1981/January 1982, p.41).

386. FIN   1975-c.
        T1:Fin
        Kew, Victoria, Australia
        F.n.k.;1975(?)-c.
        L;not found
Not seen. Mentioned in item 393 (v.1,n°2, July 1975, p.34) and in
Ulrich's, 1982. "A women's liberation magazine", articles,
reviews, poetry, graphics.

387. INTERNATIONAL WOMEN'S YEAR NEWSLETTER   1975
        T1:International Women's Year Newsletter
        Ed. The Committee on Women
        Wellington, New Zealand
        Every 4 to 6 weeks throughout 1975
        L:not found
Not seen. Listed in item 287.

388. LIBIDO   1975-?
        T1:Libido
        Ed. Sheffield University Women's Liberation Group
        Sheffield
        Monthly?;1975-?
        L:Flic
Only one issue found n°3, October 1975. A4 newsletter on

childcare, nurseries.

389. LUNA   1975-c.
       Tl:Luna:A journal of creative and critical writing
       Kew, Victoria, Australia
       F.n.k.;1975-c.
       L:not found
Not seen. Issue 3 mentioned in item 393 (v.2,n°2, July 1976 and
v.4,n°1, July 1978). Also listed in item 612 (v.10,n°4, December
1981/January 1982).

390. MANCHESTER MEN'S NEWS   1975-1977
       Tl:Manchester Men's News
       Manchester
       F.n.k.;1975-1977(?)
       L:not found
Not seen. Mentioned in item 562 (n°1, p.3) as a local newsletter
similar to item 422.

391. NORTHERN WOMAN JOURNAL   1975-c.
       Tl:The Northern Women:women's new regional journal
       T2:Northern Woman Journal
       Pub. Thunder Bay Women's Place
       Thunder Bay, Ontario, Canada
       Bi-monthly;1975-1978(?);1981-c.
       L:F, Flic (both incomplete)
A Women's Liberation newspaper concentrating on regional issues
but including national and international ones too. It seems to
have ceased around 1978 but was revived in 1981.

392. WOMEN TOGETHER   1975-1976
       Tl:Women together:A community paper for everyone who's a
       woman
       Harrow Weald, Middlesex
       Monthly?(7 issues only?);1975-1976(?)
       L:Flic (incomplete)
Local paper of concern to women in the Middlesex area. Short
informative articles, contacts, lists of groups, etc.. Not to be
confused with items 276 and 342.

393. HECATE   1975-c.
       Tl:Hecate:A Women's Interdisciplinary Journal

Ed. Carole Ferrier
Pub. English Department, University of Queensland
St Lucia, Brisbane, Queensland, Australia
Twice yearly;January 1975-c.
L:F, Flic (both incomplete)

Research journal circulating 2,500 copies (see Ulrich's, 1982),
produced by an editorial board of socialist feminist academics.
"A means of providing a forum for discussing, at a fairly
theoretical level, issues relating to the liberation of women"
(v.1,n°1, January 1975, pp.4-5). It prints historical, critical
and research articles "which employ a feminist, Marxist or other
radical methodology to focus on any aspect of the situation of
women" under capitalism and patriarchy (item 297, n°129, April
1983, p.42, advertisement). Deeming a purely feminist approach and
methodology inadequate, it aims to develop alternative critical
models of analysis. It publishes research findings, bibliographics,
interviews, literary criticism, reviews, poetry, fiction,
graphics.

394. INTERNATIONAL WOMEN'S YEAR 1975
     Tl:International Women's year:UK newsletter
     Pub. Women's National Commission, UK co-ordinating Committee
     Quarterly?;January 1975-n°3, September 1975 (n.i.c.)
     L:F (incomplete)

Two-page A4 newsletter mainly carrying a calendar of events. See
also item 346.

395. WOMANSPEAK 1975-c.
     Tl:Womanspeak
     Ed. Womanspeak Collective
     Spit Junction, Sydney, New South Wales, Australia
     5 issues per year;January 1975-c.
     L:Flic (incomplete)

A magazine with a circulation of 3,000 copies (see Ulrich's,
1982). Articles on wide-ranging national and international issues,
wide space devoted to women writers and painters, reviews,
letters, poetry and fiction. Not to be confused with item 679.

396. MANCHESTER WOMEN'S PAPER 1975-1984
     Tl:Manchester women's paper
     Manchester
     Bi-monthly;irregular;January(?) 1975-1978(?);October(?) 1983-1984

            L:F, Flic (both incomplete)
A4 printed magazine with a national circulation aimed at
women outside the Women's Liberation Movement and hence on
public sale. The collective stated "We started the paper
because we wanted to reach women who weren't highly educated
or middle-class, and also to present a kind of alternative
to the usual women's magazines which churn out the same
stereotypes and put women back in their usual place." (Collins
et al, 1978, p.107). The main concern of the collective
was to fill the gap between women in the Women's Liberation
Movement and other women. Issue 15, February/March 1978
claimed a circulation of 1,000 copies per issue. Publication
was interrupted for a few years, a new collective tried to
relaunch the paper on 1 October 1983 (see item 297, n°136,
November 1983, p.25). Yet item 438 (May 1984, p.6) mentions its
demise. The collective monitored various local and national
newspapers. They published a lot of contact addresses and short
features. The contents of the paper grew more overtly feminist
over the years. Topics covered were varied yet some areas such as
women's health, violence against women, sexuality, abortion were
given special coverage. Not to be confused with items 329 and
438.

397. SYDNEY WOMEN'S LIBERATION NEWSLETTER 1975-c.
        Tl:Sydney Women's Liberation newsletter
        Sydney, New South Wales, Australia
        10 issues per year;January 1975(?)-c.
        L:F (1 issue only:January 1975)
Self-explanatory. Latest mention found occurs in item 692 (n°12,
August/September 1983, p.29).

398. CONTACT 1975-c.
        Tl:Contact:newsletter of the National Association of Women
        Citizens
        Ed. Helen Wittick
        Crawley
        Bi-monthly;February/March 1975-c.
        L:F (incomplete)
Very thin newsletter. Mild feminism.

399. BREAD AND ROSES 1975-1977
        Tl:Bread and Roses

Leeds

Irregular (6 issues found);Spring 1975-1977(?)

L:F, Flic (both incomplete)

Printed magazine produced by a collective of "women within the
Lesbian Free Paper women's groups living in Leeds, it filled a
space between community and radical women's papers" (Noyce, 1979,
p.36). It was given away "because women's ideas are for sharing
not for selling" (item 297, n°53, July 1976, p.13) and claimed a
national circulation of about 1,000 copies. Each issue focused on
one theme e.g. rape, lesbianism, women at work, Women's Aid,
astrology but also carried news, letters, prose, poetry and
artwork.

400. RED HERRING 1975

Tl:Red herring

Edinburgh, Scotland

Irregular;Spring 1975-n°5, November 1975 (n.i.c.)

L:F (n°5, November 1975 only)

A4 newsletter produced by the Scottish Lesbian Feminists, a group
formed in reaction to the Gay Rights Congress held in Edinburgh
in December 1974. The group included among others: Margaret
Robinson and Lorna Carmichael. Latest mention found occurred in
item 400 (Winter 1976, p.12).

401. WOMEN FOR LIFE NEWSLETTER 1975-?

Tl:Women for Life newsletter

F.n.k.;Spring/Summer 1975-?

L:Flic (n°s 1 to 8)

Produced by the Feminist Anti-abortion Group. See also item 535.
Not to be confused with item 837.

402. BRISTOL WOMEN'S CHARTER 1975-?

Tl:Bristol Women's Charter

Ed. Working Women's Charter

Bristol

Irregular;March 1975-?

L:F, Flic (both one issue only)

Issue 1 was an A4 newsletter dealing with work, nursery
provisions, childcare and the Charter.

403. ROOM OF ONE'S OWN 1975-c.

Tl:Room of one's own:A feminist journal of literature and

criticism

Ed. Joanna Dean

Pub. Growing Room Collective

Vancouver, British Columbia, Canada

Quarterly;March 1975-c.

L:not found

M:UM

Not seen. Listed in item 393 (v.3,n°2, July 1977, p.14) and in
various issues of item 294. Eighty page journal with a circulation
of 1,000 copies (see Ulrich's, 1982). Feminist prose, poetry,
essays and literary criticism.

404. SEX ROLES 1975-c.

T1:Sex roles:A journal of research

T2:Research Committee on Sex Roles and Politics newsletter

UK ed. Margherita Rendel

Pub. International Political Science Association

London and New York

Quarterly;March 1975-c.

L:F

Newsletter mainly aimed at academics. It reports on the activities
of the Research Committee and provides information on forthcoming
events, current research and reviews.

405. NOTTINGHAM WOMEN'S LIBERATION NEWSLETTER 1975-1980

T1:Nottingham Women's Liberation Newsletter

Pub. Women's Centre

Nottingham

Monthly;bi-monthly;March 1975(?)-June/July 1980

L:Flic (incomplete)

Local women only newsletter. Though listed in Cadman et al, 1981,
publication was interrupted in 1980. No trace of any further
newsletters. Not to be confused with item 271.

406. BIRMINGHAM WOMEN'S PAPER 1975-1977

T1:Brum Women's Press

T2:Brum Women's Paper

T3:Birmingham Women's Paper

Monthly;April 1975(?)-July 1977 (n.i.c.)

C BY:item 658

L:F, Flic (both incomplete)

Thin offset litho paper produced by an open collective at the

Women's Centre. Listings of local groups and events, NAC news but
also some general interest features. Not to be confused with item
303.

407. SHEFFIELD WOMEN'S LIBERATION NEWSLETTER 1975-c.
     T1:Sheffield Women's Liberation Newsletter
     Sheffield
     Monthly;May 1975-c.
     L:Flic (incomplete)
Thin A4 duplicated newsletter for women only, internal to the
local Women's Liberation Movement. Not to be confused with item
637.

408. NATIONAL ABORTION CAMPAIGN NEWSLETTER 1975-c.
     T1:National Abortion Campaign (NAC) Newsletter
     Two weekly;monthly;bi-monthly;irregular;Summer 1975-c.
     L:F, Flic (both incomplete)
Multi-coloured A4 newsletter of 30 to 40 pages. News of NAC
groups and developments on the abortion front. See also item 299.
N.A.C. is a specifically feminist (though not women-only)
abortion pressure group which, together with A.L.R.A., has
successfully mobilised opposition to a succession of legislative
and administrative attempts to reduce or remove women's right to
abortion. However, internal tensions (I.M.G. influence was felt
to be disproportionately strong) led to a more-or-less friendly
split in 1983, for the fruits of which see item 900.

409. W.I.R.E.S. 1975-c.
     T1:Women's Liberation Movement National Information Service
     newsletter:WLMNIS Newsletter
     T2:W.I.R.E.S.
     Leeds;September 1975-December 1977
     York;January 1978-December 1979
     Nottingham;January 1980-December 1981
     Sheffield;January 1982-December 1983
     Oxford;January 1984-c.
     Twice-monthly
     L:F, Flic (both incomplete)
The only national internal newsletter of the Women's Liberation
Movement and the only one totally accountable to the Movement as
represented by its readers and contributors. For internal use, it
is available to women only. Its circulation has risen from 50

copies per issue to 750. It is produced by the Women's Information
Referral and Enquiry Service. W.I.R.E.S. was set up by a
volunteering group on the instruction of the May 1975 National
Women's Liberation Movement Conference to provide a central pool
of information for the Movement and to produce a newsletter. The
service moves every two years to a different town and is run by
rotating collectives in order to avoid centralization of
information and power. The style and format of its A4 newsletter
has been much improved over the years. The latter is designed to
co-ordinate activities of the Movement in Britain. It carries
articles, debates internal to the Movement, reviews, publication
of events, letters, news from conferences and campaigns all over
the country. It helps local groups keep in touch with each
other. It is valuable for being the only mouthpiece of the Women's
Liberation Movement.

410. ATLANTIS 1975-c.
        Tl:Atlantis:A Women's Studies Journal - Journal d'Etudes sur
        la Femme
        Eds. Drs Susan Clark, Margaret Conrad, Donna Smyth
        Pub. Institute for the Study of Women
        Mount Saint Vincent University, Halifax, Nova Scotia, Canada
        Twice yearly;Fall 1975-c.
        L:Flic (incomplete)
"An interdisciplinary journal devoted to critical and creative
writing in English or French on the topic of women" (v.9,n°1,
Fall 1983). Running about 150 pages, it includes scholarly
articles, essays, book reviews, short stories and poetry.

411. WRCC NEWSLETTER 1975-1983
        Tl:WRCC Newsletter:Women's Research and Resources Centre
        Newsletter
        Bi-monthly;November 1975-November/December 1983
        C BY:item 901
        L:F, Flic
A4 printed newsletter of about 10 to 16 pages, internal to members
of the centre. GLC funded, the W.R.R.C. provides information
facilities for people researching on women - a library and reading
room, a research index, women's studies news, seminars. The
newsletter aims to service and inform the W.R.R.C. membership. It
publishes calendars and reports of meetings and conferences, a
"contacts" section, letters, book reviews, new acquisitions to the

library, women's studies courses, a research index including titles of research added to the WRRC research index. Sold only through subscriptions, it claims a circulation of about 1,200 copies. Possible half the readership are women involved in academic work.

412. WOMEN'S LIBERATION CAMPAIGN FOR LEGAL AND FINANCIAL
     INDEPENDENCE NEWSLETTER 1975-1976
     Tl:Women's Liberation Campaign for Legal and Financial
     Independence newsletter
     F.n.k.;November 1975(?)-October 1976 (n.i.c.)
     L:F (2 issues only)
The London Women's Liberation Campaign for Legal and Financial Independence Group grew out of the conference held on this topic in December 1974. It published a thin A4 newsletter with news of groups around the country and a few articles about the contents of the demand and ways of campaigning.

413. IMAGES OF WOMEN NEWSLETTER 1975-1976
     Tl:Images of Women Newsletter
     2 issues only;Winter 1975-March(?) 1976
     L:Flic
Two printed newsletters produced by the women and film group including Angela Martin. Information on women in the media, lists of courses, films, feminist groups, etc., addresses for obtaining material. Not to be confused with items 457 and 578.

414. MABEL 1975-c.
     Tl:Mabel
     Australia
     Monthly;December 1975-c.
     L:Flic (n°1 only)
Women's Liberation newspaper.

415. MAKARA 1975-1978
     Tl:Makara
     Pub. (1)Pacific Women's Graphic Arts Co-operative
     Association;(2)Makara Publishing and Design Cooperative
     Vancouver, British Columbia, Canada
     Bi-monthly;quarterly;December 1975-1978(?)
     L:not found
Not seen. Listed in item 294, latest mention found in October

1978 issue.

416. CAMBRIDGE WOMEN'S LIBERATION NEWSLETTER 1975-c.
    Tl:Cambridge women's liberation newsletter
    Ed. and pub. The Newsletter group
    Cambridge
    Monthly;December 1975(?)-c.
    L:F, Flic (both incomplete)
Duplicated A4 local publication for women only. Cadman, 1981 says
it started in the early seventies. The earliest issue found was
dated December 1975. Averaging twelve pages long, it contains a
calendar of events, letters and information about activities and
issues within the Women's Liberation Movement in Cambridge of
interest to local women mainly. But it also includes some national
news and issues.

417. HERSTORY 1975-1976
    Tl:Herstory:women's liberation newsletter
    Liverpool
    F.n.k.;February(?) 1975(?)-September(?) 1976
    C BY:item 621?
    L:Flic (incomplete)
Newsletter mainly of interest to local women. See also item 490.

418. HYSTERIA 1975-?
    Tl:Hysteria
    Ed. and pub. Reading University Women's Group
    F.n.k.;1975(?)-?
    L:Flic (1 undated issue only)
Very slim A5 printed newsletter. Maybe a one-off issue. Articles
on feminist art, the menstrual taboo, the Women's Liberation
Movement.

419. KHASMIK 1975-c.
    Tl:Khasmik
    Sydney, New South Wales, Australia
    Quarterly;1975(?)-c.
    L:not found
Not seen. Mentioned in item 393 (v.1,n°1, January 1975, p.66).
Poetry periodical.

420. LONDON WORKING WOMEN'S CHARTER CAMPAIGN   1975-1977
      Tl:London Working Women's Charter Campaign newsletter
      F.n.k.;1975(?)-October 1977 (n.i.c.)
      L:Flic (incomplete)
Earliest issue seen n°3 dated 1975. Campaign newsletter devoting
much space to the question of abortion, trade unions, public
spending cuts, unemployment. See also item 453.

421. MANITOBA ACTION COMMITTEE ON THE STATUS OF WOMEN NEWSLETTER
      1975-?
      Tl:Manitoba Action Committee on the Status of Women
      newsletter
      Winnipeg, Manitoba, Canada
      Bi-monthly;1975(?)-?
      L:not found
Not seen. Only mention occurs in item 294 (v.4,n°1, February 1975,
p.46).

422. MEN'S NEWS   1975-1977
      Tl:Men's News
      F.n.k.;1975(?)-1977(?)
      L:not found
Not seen. Mentioned in item 562 (n°1, p.3). "Between the summers
of 1975 and 1977 an internal newsheet called Men's News circulated
among London groups". Successor to item 357?

423. NEWSLETTER FOR WOMEN WORKING IN PUBLISHING   1975-?
      Tl:Newsletter for women working in publishing
      F.n.k.;early 1975(?)-?
      C BY:item 679?
      L:F, Flic (both n°1 only, undated)
The women in publishing group evolved out of a conference of
women in the communications industries - newspapers, magazines,
books, film and theatre - held in January (1975?). It aimed "to
find out what work women do; to campaign for increased union
support for women's issues; to make links with isolated freelance
workers . . .; to help establish women's groups within publishing
firms . . .; to produce a newsletter". Thin A4 newsletter,
predecessor to item 679?

424. READING WOMEN'S GROUP MAGAZINE 1975-?

   Tl:Reading Women's Group Magazine

   Reading

   F.n.k.;1975(?)-?

   L:Flic (1 undated issue only)

A4 printed magazine put together by Reading Women's Group, formed
in March 1974. Some information on the local and national events
related to women's issues but wide space devoted to features on
theoretical problems. See also item 419.

425. SCARLET WOMAN 1975-1978

   Tl:Scarlet woman

   Sydney, Chippendale, New South Wales, Australia

   Quarterly;1975(?)-1978(?)

   L:not found

Not seen. Mentioned in items 393 (v.1,n°2, July 1975, p.53) and
294 (v.7, n°4, 1978, p.68). A socialist feminist magazine. Issues
frequently thematic. Articles, book reviews and movement news.
Not to be confused with items 272 and 450 and Scarlet Woman, USA
(not listed).

426. SCOTTISH WOMEN'S LIBERATION WORKSHOP NEWSLETTER 1975-?

   Tl:Scottish Women's Liberation Workshop Newsletter

   St Andrews

   F.n.k.;1975(?)-?

   C:item 340?

   L:not found

Not seen. Listed in Noyce, 1979, p.269.

427. SOURCE 1975-?

   Tl:Source

   Ed. and pub. Alberta Options for women Council

   Edmonton, Alberta, Canada

   F.n.k.;1975(?)-?

   L:not found

Not seen. Listed in item 294 (v.4,n°1, February 1975, p.46). See
also item 377.

428. VASHTI 1975-c.

   Tl:Vashti

   Fitzroy, Melbourne, Victoria, Australia

   Irregular;1975(?)-c.(?)

L:Flic (2 issues only)

Magazine produced by a collective. Only issues found: n°23, Spring
Spring/Summer 1978 and n°24, Summer 1979. "Vashti, as a
Women's Liberation newspaper, provides a forum for
radical feminist views and analysis. (They) aim to publish
writings that are pro-feminist, pro-lesbian and anti-capitalist"
(n°24, p.2). See also item 341.

429. VOW 1975-c.
    Tl:VOW:Voice of Women
    Pub. African National Congress of South Africa - Women's
    Section
    Lusaka, Zambia
    Quarterly;1975(?)-?
    L:F (1976 Fourth Quarter issue only), Flic (1979 Fourth
    Quarter issue only)

A magazine published in English, "aimed at Women's Organisations,
Solidarity Groups, Non Government Organisations and all groups and
individuals interested in women in liberation". Mainly concerned
with South African news and politics of liberation. Not to be
confused with items 676, 795.

430. WOMAN TODAY 1975-c.
    Tl:Woman today
    Pub. Port Coquitlam Area Women's centre
    Port Coquitlam, British Columbia, Canada
    Bi-monthly;1975(?)-c.(?)
    L:not found

Not seen. Mentioned in The Tribune Newsletter (n°19, 2nd quarter
1982, pp.8-9, not listed): "News about the Centre and the feminist
movement in Canada and around the world".

431. WOMEN'S INFORMATION CENTRE NEWSLETTER 1975-?
    Tl:Women's Information Centre newsletter
    Toronto, Ontario, Canada
    F.n.k.;1975(?)-?
    L:not found

Not seen. Listed in item 294 (v,4,n°2, May 1975).

432. AFRICA WOMAN 1976-c.
    Tl:Africa woman
    Ed. Ralph Uwechue

Pub. Africa Journal Ltd

Bi-monthly

L:F (incomplete)

Earliest issue found n°2, 1976. Format and style of traditional women's magazines. Moderate liberal feminism.

433. CANADIAN ADVISORY COUNCIL ON THE STATUS OF WOMEN 1976-c.

Tl:Canadian Advisory Council on the Status of Women:Annual Report - Conseil Consultatif Canadien de la Situation de la Femme:Rapport Annuel

Ottawa, Ontario, Canada

Yearly

L:not found

Not seen. Listed in Ulrich's, 1982. See also item 370.

434. CATCALL 1976-c.

Tl:Catcall:A feminist discussion paper

Irregular (16 issues published in 1984)

L:F (1 issue only), Flic

A4 duplicated newsletter available to women only. Produced by a collective of three members including Lynn Alderson, its publication has been irregular due to lack of woman power and lack of material as the group doesn't write articles. Catcall began with a national circulation of 200 copies per issue, it averaged 750 copies in 1983. Its basic aim is to provide "a non-sectarian forum for discussion, theory, and the exchange of ideas by and for women in the women's liberation movement" (n°5, 1977, p.1). It attempts to illuminate the relationship between theory and practice and to break the way theory is seen as something distant, abstract and hard. It welcomes "articles from feminists of any (or no) tendency" (n°9, March 1979, p.3). It publishes short non academic articles on matters of general interest to women in the Women's Liberation Movement. Topics covered have been wide ranging: infertility, abortion, transexualism, lesbianism, racism, nuclear power, male violence, women's health, the women's movement in Iran, etc.. Catcall does not carry fiction but includes funny cartoons.

435. E.O.C. ANNUAL REPORT 1976-c.

Tl:Equal Opportunities Commission annual report

Pub. H.M.S.O.

Annual;1976-c.

L:Flic (n°1 only)

Self-explanatory. See also items 512, 553, 570 and 873.

436. BOLTON WOMEN'S GROUP NEWSLETTER 1976-?
        Tl:Bolton Women's Group newsletter
        Bolton
        Monthly
        L:not found

Not seen. Only mention found occurs in item 438 (n°4, January/
February 1977, p.2). The group started meeting in 1971. They set
up a newletter in 1976 "basically to tell women in and around the
group about events/meetings/social events etc. around Bolton".

437. LESBIAN NEWS-LETTER 1976-?
        Tl:Lesbian news-letter
        Australia
        L:Flic (n°1, 1976 only)

Issue n°1 is a sixteen page A4 printed newsletter.

438. MANCHESTER WOMEN'S LIBERATION NEWSLETTER 1976-c.
        Tl:Manchester women's liberation newsletter
        Manchester
        Bi-monthly (up to n°20, May/June 1980);then monthly (10 issues
        per year, double issue July/August and December/January)
        C;item 329?
        L:F, Flic (both incomplete)

Earliest issue seen: n°4, January/February 1977. Circulation: 550
copies an issue (n°56, May 1984). Printed A4 newsletter eight
pages long until 1980 when the collective decided to duplicate it
for two main reasons: financial cost and lack of space. Though on
open sale, it is aimed at women only. The 1980 editorial
collective attempted "to direct the newsletter towards
communication of ideas, theories, etc. and news of practice within
the WLM in Manchester. Though this is what the newsletter set out
to do when it was first conceived, it has tended over the years to
become an introduction to the WLM rather than a journal for
discussion within it. Obviously it's extremely important that such
an introduction to feminist politics exists within Manchester and
we feel that this role is amply filled by the Manchester Women's
Paper" (n°20, May/June 1980). The newsletter covers local and
national news and miscellaneous issues within the Women's
Liberation Movement: lesbianism, Greenham Common, the Police Bill,

127

etc. have been discussed. It contains notices of events, press cuttings, listing of groups, poetry. Item 513 was distributed as an insert into the newsletter though it was produced by another collective and the group didn't always agree with its contents.

439. SPIRAL 1976-c.
    T1:Spiral
    Spiral Collective
    Wellington, New Zealand
    Irregular
    L:Flic (2 issues only)
Feminist arts journal: prose, poetry, photographs, book reviews. Circulation: 500 copies (Ulrich's, 1982).

440. WAGES FOR HOUSEWORK CAMPAIGN BULLETIN 1976-c.
    T1:Wages for Housework Campaign Bulletin
    Ed. and pub. Toronto Wages for Housework Campaign Committee
    Toronto, Ontario, Canada
    Two/Three issues per year
    L:not found
Not seen. Listed in Ulrich's, 1982. A tabloid with a circulation of 10,000 copies. See also item 286.

441. WOMEN AND COLLEGE EDUCATION 1976-?
    T1:Women and college education
    Croydon, Victoria, Australia
    Quarterly
    L:not found
Not seen. Listed in item 294 (v.6), "A journal of information on women's studies". Lists seminars, conferences, university courses, etc..

442. WOMEN AND ENVIRONMENTS 1976-c.
    T1:Women and environments international newsletter
    T2:Women and environments
    Eds. have included David Morley, Becky Peterson and Gerda Wekerle
    Pub. Faculty of Environmental Studies, York University
    Downsview, Ontario, Canada
    Quarterly;3 issues per year
    L:not found
Not seen. Listed in Feminist Periodicals (v.2,n°4, 1982, p.IX).

"Topics: planning, architecture, design; housing and community development; geography, urban sociology, environmental psychology, energy and ecology". Circulation: 500 copies (Ulrich's, 1982). "Features, notes, reviews, abstracts, course outlines, and contacts" (item 613, v.10, n°4, December/January 1982, p.46).

443. WORKING PAPERS   1976-c.
    T1:Working papers in sex, science and culture
    T2:Working papers:studies in the discourses of sex,
    subjectivity and power
    Eds. including Terry Bell, Andrew Benjamin, Elizabeth Gross,
    Paul Foss, Meaghan Morris and Graeme Tubbenhauer
    Darlington, Australia
    3 issues per year;1976-c.(?)
    L:Flic (incomplete)
Earliest issue seen v.1,n°2, November 1976. Substantial research journal edited by men and women which "critically examines the function of language, ideology and scientificity in the construction of sex theories ranging from conventional sciences to liberation movements." Some topics of feminist interest.

444. WRAG NEWSLETTER   1976-?
    T1:WRAG newsletter:Brighton Women's Rights Action Group
    newsheet
    Pub. Brighton Women's Centre
    Brighton
    Irregular
    L:Flic (only 3 issues dated 1976)
Slim A4 duplicated newsletter for local women.

445. LIVEWIRE   1976-?
    T1:Livewire
    Lewes, Sussex
    3 issues per year;early 1976-?
    L:Flic (3 issues dated 1976)
A5 duplicated local news sheet funded by the Social Services Department. The collective started working in November 1975 and the first issue came out early in 1976. Free of charge, about 1,000 copies per issue distributed to launderettes, bookshops, cornershops, clinics, etc.. Thematic issues: n°1 childcare, n°2 health, n°3 work. See Collins et al, 1978, p.106.

446. RIGHTS FOR WOMEN UNIT NEWSLETTER   1976-c.

      T1:The Collective Fund newsletter

      T2:Women's rights newsletter

      T3:Rights for Women Unit newsletter

      Ed. and pub. NCCL - Rights for Women;NCCL - Women's Rights

      Unit;NCCL - Rights for Women Unit

      Monthly;bi-monthly;January 1976-c.

      L:F, Flic (both incomplete)

Thin A4 magazine of the National Council for Civil Liberties of
the Rights for Women Unit renamed and restyled in November 1982.
The Council helps women use the law and publishes pamphlets.
The newsletter covers campaigns for women's rights in such areas
as work legislation, sexual harassment at work, abortion,
immigration, violence, E.O.C. news, etc.. No long features. Not to
be confused with item 515.

447. CHILEAN WOMEN   1976

      T1:Chilean women

      Ed. and pub. Women's Campaign for Chile

      F.n.k.;February 1976

      L:Flic (n°1 only)

Issue 1 was not a "genuine" newsletter but rather a pamphlet.
Brought out by a group of Chilean and English women within the
Chilean Solidarity Campaign, it reported on the role of women in
the Chilean people's liberation struggle. Though the group
announced future newsletters, it seems to have been a one-off
issue.

448. WOMEN'S NATIONAL COMMISSION   1976-1978

      T1:Women's National Commission:international news sheet

      Ed. Dr Grace Thornton

      Irregular;Spring 1976-1978 (n.i.c.)

      L:F (issues 1 to 6), Flic (incomplete)

A4 news sheet used to put across news of the Commission: reports
of international visits, meetings, forthcoming events, etc..
Faint feminist leanings. See also item 274.

449. GLASGOW WOMEN'S CENTRE NEWSLETTER   1976-c.

      T1:Glasgow Women's Liberation newsletter

      T2:Glasgow Women's Centre newsletter

      Glasgow

      Monthly;April 1976(?)-c.

L:Flic (incomplete)
Practical and informative A4 duplicated newsletter for women only.
Mainly of interest to local women: listings of local groups and
events but no genuine features.

450. SCARLET WOMEN   1976-1982
     T1:The scarlet woman or revolt
     T2:Scarlet women:newsletter of the socialist feminist current
     of the Women's Liberation Movement
     T3:Scarlet Women:journal of the socialist feminist current
     of the Women's Liberation Movement
     North Shields, Tyne and Wear (printed in Manchester)
     Irregular;May 1976-n°14, January 1982
     L:F (n°1 missing);Flic (n°1 and 2 missing)
Scarlet Women was started by Tyneside Coast women as a first step
towards rebuilding the socialist-feminist current within the
women's movement after discussions at the 1975 Women's Liberation
Conference in Newcastle. Originally a thin duplicated A4 bulletin,
it was printed and expanded with issue 5. It became a full
discussion journal less news oriented and dealt with more
theoretical issues. In 1978 the organisational structure was
changed. It was decided to circulate the production of the
newsletter around the country thus predominantly reflecting the
concerns of the regions. A national editorial collective would
provide continuity. The latter included among others:Ruthie Petrie
and Anne Torodo. Before this, editorial decisions were taken by
the North Shields Scarlet Women Collective. The 1978 national
collective worked out a statement reprinted in each issue about
what it thought the basic concerns of socialist feminism were and
what this meant for the newsletter: "Socialist Feminism is a
distinct revolutionary approach, a challenge to the class
structure and to patriarchy. By the patriarchy we mean a system in
which all women are oppressed, an oppression which is total,
affecting all aspects of our lives . . . The struggle is about a
change in total social relations" and not in the economic
structure alone. "What we are looking for is nothing less than a
total redefinition of socialist thought and practice." Scarlet
Women carried "papers, letters, articles and ideas that developed
the thought and effectiveness of socialist feminism . . .
Contributions were based on the belief in an autonomous Women's
Liberation Movement . . ." Each issue had contributions about
practice and theoretical articles. But in its own word the

collective did not see itself as "engaging in academic debates
. . . The journal belonged to the women's movement rather than
the universities. Thematic issues covered: reproduction, women's
independent income, fascism, violence against women, Irish
feminists, imperialism, sexuality, women and new technology, etc..
The journal was not visually attractive but contents were solid
and interesting. Subscriptions were available to women only but
the journal was on open sale to reach more women. Issue 13 on
sexuality was sold to women only. Not to be confused with items
272 and 426.

451. WOMEN AND EUROPE 1976-c.
    T1:Women and Europe:news and views on European affairs of
    special interest to women and their organisations
    T2:Women and Europe:news and views on European affairs of
    special interest
    Eds. Kay Fox (President of the National Council of Women)
    and Kay Bolton (Chairman of the National Commission of
    Standing Conferences of Women's Organisations)
    Pub. The European Movement
    Bi-monthly;May/June 1976-c.
    L:F, Flic (incomplete)
Four page A4 bulletin very neatly printed, edited by two members
of the National Council of the European Movement and sponsored by
the European Movement. Launched on 4 May 1976 during Europe week
because women's lives are increasingly influenced by Europe but
women are inadequately represented as policy makers and top
executives. Official publication aimed at "not only officers and
national committees but also members of branches, institutes,
guilds, clubs and standing conferences throughout the UK" (v.1,n°2
n°2, July/August 1976, p.1). Free of charge for women's
organisations. Not to be confused with item 548.

452. WOMEN'S ACTION 1976-1979
    T1:Women's action
    Ed. Belfast Women's Collective
    Belfast
    Bi-monthly;irregular;June 1976-v.3,n°3, 1979 (n.i.c.)
    L:F, Flic (both incomplete)
Put out by socialist women who believe the oppression of Irish
women is political and "related both to National and Class
oppression" (Statement of Aims, v.2,n°3, August /September 1978).

132

Strongly feminist contents mainly concerned with publicising Irish
women's oppression and struggle: Northern Ireland Women's Aid,
sexuality, contraception, education opportunities, the right to
work, the Catholic Church, etc..

453. WOMEN'S CHARTER 1976-?
    Tl:Women's Charter:newspaper of the Working Women's Charter
    Campaign
    Bi-monthly;Summer 1976-?
    L:F, Flic (both issue n°1 only)
Eight page organisational newspaper of the campaign carrying
industrial disputes, case histories of sex discrimination, etc..
See also items 420 and 485.

454. WOMEN IN TOWER HAMLETS 1976-?
    Tl:Women in Tower Hamlets:information and gossip for women
    in the East End
    Eds. Janice Giffen and Christine Smith
    Pub. Oxford House
    F.n.k.;August 1976-?
    L:F, Flic (both issue n°1 only)
A one-off publication? Very well produced twenty page tabloid.
Dealt with local and national issues. Main topics covered
childcare, work, health.

455. WAGES FOR HOUSEWORK 1976-c.
    Tl:Wages for Housework:campaign bulletin
    Ed. Toronto Wages for Housework Committee including Judith
    Ramirez
    Pub. CASH:Committee to Advance the Status of Housework
    Toronto, Ontario, Canada
    Quarterly;Fall 1976-c.
    L:F (v.2,n°1, Fall 1977 only)
CASH was founded in 1975 to upgrade the economic, social and legal
status of housework. Its 4-page tabloid campaigns for the
recognition of housework as productive work. See also items 286
and 495.

456. OWWTA NEWSLETTER 1976-1978
    Tl:OWWTA newsletter
    Pub. Organized Working Women Toronto Association
    Co-ordinators:Elizabeth Smith;Deirdre Gallagher

Don Mills, Ontario, Canada
Monthly;September 1976-1978 (n.i.c.)
C BY:item 589
L:not found
Not seen. Latest trace found item 294 (v.7,n°4, 1978, p.52).

457. IMAGES   1976-c.
Tl:Images:Kootenay Women's Paper
Nelson, British Columbia, Canada
Bi-monthly;September/October 1976(?)-c.
L:not found
Not seen. Item 294 (v.6,n°l, February 1977, p.79) mentions issue
September/October 1976. "A collectively produced women's paper
which features thematic issues often built around rural concerns"
(see item 294, v.6,n°3, October 1977, p.87). Not to be confused
with items 413 and 578.

458. COMING AGE   1976-c.
Tl:The coming age:The maqazine of Lux Madriana
T2:The coming age:The magazine of the living matriarchal
community
T3:The coming age:The definitive introduction to matriarchy
and the feminine tradition
Pub. Lux Madriana
Various locations:Oxford, Wirral, Todmorden, Burtonport
Quarterly;December 1976-c.
L:not found
Funded by the organisation Lux Madriana, The Coming Age is the
organ of the An Droichead Beo matriarchal Community as
representative of British matriarchal communities as a whole. The
magazine is "a veritable encyclopaedia of the matriarchal
tradition" (n°12, p.31). It discusses any aspect of life - social
structure, politics, life-style, psychology, nuclear technology,
art, animals, religion, astronomy, etc. - from the standpoint of
the matriarchal tradition. In addition, each issue contains
material on the seasonal festivals, old Rhennish songs, a
matriarchal story. The community totally rejects the modern
materialist patriarchal world and struggles for a return to
absolute matriarchy. Circulation has risen from 200 copies in 1976
to about 1,000 in 1983. "An Droichead Beo" means "The bridge of
life" in Gaelic.

459. EXECUTIVE SECRETARIES ASSOCIATION NEWSLETTER   1976-c.
    Tl:ESA:The Executive Secretaries Association
    T2:The Executive Secretaries Association newsletter
    Eds. rotating each year (S. J. Vick, S. Parissien, etc.)
    London;Gosfield, nr Halstead (Essex)
    3 issues per year;December 1976(?)-c.
    L:F (incomplete)
Thin A4 newsletter. Self-explanatory. Short articles, book
reviews.

460. ASTMS NEWSLETTER   1976-?
    Tl:ASTMS newsletter
    Ed. and pub. Division 15 Action Committee on Sex
    Discrimination including Pat Dawson and Angela Martin
    Bi-monthly;1976(?)-?
    L:Flic (incomplete)
Extremely thin A4 newsletter published by the Committee
established in October 1974. Funded by the Divisional Council of
the Association of Scientific, Technical and Managerial Staffs.
Focuses on women and work, but also includes book reviews. Not to
be confused with the ASTMS Journal (not listed).

461. BANSHEE   1976-1978
    Tl:Banshee:journal of Irishwomen United
    Ed. and pub. Irish United Women
    Dublin
    Bi-monthly;irregular;1976(?)-1978(?)
    C BY:item 560
    L:F, Flic (both incomplete)
    M:Harvester
A4 printed magazine put together by Irish United Women, a group
formed in April 1975 and composed "of women's liberationists who
believe that the best perspective for struggle against women's
oppression in Ireland lies in an ongoing fight around the charter
of demands printed" on issue 1 p.1. The title means "fairy woman".
Articles, news, letters, book reviews, poems, cartoons. Strongly
feminist contents. Miscellaneous issues covered: contraception,
equal pay, wages for housework, prostitution, etc.. A regular
"Father Church" section criticizes Catholicism.

462. BLUESTOCKING   1976-c.
    Tl:Bluestocking:National Newsletter of the Australian

Women's Education Coalition
Pub. National Coordinating Committee of the AWEC
Various locations:Leichhardt, New South Wales, etc.,
Australia
Bi-monthly;1976(?)-c.
L:Flic (incomplete)

Thin professionally produced newsletter of the AWEC, a coalition
of women's education and other groups aiming "to advance women's
issues in education and to promote equality of access and outcomes
in education for women" (n°40, November/December 1982, p.1). It
keeps its membership informed on current developments and
policies relating to women's and girls' education and on
non-sexist education material and programmes.

463. CARDIFF WOMEN'S LIBERATION NEWSLETTER 1976-c.
    T1:Cardiff Women's Action Group Newsletter
    T2:Cardiff Women's Liberation Newsletter
    Cardiff
    Monthly;1976(?)-c.
    L:Flic (incomplete)

Internal newsletter for Cardiff. Mentioned in item 589 (n°5, 1979,
p.8) and in Kanter et al, 1984.

464. EQUAL TIMES 1976-?
    T1:Equal times:New Brunswick's only women's newspaper
    New Brunswick, Canada
    F.n.k.;1976(?)-?
    L:not found

Not seen. Listed in item 294 (v.5,n°1, February 1976, p.28).

465. GAYZETTE 1976-?
    T1:Gayzette
    Edinburgh
    Monthly;1976(?)-?
    L:not found

Not seen. Mentioned on a list of current periodicals published by
Wires (see item 409) and dated 11/5/1977. "For lesbians in
Scotland".

466. LONDON NURSERY CAMPAIGN NEWSLETTER 1976-?
    T1:London Nursery Campaign newsletter
    F.n.k.;1976(?)-?

L:Flic (n°3, 1976 only)

Self-explanatory. See also item 770.

467. NATIONAL ASSEMBLY OF WOMEN NEWSLETTER   1976-?

    Tl:National Assembly of Women newsletter

    F.n.k.;1976(?)-?

    C BY:item 698

    L:not found

Not seen. Included by Wires in its list of periodicals dated
11/5/1977. "Duplicated, some feminist items". See also item 701.

468. NOTTING HILL WOMEN'S PAPER   1976-?

    Tl:Notting Hill Women's Paper

    F.n.k.;1976(?)-?

    L:Flic (1 undated issue)

Self-explanatory.

469. ROMAN CATHOLIC FEMINISTS   1976-c.

    Tl:Roman Catholic feminists

    Irregular;1976(?)-c.

    L:F, Flic (both incomplete)

Extremely thin newsletter running from half a page to eight pages.
Earliest issue seen: n°5, December 1977. The London group is part
of an international movement for the liberation of women in the
Church. The newsletter gives information on the network of
national and international groups which attempt to integrate
feminism and Catholicism. No features.

470. SCARLET WOMEN   1976-c.

    Tl:Scarlet Women:A Socialist Feminist Magazine

    Chippendale, New South Wales, Australia

    Quarterly;twice yearly;1976(?)-c.

    L:F (n°5, March 1977 only)

A mixture of articles discussing theoretical issues and of reports
on the women's liberation struggles. Not to be confused with item
450.

471. SHEFFIELD CHILDBIRTH GROUP NEWSLETTER   1976

    Tl:Sheffield Childbirth Group Newsletter

    Sheffield

    F.n.k.;1976(?)-?

    L:not found

Not seen. An article in item 297 (n°66, January 1978, p.20) says
the group was formed in spring 1976 and quotes issues 1 and 3.

472. SOUTH LONDON WOMEN'S CENTRE NEWSLETTER 1976-?
     Tl:South London Women's Centre Newsletter
     F.n.k.;1976(?)-?
     L:Flic (issues 4 to 19)
Self-explanatory.

473. SUSAN SAXE DEFENSE COMMITTEE NEWSLETTER 1976-1977
     Tl:Susan Saxe Defense Committee Newsletter
     F.n.k.;1976(?)-1977(?)
     L:Flic (n°5, February 1977 only)
Self-explanatory.

474. TIGHTWIRE 1976-c.
     Tl:Tightwire
     Pub. Kingston women prisoners
     Kingston, Ontario, Canada
     Bi-monthly;1976(?)-c.
     L:not found
Not seen. Earliest mention found in item 294 (v.5,n°3, October
1976, p.71). Still listed in item 612 (v.9,n°4, December 1981/
January 1982, p.45).

475. WINGS 1976
     Tl:Wings
     Ed. and pub. Bath Gay Awareness Group
     Irregular;1976(?)-?
     L:not found
Not seen. Mentioned in item 363 (n°21, September 1976, p.14). A
local newsletter for gay women in Bath and the surrounding
district.

476. WOMEN IN MEDICINE 1976-1978
     Tl:Women in medicine:newsletter of Medical Women's Federation
     Ed. n°s 8 and 10:Dame Albertine Winner
     Pub. Medical Women's Federation, n°8 President:Mary Jones
     Irregular;1976(?)-n°11, July 1978 (n.i.c.)
     L:F (incomplete)
Thin printed newsletter with faint feminist leanings. Earliest
issue seen: n°8, August 1977. Not to be confused with WIM (Women

138

in Medicine), a national group of feminist doctors and medical students.

477. WOMEN'S BUREAU NEWSLETTER 1976-c.
     Tl:Women's Bureau newsletter
     Ed. and pub. Ontario Women's Bureau
     Toronto, Ontario, Canada
     Quarterly;1976(?)-c.
     L:not found
Not seen. Free government publication listed in item 294 (v.5,n°3, October 1976, p.71) and in item 612 (v.10,n°4, December 1981/ January 1982, p.47). See also item 332.

478. CAMBRIDGE SCARLET WOMEN 1977-?
     Tl:Cambridge scarlet women.
     Cambridge
     Monthly?
     L:Flic (n°2, May 1977 only)
Thin A4 local newsletter. Not to be confused with items 450 and 272.

479. CONVENTION NOTES 1977-?
     Tl:Convention notes
     Honorary Secretary:Betty Pepper
     Pub. Scottish Convention of Women
     Tranent, East Lothian
     L:not found
Not seen. Listed in item 612 (v.9, n°4, December 1980/January 1981, p.45). "Begun in 1977, the Convention engages a variety of practical activities such as sponsored reports, seminars and research" and publishes Convention Notes.

480. EMOTAN 1977-c.
     Tl:Emotan
     Ibadan, Nigeria
     Monthly;1977-c.
     L:not found
Not seen. Listed in item 613 (v.10,n°4, December 1981/January 1982, p.49). "A general women's magazine".

481. INFORMATION:STATUS OF WOMEN 1977-c.(?)
     Tl:Information:Status of Women/Situation de la Femme

Pub. Office of the Status of Women
Ottawa, Ontario, Canada
Quarterly;1977-c.(?)
C:item 346
L:not found
Not seen. Listed in item 294 (v.6,n°3, October 1977, p.87). Free
official bulletin published in English and in French.

482. LONDON HOMEWORKING CAMPAIGN BULLETIN 1977-1978
    Tl:London Homeworking Campaign bulletin
    F.n.k.;1977-n°11, December 1978 (n.i.c.)
    L:Flic (2 issues only)
Newsletter of the campaign against the exploitation of
homeworkers. Earliest issue found n°4, 1977.

483. MAMA 1977-1979
    Tl:Mama:Women Artists Together
    Ed. and pub. Mama Collective
    Birmingam
    F.n.k.;1977-1979 (n.i.c.)
    L:Flic (incomplete)
    M:Harvester
The group concerned with male dominance of art, worked to
establish a place for women in art. In their own words, "it is
difficult to become a serious artist if you are a woman. The idea
is a contradiction in terms for most people, culture is created
by men for men . . . The role of women in art has been that of the
model, the idealized object . . ." (see Thomas, 1981, p.15).
Published essays, poems, pictures. Contributors included: Ann
Berg, Beverly Skinner, Roslyn Smythe, Monica Sjoo.

484. SOCIALIST INTERNATIONAL WOMEN BULLETIN 1977-c.
    Tl:Socialist International Women Bulletin
    Bi-monthly;v.23, 1977-c.
    C:item 290
    L:not found
Continuation of item 290. Circulation: 10,000 (Ulrich's, 1982).

485. WOMEN'S FIGHT 1977-?
    Tl:Women's Fight:paper of the Working Women's Charter
    Campaign
    Bi-monthly

C:item 453

L:F (issues 2 and 3 only), Flic (issue 2 only)

Printed in newspaper format. See also items 420 and 453. Not to be confused with item 682.

486. WOMEN'S LIBERATION 1977-?

Tl:Women's Liberation:journal of Women's Liberation Front

C:item 250?

L:Flic (issue 1 only)

Self-explanatory.

487. WOMEN'S STUDIES NEWSLETTER 1977-c.

Tl:Women's Studies Newsletter

Founding ed. Carolyn Brown;then Ally Jones

Pub. (a)Workers' Education Association (W.E.A.);(b)Women's Education Advisory committee (W.E.A.C.), W.E.A. Stourbridge

Quarterly;irregular;twice yearly

L:F, Flic, BM;P 521/3483 (all incomplete)

The W.E.A. is a national voluntary body running courses in adult education for men and women. Over the past years, it has developed many classes in women's studies and the W.E.A.C. was created. The publication of Women's Studies is only part of the work of W.E.A.C. members. The twelve pages or so of this A4 national newsletter are very neatly produced and aim to disseminate information about the activities of the various branches of the association. Contents include news, conference reports, articles, lists of future events and of the women's studies courses available, together with poems, fiction, film and book reviews. Features focus on sex role stereotyping of women and on the importance and contents of women's education. After a temporary hiatus, the newsletter was relaunched on 10 May 1984.

488. WOMEN'S VOICE 1977-1982

Tl:Women's voice:women's magazine of the Socialist Workers' Party

Darlington (Durham);London

Monthly (65 issues)

C:item 290

C BY:Socialist Review (not listed)

L:F, Flic (both incomplete)

Women's Voice was the national women's organisation of the Socialist Workers' Party with local groups all over the country.

An editorial board, including among others Eunice Sharples and
Yolanda Bystram, published an A4 printed magazine, 28 pages long.
Contents included regulars such as letters, health, industrial
news, reviews. The features had a strong socialist stand. They
focused on women working, on industrial disputes and on the Tory
attacks against the working class in matters of education,
housing, social facilities, etc.. Women were encouraged to join
trade unions. Revolution, not reform, was advocated. Racism and
imperialism were condemned and though issues concentrated on Great
Britain, the struggle for socialism and for women's liberation was
considered as a world-wide struggle. Women's oppression was seen
as part of general oppression. The editorial board attempted to
put across to the traditional left some of the ideas of the
women's movement. But analyses remained more socialist than
feminist. However, the SWP disbanded the organisation in late
1981. For the latter, the concept of Women's Voice proved to be
"an ineffectual compromise between separatism and the Marxist
tradition" (item 297, n°114, January 1982, p.10). The magazine was
maintained for a short while and then had to fold. The official
reason for the discontinuation of publication was the scarcity of
resources. In fact its demise was the result of the Party's
opposition to any kind of autonomous women's movement. Women's
separatism could divide the working class struggle.

489. WOMEN IN EASTERN EUROPE NEWSLETTER   1977-c.
       Tl:Women in Eastern Europe newsletter
       Ed. Women and Eastern Europe Group
       Birmingham
       Irregular (n°5 Winter 1982-83);January 1977-c.
       L:F, Flic (both incomplete)
Newsletter that grew out of a conference in Birmingham in October
1976. Issue n°1 was sent to some 50 people or groups only. The
producing group has included: Barbara Holland, Alix Holt, Barbara
Brown, Vicky Spark, etc. and the CREES of the University of
Birmingham helps towards production cost. The last issue seen n°5,
Winter 1982-83 well produced newsletter 32 pages long. The group
believes that "the women's movement has not traditionally paid
much attention to Eastern Europe (editorial, n°2, June 1979,
p.(2)). The newsletter carries "news and articles on the position
of women in Eastern Europe, government policies and their effects
on women and the views of East European women themselves on the
situation there" (ibid.). "As ideas about socialism are often

informed by distorted perceptions of Eastern Europe and the Soviet
Union, (the group members) aim to offer an alternative approach
based on sharing (their) work and personal experiences"
(editorial, n°5, Winter 1982-83, p.(2)). They offer a socialist
feminist approach to women's lives in Eastern Europe and in the
Soviet Union. They highlight how the latter are shaped by the
socio-economic and political structures. In their own words, "the
countries of Eastern Europe call themselves socialist and assert
that they have solved 'the woman question' . . . This is untrue
. . . the subordinate position of women is as integral to the
political system in the East as it is in the West (n°2, June 1979,
p.(2)). Patriarchy has survived too. The newsletter is valuable
both as reference document and as communication network.

490. MERSEYSIDE WOMEN'S PAPER   1977-c.
     Tl:Merseyside women's paper:A Women's Liberation magazine
     Liverpool
     10 issues per year;from 1978 onwards quarterly;January(?)
     1977-c.
     L:F, Flic (both incomplete)
Interesting A4 printed paper sixteen pages long and sold publicly.
It is produced by a collective which has included among others:
Sue Aldridge, Naomi Frisch, Wendy Owens, Sue Ryrie, Hilary
Williams. Contents cover information about the local Women's
Liberation Movement and local issues but also national and
international news. They include features, letters, contact
addresses, a diary of events, poems, fiction, book reviews,
crosswords and cartoons. See also item 622.

491. ABOUT WOMEN   1977-c.
     Tl:About women
     Regina, Saskatchewan, Canada
     Ed. and pub. Women's Division of the Saskatchewan Department
     of Labour
     Bi-monthly;quarterly;February 1977-c.
     L:not found
Not seen. Listed in item 613 (v.10,n°4, December 1981/January
1982, p.39). "News on the status of women and new materials in the
Resource Centre". Free. Circulation: 5,000 (Ulrich's, 1980). Not
to be confused with item 729.

492. LONDON WOMEN'S LIBERATION NEWSLETTER   1977-c.

   T1:A Woman's Place newsletter
   T2:London Women's Liberation newsletter
   Weekly;February 1977-c.
   C:item 249
   L:F, Flic (both incomplete)

Continuation of item 249, it is the oldest surviving newsletter in
the British Women's Liberation Movement and the only one to be
published weekly. Produced by a collective operating from A
Woman's Place, this duplicated multicoloured A4 newsletter is
"internal to the Women's Liberation Movement and is not to be read
by men". It is of interest to feminists in London only. It ran to
about 15-20 pages in 1983 and claimed a circulation of 650 copies
(n°298, 4 January 1983). It provides an up-to-date source of
information concerning events, groups, courses. It also carries
accommodation lists, "for sale" and job ads. It could enable women
to air their views on current events rather quickly compared to
the other less frequent feminist publications. Yet little space is
left for opinion pages.

493. LEICESTER WOMEN'S LIBERATION NEWSLETTER   1977-c.

   T1:Leicester Women's Liberation Newsletter
   Leicester
   Bi-monthly;February/March 1977(?)-c.
   L:Flic (incomplete)

Local women only newsletter.

494. WAGES FOR HOUSEWORK   1977-c.

   T1:Wages for Housework:campaign bulletin
   Ed. Selma James
   Quarterly;irregular;Spring 1977-c.
   C:item 286?
   L:F (incomplete)

Free four page bulletin printed in A4, then tabloid format. Gives
news of the Wages for Housework Campaign internationally.
Campaigns for recognition and payment of housework, a demand
disapproved of by many feminists. Highlights women's struggle
against rape, the prostitution and immigration laws. Most
contributions by Black Women for Wages for Housework, the English
Collective of Prostitutes, the US Prostitutes Collectives, Wages
Due Lesbians UK and USA, British Women Against Rape groups, Boston
Rape Action Project, Housewives in Dialogue, etc.. See also items

286 and 354.

495. CAMDEN WOMEN'S CENTRE NEWSLETTER   1977-?
     Tl:Camden Women's Centre newsletter
     Monthly;30 March 1977-?
     L:Flic (incomplete)
Local and very slim A4 duplicated newsletter. It aims "to
facilitate communication among all the women involved in the
centre" (n°1) and to let local women know about the centre's
activities. Calendar of events, reports on conferences, groups.

496. CITY OF LONDON POLY:WOMEN'S NEWS SHEET   1977-?
     Tl:City of London Poly:women's news sheet
     Monthly?;April 1977(?)-?
     L:F (April 1977 only)
Self-explanatory.

497. LONDON COMMUNIST WOMEN'S BULLETIN   1977-1978
     Tl:London Communist Women's bulletin
     About every two months;April(?) 1977-n°7, February 1978
     (n.i.c.)
     L:F, Flic (both incomplete)
Thin A4 printed bulletin focusing on the Communist Party meetings,
the Communist University of London. Issue 2 dated June 1977.

498. ANARCHIST FEMINIST NEWSLETTER   1977-1980
     Tl:Anarchist Feminist Newsletter
     York;London;Dublin
     Bi-monthly;irregular;May 1977-n°8, October 1980 (n.i.c.)
     L:Flic
A woman only newsletter which grew out of the 1977 National
Women's Liberation Conference. Edited by various regional groups.
Contact person: Sophie Laws. Could be the same as item 504.

499. SCOTTISH WOMEN'S LIBERATION JOURNAL   1977-1978
     Tl:Scottish Women's Liberation Journal
     T2:Whatever happened to the Scottish Women's Liberation
     Journal?
     Edinburgh
     Irregular;May 1977-n°4, April 1978
     C BY:item 564
     L:F, Flic (both incomplete)

145

M:Harvester

The idea of publishing a newsletter emerged at the Scottish
Women's Liberation Conference in Glasgow in 1976 and the first
issue was launched at the next one held in Aberdeen in May 1977.
It was run by an open editorial collective whose members came from
several areas in an attempt to represent the whole of Scotland:
Aberdeenshire, Dundee, Edinburgh, Glasgow and St Andrews. A
variety of political opinions were represented in the group which
included among others: Kate Arnot, Sally Henry, Joan McLellan.
Stephanie Markman, Lorna Mitchell, Ingrid Muir, Alison Scott. The
newsletter had come into existence to fulfil needs arising from
the growth of the Women's Liberation Movement in Scotland. It was
"intended to be a forum for discussion for women in Scotland"
(n°2, 1977, p.2). Its contents examined feminist issues in the
light of the situation in Scotland and focused on the influence of
Scottish culture, politics and laws on women's oppression. Each
issue carried news items, consistent features, poetry, graphics,
book reviews. Topics covered included abortion, women in Eastern
Europe, in rural Scotland, in trade unions, etc.. Publication was
irregular due to production cost and a small circulation. The
editorial of issue 1 claimed that the journal would be
"non-sectarian . . . and open to all shades of political opinion
contained in the Women's Liberation Movement". Its politically
"mixed" collective would produce a broad-based journal. Yet
ideological differences between socialist and radical feminists
caused the dissolution of the collective. Issue 4 entitled
Whatever happened to the Scottish Women's Liberation Journal? was
produced by radical feminists who were "dissatisfied with the
political practice of some members of the old SWLJ collective, and
the members of the new Msprint collective" (n°4, April 1978, p.1).

500. UNIVERSAL WOMAN   1977-?
     Tl:The universal woman:newsletter of the Young Women's
     Spiritual Association
     Liverpool;London
     Irregular;May 1977-?
     L:Flic (incomplete)
Thin A4 duplicated newsletter brought out by YWSA "a movement
which aims to unite all women in spiritual Sisterhood". "YWSA is a
group of women throughout England who are working to create a
visible synthesis between spiritual visions for a new society and
concrete social action". Women's "liberation will not come by

struggling to match male standards, but rather by realizing their own inner strength and divine qualities. YWSA aims at the liberation of women in all spheres of life, with a spiritual view of life as the base and direction for this movement" (n°1, May 1977, p.1).

501. WOMEN AND WORK 1977-c.
     T1:Women and Work newsletter
     T2:Women and work
     Ed. Tina Falk
     Pub. Women's Bureau, Dept of Employment and Industrial
     Relations;then Dept of Employment and Youth Affairs
     Victoria;Canberra, Australia
     Quarterly;May 1977-c.
     L:F (incomplete)
Free, slim newsletter for working women - articles on equal opportunities, non-traditional occupations, etc.. Circulation: 10,000 copies (Ulrich's, 1982). Not to be confused with item 725.

502. BREAKING CHAINS 1977-c.
     T1:Breaking chains:The newspaper of ALRA - The Abortion Law
     Reform Association
     Bi-monthly;May/June 1977-c.
     C:item 239
     L:F, Flic (both incomplete)
Thin A4 printed newspaper put together by an editorial committee which has included Judy Cottam, David Flint, Colin Francome, Sue Heal, Hilary Jackson, Marion Newman, Barbara Nicholls, Sharon Spiers, et al. Founded as a single issue publication about ALRA and a Woman's Right to Choose campaigns. Contents are less reformist and more strongly feminist than its predecessor's. The editorial committee hopes their publication will contribute to the unity of the pro-choice movement "by bringing together views and comment from people involved in the fight, in the NHS, the Trades Unions, the women's and students' movements, the political parties and all the groups and individuals who are active in this particular struggle. (It aims) to highlight and discuss aspects of abortion and related issues and to supply up-to-date information on international news, statistics, campaigns developments . . . plus details of relevant literature" (editorial, n°1, p.2). Contributions are short but the publication is a very useful source of information.

147

503. LANCASTER WOMEN'S CENTRE NEWSLETTER 1977-1978
     Tl:Lancaster Women's Centre Newsletter
     Lancaster
     B-monthly;monthly;irregular;May/June 1977(?)-May 1978
     (n.i.c.)
     C BY:item 647
     L:Flic (incomplete)
Local women only newsletter. Publication seems to have ceased
between 1978 and 1980 but was resumed as item 647.

504. ANARCHA FEMINIST NEWSLETTER 1977-1980
     Tl:Anarcha Feminist Newsletter
     Lancaster
     Irregular;June 1977-January 1980 (n.i.c.)
     C:item 292
     L:Flic (incomplete)
Replaces the Libertarian Women's Network Newsletter. Carries news
of the Anarchist Women's Network and short articles. Contact
person: Sue Smith. Same as item 498?

505. OPPRESSION OF SOUTH ASIAN WOMEN 1977-?
     Tl:Oppression of South Asian Women
     F.n.k.;June 1977-?
     L:not found
Not seen. A list established by W.I.R.E.S. in 1980 refers to it as
a proposed new paper. A bulletin of comment came out on 1 June
1977. Contributors included A. Begum.

506. ZERO 1977-1978
     Tl:Zero:anarchist/anarca-feminist monthly
     Bi-monthly;June 1977-n°8, 1978 (n.i.c.)
     L:F, Flic (both incomplete)
Tabloid produced by a mixed collective of anarchists and
anarca-feminists mainly from East London, the first issue had a
print run of 3,000 copies. "Anarca-feminism consists in
recognising the anarchism of feminism and consciously developing
it" (n°1, June 1977, p.7). Anarchist feminists "don't just want
the overthrow of capital but full Sexual-social revolution, the
simultaneous overthrow of capital, patriarchy and state" (ibid.,
p.6). National and international news, articles, lists of events,
contacts and publications, letters, agitprop. Not to be confused
with item 499.

507. P.R.O.S. 1977-?

    Tl:P.R.O.S. bulletin

    Ed. and pub. Programme for the Reform of the Soliciting Laws

    Birmingham

    F.n.k.;June(?) 1977-?

    L:not found

Not seen. Publication announced in item 363 (n°27, May 1977, p.4).
Put together by a group of prostitutes, social workers and lawyers
in the Birmingham area.

508. BEYOND PATRIARCHY PUBLICATIONS 1977

    Tl:Beyond patriarchy publications

    2 issues only numbered 1 and 3;August 1977-December 1977

    L:not found

    M:Harvester

Interesting though short-lived publication. It analysed the notion
of patriarchy, fought to abolish it and proposed its replacement
by a "gynandry". Contributors included Mary Coghill, Pauling Long
and Diana Scott. See Thomas, 1981, pp.14-15.

509. NORTH STAFFORDSHIRE WOMEN'S ACTION GROUP NEWSLETTER 1977-
    1978

    Tl:North Staffordshire Women's Action Group Newsletter

    North Staffordshire

    Monthly;August(?) 1977-April 1978 (n.i.c.)

    L:Flic (n°9, April 1978 only)

A4 newsletter carrying not only listings but also short features.

510. BRISTOL ANTI-RAPE GROUP NEWSLETTER 1977-?

    Tl:Bristol Anti-Rape Group newsletter

    Pub. Women's Centre

    Bristol

    Monthly;September 1977-?

    L:Flic (n°1 only)

A four-page A4 news sheet sent to all anti-rape groups. Topics
covered:prostitution, the relationships between race, class and
rape, pornography, the seventh demand (freedom for all women from
intimidation by the threat or use of violence or sexual coercion,
regardless of marital status. An end to all laws, assumptions and
institutions that perpetuate male dominance and men's aggression
towards women).

511. LIP   1977-c.

     T1:LIP:journal of women in the visual arts

     Co-ordinator Suzanne Spunner

     Carlton;then Parkville, Victoria, Australia

     Annual;October 1977-c.

     L:Flic (incomplete)

Put together by a collective of women working in the arts and media. Primarily concerned with the visual arts, LIP also includes features on culture and politics, performance, theatre, film, media and music, plus reviews and photos.

512. EOC DOCUMENTS BULLETIN   1977-1978

     T1:EOC Information Centre Documents Bulletin

     Ed. and pub. Equal Opportunities Commission

     Manchester

     Twice monthly?;11 November 1977-n°30, 1978 (n.i.c.)

     L:F

Internal bulletin.

513. MANCHESTER LESBIAN EXPRESS   1977-?

     T1:Manchester lesbian express

     Manchester

     Monthly;November 1977(?)-?

     C BY:item 614

     L:Flic (2 issues only;November and December 1977)

Local printed newsletter for lesbians.

514. RIGHTS OF WOMEN BULLETIN   1977-c.

     T1:R.O.W. bulletin

     T2:Rights of Women bulletin

     Bi-monthly;quarterly;December(?) 1977-c.

     L:F, Flic (both incomplete)

News sheet mainly for internal use put together by a collective of women working in the legal profession or interested in the law, formed in 1974. They oppose the many man-made laws, act as a pressure group and run a Women's Legal Resource Centre advising women on legal problems. The bulletin carries information on the centre activities, details of new and proposed legislation, tribunal and court decisions affecting women, features, analyses of publications and cartoons. Not to be confused with item 446.

515. BREAKTHROUGH   1977-?

   Tl:Breakthrough
   Pub. York University
   Downsview, Ontario, Canada
   5 issues per year;1977(?)-?
   C BY:item 814
   L:not found
Not seen. Listed in item 294 (v.6,n°3, October 1977, p.85).

516. BRIDGES   1977-c.

   Tl:Bridges:between Manitoba women
   Pub. the YWCA of Winnipeg
   Winnipeg, Manitoba, Canada
   Quarterly;3 times a year;1977(?)-c.(?)
   L:not found
Not seen. A tabloid listed in item 294 (v.6,n°3, October 1977,
p.85) and in item 612 (v.10,n°4, December 1981/January 1982, p.39).

517. BRIGHTON LESBIAN GROUP NEWSLETTER   1977-c.

   Tl:Brighton Lesbian Group Newsletter
   Brighton
   F.n.k.;1977(?)-c.
   L:not found
Not seen. Earliest mention found occurs in item 409 (n°31, October
1977, p.32), latest one in Gay News (n°260, 3-16 March 1983, p.30;
not listed).

518. BROKEN RIB   1977-?

   Tl:Broken rib:Edinburgh Women's Aid newsletter
   Ed. and pub. Edinburgh Women's Aid
   Edinburgh
   Monthly;1977(?)-?
   L:not found
Not seen. Item 409 (n°31) reprints an article from it. Most
contributions from women in the refuge. See also item 539.

519. CANADIAN HOUSEWIVES' REGISTER NEWSLETTER   1977-c.

   Tl:Canadian Housewives' Register newsletter
   Rexdale, Ontario, Canada
   F.n.k.;1977(?)-c.(?)

        L;not found
Not seen. Mentioned in item 294 (v.6,n°1, February 1977). See also
item 238.

520. CANADIAN PSYCHIATRIC ASSOCIATION TASK FORCE ON WOMEN'S ISSUES
     NEWSLETTER 1977-c.
     Tl:Canadian Psychiatric Association Task Force on Women's
     Issues Newsletter
     Ed. Dr Sue Stephenson;then Dr Margaret D. Whitfield
     Vancouver, British Columbia;Toronto, Ontario, Canada
     F.n.k.;1977(?)-c.
     L;not found
Not seen. Listed in item 294 (v.6,n°3, October 1977, p.86) and in
item 612 (v.10,n°4, December 1981/January 1982, p.40).

521. COVENTRY WOMEN'S LIBERATION NEWSLETTER 1977-?
     Tl:Coventry Women's Liberation newsletter
     Coventry
     F.n.k.;1977(?)-?
     L:not found
Not seen. Mentioned on a list of publications dated 11 May 1977
established by W.I.R.E.S. (see item 409).

522. DAY CARE 1977-c.
     Tl:Day care/Garde de jour
     Ed. and pub. National Day Care Information Centre
     Ottawa, Ontario, Canada
     Quarterly;1977(?)-c.
     L:not found
Not seen. Earliest mention found in item 294 (v.6,n°3, October
1977, p.86). Bilingual, free of charge.

523. FEDERATION OF WOMEN TEACHERS' ASSOCIATIONS OF ONTARIO
     NEWSLETTER 1977-c.
     Tl:Federation of Women Teachers' Associations of Ontario
     newsletter
     Toronto, Ontario, Canada
     Twice yearly;7 then 5 issues during the school year 1977(?)-c.
     L:not found
Not seen. Listed in item 294 (v.6,n°3, October 1977, p.86) and in
item 612 (v.10,n°4, December 1981/January 1982, p.42).

524. HORNSEY WOMEN'S CENTRE NEWSLETTER   1977-?

    T1:Hornsey Women's Centre Newsletter

    F.n.k.;1977(?)-?

    L:Flic (issues 2 and 6, undated)

Self-explanatory. Mentioned on a list established by W.I.R.E.S.
dated 11 May 1977 (see item 409).

525. JOIN HANDS   1977-?

    T1:Join hands

    Sydney, New South Wales, Australia

    F.n.k.;1977(?)-?

    L:not found

Not seen. Listed in item 393 (v.3,n°1, February 1977, p.121). "The
journal of the Women's Collective of the CPA".

526. KINESIS   1977-c.

    T1:Kinesis:The feminist news

    T2:Kinesis:Vancouver Status of Women newspaper

    Ed. and pub. Vancouver Status of Women

    Vancouver, British Columbia, Canada

    10 issues per year;1977(?)-c.

    L:not found

Not seen. Earliest mention found occurs in item 294 (v.6,n°1,
February 1977, p.79). "Women's newspaper, focusing on B.C. news
but providing coverage of other areas and issues as well" (item
613, v.10,n°4, December 1981/January 1982, p.43).

527. LIBERTARIAN WOMEN'S NETWORK NEWSLETTER   1977-?

    T̄1̄:Libertarian Women's Network Newsletter

    Dundee

    Irregular;1977(?)-?

    L:F, Flic (both incomplete)

Listed in item 294 (v.6,n°1, February 1977, p.85).

528. MANCHESTER MEN'S GROUPS NEWSLETTER   1977-?

    T1:Manchester men's groups newsletter

    Manchester

    F.n.k.;1977(?)-?

    C:item 390

    L:F (autumn 1977 only)

The only issue seen was produced by some of the Whatley Range

Group and a few male friends.

529. MATCH NEWSLETTER   1977-c.
     Tl:Match newsletter
     Pub. Match International Centre
     Ottawa, Ontario, Canada
     Bi-monthly;1977(?)-c.
     L:not found
Match International Centre is a non-governmental organisation
which grew out of the World Conference in Mexico. It provides a
clearinghouse for Canadian and Third world women (see item 294,
v.6,n°3, October 1977, p.88 and item 613, v.10,n°4, December 1981/
January 1982, p.43).

530. NORWICH WOMEN'S LIBERATION NEWSLETTER   1977-c.
     Tl:Norwich Women's Liberation Newsletter
     Norwich
     F.n.k.;1977(?)-c.
     L:not found
Not seen. The group introduced itself in item 374 but did not
mention the publication of a newsletter. The earliest mention
found occurred on a list established by W.I.R.E.S. dated 11 May
1977 (see item 409). Latest mention found in Cadman et al, 1981.
Local, available to women only. The 1977 contact was Doris Booth.
See also items 373 and 374.

531. OCSW NEWSLETTER   1977-c.
     Tl:Ontario Committee on the Status of Women newsletter
     Toronto, Ontario, Canada
     3 issues per year;1977(?)-c.
     L:not found
Not seen. Listed in item 294 (v.6,n°3, October 1977, p.88) and in
item 612 (v.10,n°4, December 1981/January 1982, p.44).

532. OPTIMIST   1977-c.
     Tl:The Optimist
     Pub. Yukon Status of Women Council
     Whitehorse, Yukon Territories, Canada
     Bi-monthly;quarterly;1977(?)-c.(?)
     L;not found
Not seen. Local newsletter. Earliest trace found occurs in item
294 (v.6, February 1977). Still listed in item 612 (v.10,n°4,

December 1981/January 1982).

533. OWLA NEWSLETTER 1977-1978
    Tl:OWLA:Ontario Women and the Law Association Newsletter
    Ed. Osgoode Women's Caucus
    Pub. Osgoode Hall Law School, York University
    Downsview, Ontario, Canada
    Quarterly;1977(?)-1978(?)
    L:not found
Not seen. Earliest mention found in item 294 (v.6,n°1, February
1977, p.89). No longer published says item 294 (v.3,n°4, 1978,
p.52).

534. OXFORD WOMEN'S LIBERATION NEWSLETTER 1977-c.
    Tl:Oxford Women's Liberation Newsletter
    Oxford
    Monthly;1977(?)-c.
    C:item 260?
    L:not found
Not seen. Local, women only newsletter. Earliest mention found on
a list drawn by W.I.R.E.S. and dated 11 May 1977 (see item 410).
Latest mention occurs in Cadman et al, 1981.

535. S.P.U.C. NEWSLETTER 1977-?
    Tl:S.P.U.C. Newsletter
    Ed. and pub. Society for the Protection of the Unborn Child
    F.n.k.;1977(?)-?
    L:Flic (2 undated issues)
S.P.U.C. founded by Sir William Liley, in the 1960s fights against
the third demand of the Women's Liberation Movement i.e. "Free
contraception and abortion on demand".

536. SYBIL 1977-c.
    Tl:Sybil:A Newsletter for Women in Western Australia
    Nedlands, West Australia, Australia
    F.n.k.;1977(?)-c.
    L:not found
Not seen. Earliest mention found occurs in item 393 (v.3,n°1,
February 1977, p.5). Also listed in item 612 (v.10,n°4, December
1981/January 1982, p.63).

537. UPSTREAM   1977-c.

    T1:Upstream:An Ottawa women's publication

    Ed. and pub. Feminist Publications of Ottawa

    Ottawa, Ontario, Canada

    25 issues per year;monthly;1977(?)-c.(?)

    L:not found

Not seen Earliest mention found in item 294 (v.6,n°1, February
1977). Latest mention occurs in <u>Feminist International</u>, Japan, not
listed (n°2, 1980, p.76). At first published in English only,
then became bilingual. News, features, arts, sports.

538. WOMEN'S AID FEDERATION NEWSLETTER   1977-c.

    T1:National Women's Aid Federation newsletter

    T2:Women's Aid Federation (England) Newsletter

    F.n.k.;1977(?)-c.

    L:not found

Not seen. Mentioned on a list established by W.I.R.E.S. dates
11 May 1977 (see item 409) and in Cadman et al, 1981. See also
item 352.

539. WOMEN'S NEWS SERVICE   1977-c.

    T1:Women's News Service

    Ed. Women's Officer

    Pub. Australian Union of Students, Women's Department

    Carlton, Victoria, Australia

    8 issues per year;1977(?)-c.

    L:F, Flic (both incomplete)

Earliest mention found in item 394 (v.3,n°1, February 1977).
Informative A4 printed newsletter of approximately 40 pages. It
offers a news service of events and women's issues by providing
"copy and graphics for campus newspapers and the alternative
press". News items and theoretical articles on wide ranging
feminist issues and on women's liberation struggles in Australia
and overseas. See also item 595.

540. CCLOW NEWS   1978-c.

    T1:Connections:CCLOW News

    T2:CCLOW News

    Ed. Mary Corkery

    Pub. (a)Canadian Committee on Learning Opportunities for
    Women;(b)Canadian Congress for Learning Opportunities for
    Women

Toronto, Ontario, Canada

F.n.k.;1978(?)-c.

L:not found

Not seen. Mentioned in item 294 (v.7,n°4, 1978, p.49) and in item
612 (v.10,n°4, December 1981/January 1982, p.40).

541. GEMMA   1978-c.

Tl:Gemma (lesbians with/without disabilities, all ages)

Newsletter

Quarterly

L:Flic (incomplete)

Gemma is a national self-help group of homosexual women with and
without physical handicap, all ages, formed in 1976 through
Sappho magazine (see item 293) and with help and encouragement
from Bill Stewart of Sexual Problems of the Disabled and from
Trevor Thomas who then held CHE's folio for disabled gays. In its
own words, it aims to lessen the isolation of disabled lesbians
who have no access to gay publications or groups and who do not
wish to "come out" to family, heterosexual friends, etc. and to
increase awareness of their needs in the lesbian/gay community and
in society in general. Membership in December 1979 was 80. The
newsletter mainly carries listings (of groups, penfriends, etc.)
and is available in print or on tape.

542. INTERNATIONAL FEMINISM AND NONVIOLENCE NEWSLETTER   1978-c.

Tl:International Feminism and Nonviolence Newsletter/
Feminisme et Non violence/Feminismus und Gewaltfreiheit

Manchester

Bi-monthly

L:not found

Not seen. Item 294 (v.7,n°4, 1978, p.63) mentions the publication
of issue 1. Latest mention found occurs in item 612 (v.10,n°4,
December 1981/January 1982, p.54). Women only newsletter put
together by Jenny Jacobs and Lesley Merryfinch and published in
English, French and German. Contents include news, short articles
and listings of contacts, of relevant books and periodicals.

543. WOMEN IN STRUGGLE   1978

Tl:Women in struggle

L:F (1 issue only)

A one-off publication produced by anarchist feminists. Focuses on
the oppression of Third World nations by the imperialist

countries. Imperialist domination uses millions of oppressed
people "as a source of cheap labour" and "imposes their own alien
culture on the oppressed countries". The system is "especially
oppressive to women".

544. WOMEN IN THE NUT 1978-c.
     Tl:Women in the NUT
     Ed. and pub. WINUT (Women In the National Union of Teachers)
     Irregular
     L:F, Flic (both incomplete)
Well produced A4 newsletter put out by a collective including
Carole Regan. The organisation has members in most areas of the
country and aims at pushing the National Union of Teachers to
defend and extend women's rights in education, employment and the
union. The newsletter carries organisational news, tackles the
question of women's representation in the union, of the position
of women within teaching (job protection, equal pay, promotion,
etc.), campaigns for equal access to all areas of the curriculum
for girls and boys and for issues which affect women as such: a
woman's right to choose and to control her own body, increased
access to nursery and childcare facilities. It condemn's NUT's
passivity and suggests positive action.

545. WOMEN'S ELECTORAL LOBBY NATIONAL BULLETIN 1978-c.
     Tl:Women's Electoral Lobby National bulletin
     O'Connor, Australia
     Every 3 weeks
     L:not found
Not seen. Listed in Ulrich's, 1982.

546. NOOL NEWS 1978-?
     Tl:Nool news
     Editorial collective including Sue Allen, London
     Pub. NOOL, York
     Monthly;14 January 1978-?
     L:Flic (incomplete)
The National Organization Of Lesbians was set up "to break the
isolation of women approaching lesbianism but also to go out and
smash the negative image of lesbians, through political action"
(item 297, n°66, January 1978, p.24). Its national newsletter
carries organisational news, reports on conferences, listings.

158

547. INTERNATIONAL JOURNAL OF WOMEN'S STUDIES 1978-c.

    Tl:International Journal of Women's Studies

    Ed. Sherri Clarkson

    Pub. Eden Press Women's Publications

    Montreal, Quebec, Canada

    5 issues per year;January/February 1978-c.

    L:F (incomplete)

    M:UM

Academic research journal of women's studies of about 100 pages covering "all aspects of women and their role in society, past, present and future" (v.1,n°1). Interdisciplinary, theoretical, historical, critical articles, abstracts of articles, book reviews. Circulation: 1,200 (Ulrich's, 1982).

548. WOMEN OF EUROPE 1978-c.

    Tl:Women of Europe:Femmes d'Europe

    Ed. Fausta Deshormes

    Pub. Commission of the European Communities

    Brussels, Belgium

    Bi-monthly;January/February 1978-c.

    L:F, Flic (both incomplete)

Free bulletin of about 20 pages, published in seven languages, mainly aimed at women's organisations and the press. Deals with the various aspects of women's lives: health, education, work, etc.. Includes statistics, news, contact addresses from each EEC member country; reports on debates concerning women in the European Parliament, on cases taken to the European Court, on the activities of women's organisations in Europe. Several substantial thematic supplements have been published. Not to be confused with item 452.

549. M/F 1978-c.

    Tl:M/F:A feminist journal

    One or two issues per year;February 1978-c.

    L:BM;B 79-15824;P 521/3241, F, Flic (incomplete)

    M:Harvester

A theoretical journal of 80-100 pages, put together by an editorial group which has included: Parveen Adams, Beverly Brown, Rosalind Coward (issues 1 and 2) and Elizabeth Cowie. It claimed a circulation of 1,200 copies in 1982. M/F aims to develop feminist theory and practice in relation to existing socialist and feminist politics. It examines Marxist-feminist positions. The first issues were influenced by the work of the French structuralist Marxist, Louis Althusser. Latter ones referred to Paul Hirst and Barry Hindess. M/F also attempts to use the work of the French historian and philosopher Michel Foucault. Finally it tries to develop the relevance of psychoanalysis to the Women's Liberation Movement and its coverage of issues includes Lacanian psychoanalytic thought. Though "theory has been the traditional preserve of men", the editorial board accepts to publish articles by men because "theory is not sexually differentiated" (n°2, p.3). However, the group "wishes to emphasise the importance of the appropriation and production of theory by women for women. Hence the basis on which men contribute to M/F raises a number of difficulties" (n°2, p.3). Contributors have included: Irene Bruegel, Mark Cousins, Paul Hirst, Julia Kristeva, Susan Lipshitz, Michele Montrelay, et al. Contents consist entirely of long articles followed by extensive notes and bibliographies, book reviews and some letters. Hence, though defining itself "as a journal within the Women's Movement and addressed to it" (n°2, p.3), its contents, language complexity and austere format make it difficult to read for women without previous knowledge of the theories referred to.

550. MOTHER'S MONEY Spring 1978
    T1:Mother's Money:Special Bulletin-Mother's Day
    Ed. and pub. International Wages for Housework Campaign
    L:F
Very thin one-off publication. Campaign news.

551. WOMEN'S STUDIES INTERNATIONAL FORUM 1978-c.
    T1:Women's Studies International Quarterly:
    Multidisciplinary Journal for the Rapid Publication of
    Research Communications and Review Articles in Women's
    Studies
    T2:Women's Studies International Forum:A Multidisciplinary
    Journal
    Ed. Dale Spender (London)
    Pub. Pergamon Press, Oxford
    Quarterly;bi-monthly;Spring 1978-c.
    L:BM;P 521/3189, F, Flic
Substantial theoretical journal with an academic approach to feminism, set up to help the rapid distribution and exchange of feminist research works in the multidisciplinary area of Women's

Studies world-wide. Published in the UK, it is also distributed in the US, Canada, Australia and New Zealand. It has a circulation of 2,000 copies (Standard Periodical Directory 1983). Topics covered are wide-ranging but guest editors are sometimes commissioned to put together thematic issues e.g. women and writing, women and media, men and sex. Though openly directed at academic women, articles are readable. However the subscription rates are off-putting.

552. BUREAU OF WOMEN'S AFFAIRS NEWSLETTER 1978
      Tl:Bureau of Women's Affairs Newsletter
      Kingston, Jamaica
      l issue only;March 1978
      C BY:item 863
      L:not found
Not seen. Mentioned in item 863 (n°1, May 1983, p.1). Number 1 was the only issue due to lack of money.

553. EOC NEWS 1978-1982
      Tl:EOC News
      Pub. Equal Opportunities Commission
      Manchester
      Bi-monthly;March 1978(?)-March/April 1982
      L:F, Flic (both incomplete)
Free tabloid newspaper. Print run approximately 30,000 copies. Organisational news. See also item 435, 512, 570 and 873.

554. HEROINE 1978
      Tl:Heroine:Women's Comik
      Pub. Arts Lab Press
      Birmingham
      F.n.k.;March 1978(?)-?
      L:Flic (March 1978 only)
A one-off publication? Feminist comic. Latest mentions occur in Spare Rib 1981 and 1982 diaries.

555. WORKING CLASS WOMEN'S LIBERATION NEWSLETTER 1978-1979
      Tl:Working Class Women's Liberation Newsletter
      Bradford;London
      Bi-monthly approx.;March(?) 1978-n°7, February/March(?) 1979
      L:Flic
Thin duplicated A4 newsletter available to women only. Brought out

161

by working class women "dissatisfied with publications dominated by middle class women and by their neglect of issues of immediate concern to working class women", the newsletter is valuable as being one of the rare attempts of this kind though unfortunately short-lived. "Working class women don't feel at home in the Movement. They say the women's movement is non hierarchical. Jargon" (n°5). "The Women's Movement must base itself on working class women and women of the oppressed nationalities, women who - in alliance with the labour movement, the Black movement, and others - have the social power to bring about change".

556. SEQUEL 1978-1983
    Tl:Sequel
    Eds. Tamarin, Sacha-Savannah
    Bi-monthly (33 issues);May 1978-1983
    L:BM;B79-19852 and P.512/3253, F, Flic (all incomplete)
Well produced national magazine of 28 pages aimed at isolated lesbians. It was available to women only in print and on tape in 1983, and sold mainly through subscriptions. Produced by two editors and two other collective members, Marie Banks and Jean Wilcox, it claimed a circulation of 1,000 copies in 1982. Its main function was to help lesbians feel less alone. The publication carried insert pages with "lonely heart" advertisements to pair up women. Contents also included news items, articles, poetry, book, film and play reviews, letters, graphics. Sequel was affiliated to the National Council of Civil Liberties. It worked closely with Gemma (see item 542), supported the Women's Liberation Movement, the ecology and animal liberation movements and campaigned against nuclear power and all forms of violence. It also encouraged vegetarianism and veganism.

557. ASSOCIATION OF RADICAL MIDWIVES NEWSLETTER 1978-c.
    Tl:Association of Radical Midwives newsletter
    Co-ordinators have included Jenny Spinks, Jen Flintham, Billie Hunter
    Pub. ARMS (Association of Radical Midwives)
    Sheffield;Cambridge;London
    Quarterly;June 1978-c.
    L:F, Flic (both incomplete)
A4 printed newsletter brought out by different groups around the country. The Association aims "to restore the role of the midwife for the benefit of the childbearing woman and her baby" and "to

re-establish the confidence of the midwife in her own skills"
(Summer 1983, p.1). The newsletter includes minutes from ARMS
quarterly meetings, is a vehicle for announcements, news and
shared technical information. It focuses on reporting current
childbirth practices and alternatives in the United Kingdom and
abroad. It also prints book and film reviews, lists useful books
and addresses.

558. STOKE WOMEN'S ACTION NEWSLETTER 1978-?
     Tl:Stoke Women's Action newsletter
     Stoke
     Monthly?;June 1978-?
     L:Flic (n°1 only)
Local women's liberation newsletter.

559. WICCA 1978-c.
     Tl:Wicca:A monthly feminist magazine
     T2:Wicca:"Wise Woman":Irish feminist magazine
     Coordinator:Wendy Wells;then Liz Holmes
     Dublin
     Monthly;June 1978-c.
     L:F, Flic (both incomplete)
A4 collectively run magazine of some twenty pages set up to fill
the gap left by the demise of item 461. Being aimed at "women in
all parts of Ireland, of all ages, in all spheres fo life" and not
at feminists only (see n°1), it is on public sale. Dedicated to
ending sexism and capitalism, it carries news, articles on the
experiences of women, contraception, childcare, marriage,
political struggles, the WLM, plus poetry, fiction, drawings,
photos, cartoons, book reviews and listings.

560. WOMEN AND MANUAL TRADES NEWSLETTER 1978-c.
     Tl:Women in manual trades Newsletter
     T2:Women and manual trades Newsletter
     Nottingham;Manchester;London
     F.n.k.;June 1978-c.
     L:Flic (incomplete)
Newsletter put together by women training or working in
traditionally male jobs such as building, gardening and mechanics.
Production seems to have been rotated among the various groups in
the country.

561. WOMEN'S CAUCUS NEWSLETTER   1978-c.

   T1:British Sociological Association:Women's Caucus Newsletter
   Eds. in 1982:Audrey Middleton and Linda Imray
   Pub. Sociology Department, York University, thereafter
   Postgraduate School of Analysis, University of Bradford
   York, Bradford
   Quarterly?;June 1978(?)-c.
   L:Flic (incomplete)

A4 newsletter for women only. Mainly covers issues of interest to
women in sociology, includes research reports, lists of events
and contacts.

562. ACHILLES HEEL   1978-1982

   T1:Achilles heel:A magazine of men's politics
   T2:Achilles heel
   One or two issues per year;Summer 1978-n°6/7, November 1982
   (n.i.c.)
   L:F

Substantial anti-sexist men's magazine. Produced by "a group of
men committed to supporting one another in writing and publishing
material about men's politics and socialism" (n°3, 1980, p.40),
it was the only public forum for discussion about masculinity in
the United Kingdom when it started. The group supported "the aims,
perspectives and demands of the Women's Liberation Movement" (n°3,
p.3). The men involved aimed to redefine and change the nature of
their relationships with women and with each other as men (n°1,
p.3). Articles discussed the issues raised in men's consciousness
raising groups. Among the topics covered were sexuality, family,
patriarchy, masculinity and violence, etc.. Achilles Heel also
included letters, lists of men's groups, poems. Issue 6/7 claimed
a circulation of 3-4,000 copies per issue.

563. FAN   1978-c.

   T1:FAN:Feminist Arts Newsletter
   T2:FAN:Feminist Artists Newsletter
   T3:FAN:Feminist Art News Magazine
   T4:FAN:Feminist Artists News
   T5:FAN:Feminist Arts News
   Birmingham
   Quarterly;3 to 4 issues a year;Summer 1978-c.
   L:F, Flic (both incomplete)

An art magazine by, for and about women artists, writers, poets,

photographers, art historians, etc., set up at the 1978 national
Women's Liberation Conference held in Birmingham. Originally a
subscribers-only duplicated news sheet with a circulation of
300/500 copies, it has been printed since 1980 and available on
tape since 1982. It claims a circulation of 1,200/1,500 copies.
The thematic part of each issue is produced by a different
regional collective of women working in the field on art, craft
and design. "Producing an issue often becomes a creative and
consciousness-raising experience and as such often needs more time
than arbitrary deadlines allow" (n°6, 1982, p.2). So in 1982/83
deadlines were abandoned. Three to four issues come out per year
depending on finances and the time it takes a production
collective to develop its theme and material. Photography, art
history, women's craft, women's space have been some of the themes
dealt with so far. The basic administrative structure e.g.
advertising, finance, distribution, subscription and long-term
planning is run by an open business collective of readers. The
latter composed of eight permanent members, has included: Kate
Walker, Sol Jorgensen, Gillian Elinor, Michele Furier, Erika
Matlow, Monica Ross, Sue Scott, Julie Harper, etc.. The business
collective also deals with news and events, letters, commentary
and review pages. FAN is valuable as it is the only British
magazine entirely devoted to covering the arts from a feminist
perspective. It fills a gap in the market. In the collective's own
words, the male dominated art world needs to be made aware of the
Women's Art Movement. FAN's main functions are education,
information, support, contact.

564. MSPRINT   1978-c.
    Tl:Msprint
    Dundee;Glasgow
    Irregular;August 1978-1980(?);May(?) 1983-c.(?)
    C:item 499
    L:F (incomplete), Flic (issues 1 to 7)
    M:Harvester
Msprint superseded item 499 after the ideological split in the
latter's collective. Its first editorial collective - Esther
Breitenbach, Fiona Forsyth, Joanna Haynes, Sally Henry, Marion
Keogh, Geri Smyth and Nina Woodcock - had many members from the
previous publication. Its members were spread across Scotland.
Less formal and more illustrated and attractive than item 499.
Msprint aims to fill a vacuum by providing Scottish women with a

magazine concentrating on the concerns and the aims of women
living and working in Scotland. It develops a socialist feminist
analysis of the legal, social and cultural position of women in
Scotland and the role of women in Scottish politics. Together with
feature articles, contents include letters, book, film and play
reviews, poetry, fiction. Issue 7 had a circulation of 1,000
copies. Afterwards, financial difficulties demoralised the
collective and led to its breakdown. Publication was interrupted
for almost two years. A new collective including Mairon Keogh
and Anne Kane was formed. As a means of re-introducing Msprint
to women, a special 4 page supplement was brought out for
International Women's Day and given at the Faslane women's
demonstration on 6 March 1983 (item 449, April 1983). It was to be
followed up by a full length edition of Msprint. No further
information.

565. CANADIAN WOMAN STUDIES 1978-c.
      Tl:Canadian Women's Studies:Les Cahiers de la Femme
      T2:Canadian Woman Studies:Les Cahiers de la Femme CWS/CF
      Eds. Shelagh Wilkinson and Mair Verthuy
      Scarborough;then Downsview, Ontario, Canada
      Quarterly;Fall 1978-c.
      L:F, Flic (both 1 issue only)
An interdisciplinary research journal "for all women who are
teaching and learning together" (v.1,n°1, p.2). It is designed to
provide information and debate on educational issues affecting
women, details of research work in progress. Contents consist of
articles in English and in French, interviews, poetry, book
reviews. Circulation: 2,000 copies per issue (Standard Periodical
Directory, 1983).

566. FIREWEED 1978-c.
      Tl:Fireweed:A women's cultural journal
      T2:Fireweed
      Toronto, Ontario, Canada
      3 issues per year;Fall 1978-c.
      L:Flic (incomplete)
Substantial literary and cultural journal brought out with the
financial assistance of the Canada Council and the Ontario Arts
Council Circulation: 1,500 copies (see Ulrich's, 1982). The
editorial collective has included among others: Sheilagh Crandall,
Pamela Godfree, Nila Gupta, Edie Hoffman, Joss Maclennan, Makeda

Silvera and Rhea Tregebov. Its members are committed to publishing on all aspects of women's culture. Fireweed includes essays, political commentary, personal experiences, poetry, fiction, reviews, drawings, photographs. Although it focuses on Canadian resources, it also prints works from American and British women. Some issues are thematic. Issue 10 (Spring 1981) focused on women's writing, issue 13 (1982) on lesbianism. Some are guest edited, for instance n°16 (Spring 1983) which was devoted to women of colour. Not to be confused with Fireweed, Lancaster, UK (not listed).

567. REVOLUTIONARY AND RADICAL FEMINIST NEWSLETTER 1978-c.
    Tl:Revolutionary and radical feminist newsletter
    Leeds
    Irregular (12 issues by 1983);Autumn 1978-c.
    L:Flic (incomplete)
A4 occasional newsletter averaging thirty pages and available to women only. It grew out of the Revolutionary and Radical Feminist Conference. Its collective, composed of eight to eleven members (mainly lesbians) has included Dee Aheane, Lal Coveney, Marianne Hester, Leslie Kay, Sandra McNeill, and Annie Smith, among others. In its own words, "it aims to promote discussion of revolutionary and radical feminist politics which sees male supremacy as the root cause of women's oppression with the ultimate objective of overthrowing male power". Contents carry articles, letters, short stories, poetry, book reviews, graphics from a sex class perspective. Features provide strong coverage of the Women's Liberation Movement, lesbianism, violence against women, etc.. From issue 7 onwards, the newsletter has been available on tape for blind women. Its circulation has risen from 200 copies for the first issue up to some 800 copies in 1983.

568. WOMAN'S FINANCIAL LETTER 1978-1980
    Tl:Woman's financial letter
    Ed. Sheila Black
    Pub. Stonehart and Charity Ltd
    F.n.k.;November 1978-1980 (n.i.c.)
    L:F (incomplete)
Newsletter produced by a woman financial journalist. Available by subscriptions only. Faint feminist leanings.

569. CHRISTIAN PARITY GROUP NEWSLETTER   1978-1980
    Tl:Christian Parity Group Newsletter
    F.n.k.;November 1978(?)-August 1980 (n.i.c.)
    L:Flic (incomplete)
Self-explanatory.

570. EOC RESEARCH BULLETIN   1978-1983
    Tl:EOC Research Bulletin
    Ed. and pub. Equal Opportunities Commission
    Manchester
    Irregular;Winter 1978/79-n°7, 1983 (n.i.c.)
    L:F, Flic
Bulletin reporting on current research on sex discrimination and
equality of opportunity. Free of charge. Circulation of about
800 copies in 1982. See also items 435, 512, 553 and 875.

571. ACTION   1978-c.
    Tl:Action
    Ed. and pub. Manitoba Action Committee on the Status of Women
    Winnipeg, Manitoba, Canada
    10 issues per year;1978(?)-c.
    L:not found
Not seen. Earliest mention occurs in item 294 (v.7,n°4, 1978, p.47)
p.47). Also listed in Standard Periodical Directory, 1983.

572. BRADFORD WOMEN'S LIBERATION NEWSLETTER   1978-1981
    Tl:Bradford Women's Liberation Newsletter
    Bradford
    Monthly?:1978(?)-1981(?)
    C BY:item 817
    L:not found
Not seen. Described in ISIS (n°16, 1980, p.35) as a local women
only newsletter set up a few years ago. Internal to the Bradford
area Women's Liberation Movement. Production rotates among the
different local action groups.

573. CANADIAN WOMEN'S HISTORY COMMITTEE NEWSLETTER   1978-?
    Tl:Canadian Women's History Committee Newsletter - Bulletin
    du Comite Canadien de l'Histoire des Femmes
    Coordinators:Joyce Parr and Marie Lavigne
    Vancouver, British Columbia and Quebec, Quebec, Canada
    Irregular;1978(?)-?

L:not found

Not seen. Only trace found item 294 (v.7,n°4, 1978, p.49).

574. CHRISTIAN FEMINIST NEWSLETTER   1978-c.
     T1:Christian Feminist Newsletter
     T2:Christian Feminist Newsletter:the Newsletter of the
     Christian Women's Information and Referral Service and the
     Christian Movement
     T3:Christian Feminist Newsletter (n°9)
     T4:Christian Feminist Newsletter:the Newsletter of the
     Christian Women's Information and Referral Service and the
     Christian Movement
     T5:Christian Feminist Newsletter
     3 issues per year approx.;1978(?)-c.
     L:F, Flic (both incomplete)
Earliest issue seen: n°9, March 1980. A4 duplicated national
Newsletter produced by women members of the Christian Movement,
"who wish to look at feminist issues from a Christian standpoint
and to challenge sexism within and outside the Church" (n°9, p.1).
Internal to the Movement, n°21, 1983, was sent to over 200 women.
Editorial and production responsibility was held by Sheelagh
Robinson until 1982. Now it is edited by different regional
Christian Feminist groups. Members of the 1982-83 administration
were: Sue Dowell, Linda Hurcombe and Sara Maitland. Contents
include articles, news of groups, reports from conferences,
information on forthcoming events, contact addresses, book
reviews. Articles focus on issues relating to feminist theology
and to the different trends within Christian Feminism.
Contributions are from women in the network mainly. See also item
841.

575. CLOSE ENCOUNTERS OF THE LESBIAN KIND   1978(?)
     T1:Close encounters of the lesbian kind
     Aberdeen
     F.n.k.;1978-?
     L:F, Flic
Printed magazine produced by the Aberdeen Lesbian group "to
publicise the existence of the group" formed in August 1977.

576. CONNECTIONS   1978-c.
     T1:Connections - Newsletter for Women in Canadian Schools of
     Social Work

Ed. and pub. (a)Women's Group at the Maritime School of
Social Work, Halifax, Nova Scotia, Canada;(b)Connections
Editorial Collective, School of Social Work, Hamilton,
Ontario, Canada
3 issue per year;1978(?)-c.
L:not found
Not seen. Mentioned in item 294 (v.7,n°4, 1978, p.49) and in item
612 (v.10,n°4, December 1981/January 1982, p.41).

577. CPA SECTION ON WOMEN AND PSYCHOLOGY NEWSLETTER   1978-1980
Tl:CPA Interest Group on Women and Psychology:newsletter
T2:CPA Section on Women and Psychology newsletter
Eds. Jeri Wine, Marti Syme, Barbara Moses
Pub. Canadian Psychological Association (Dept of Applied
OISE)
Toronto, Ontario, Canada
3 issues per year;1978(?)-1980(?)
C BY:item 791
L:not found
Not seen. Listed in item 294 (v.7,n°4, 1978, p.49).

578. IMAGES OF WOMEN   1978-?
Tl:Images of women
Ed. Centre for Contemporary Cultural Studies
Pub. University of Birmingham
Birmingham
F.n.k.;1978(?)-?
L:not found
Not seen. Listed in item 294 (v.7,n°4, 1978, p.62). "Collectively
produced by women at the C.C.C.S.". Not to be confused with items
419 and 457.

579. INDIAN RIGHTS FOR INDIAN WOMEN   1978-c.
Tl:Indian rights for Indian women:newsletter
Ed. Bella Shenfield
Edmonton, Alberta, Canada
Monthly;1978(?)-c.
L:not found
Not seen. Listed in item 294 (v.7,n°4, 1978, p.50). Organisation
founded in 1971 and "fighting for native women's rights and
against the sexual discrimination of Section 12 of the Indian
Act". Latest mention found occurs in item 612 (v.10,n°4, December

1981/January 1982, p.42).

580. MELBOURNE WOMEN'S LIBERATION NEWSLETTER   1978-c.
     Tl:Melbourne Women's Liberation Newsletter
     Melbourne, Victoria, Australia
     Monthly;1978(?)-c.
     L:Flic (incomplete)
Internal newsletter carrying news items, theoretical articles,
letters, etc.. Mentioned in item 612 (v.10,n°4, December 1981/
January 1982, p.62).

581. NATIONAL NEWSLETTER OF THE CANADIAN RAPE CRISIS CENTRES
     1978-?
     Tl:National newsletter of the Canadian Rape Crisis Centres
     Montreal, Quebec, Canada
     F.n.k.;1978(?)-?
     L:not found
Not seen. Only mention occurs in item 294 (v.7,n°4, 1978, p.51).
National coordinator, Joanie Vance.

582. NATIONAL W   1978-?
     Tl:National W
     Pub. Australian Union of Students, Women's Department
     Carlton, Victoria, Australia
     F.n.k.;1978(?)-?
     L:F (issue dated 4 September 1978 only), Flic
Interesting tabloid put together by an editorial collective. Wide
ranging topics: abortion, schooling, sexism, racism, health. See
item 539 (n°21, 1978).

583. NETWORK OF SASKATCHEWAN WOMEN   1978-c.
     Tl:Network of Saskatchewan Women
     Pub. Saskatchewan Action Committee on the Status of Women
     Prince Albert/Davidson, Saskatchewan, Canada
     Bi-monthly;monthly;1978(?)-c.
     L:not found
Not seen. Earliest mention found in item 294 (v.7,n°4, 1978, p.51),
latest one in item 612 (v.10,n°4, December 1981/January 1982,
p.44). Eight page tabloid reporting on the activities of the
Committee, reviews, articles, calendar of events.

584. NEWS SHEET 1978-c.

    Tl:Advisory Committee on Women's Affairs:news sheet

    Pub. ACWA

    Wellington, New Zealand

    Quarterly approx.;1978(?)-c.

    L:Flic (incomplete)

The Advisory Committee on Women's Affairs has replaced the former
Committee on Women as the official advisory body to the New
Zealand government on women's affairs. The news sheet reports on
the activities of official bodies, on governmental policies, etc.,
affecting women.

585. POWERHOUSE GALLERY 1978-c.

    Tl:Powerhouse gallery

    Montreal, Quebec, Canada

    Bi-monthly;1978(?)-c.

    L:not found

Not seen. Bilingual art newsletter. For further information, see
item 294 (v.7,n°4, 1978, p.52) and item 612 (v.10,n°4, December
1981/January 1982, p.44).

586. PRAIRIE WOMEN 1978-?

    Tl:Prairie women - A newsletter of Saskatoon Women's
    Liberation

    Saskatoon, Saskatchewan, Canada

    Monthly;1978(?)-?

    C:item 378?

    L:not found

Not seen. Listed in item 294 (v.7,n°4, 1978, p.52).

587. REVOLTING WOMEN 1978-?

    Tl:Revolting women

    Vancouver, British Columbia, Canada

    F.n.k.;1978(?)-?

    L:not found

Not seen. Anarchist feminist publication. Only one reference
found: item 294 (v.7,n°4, 1978, p.52).

588. RHIANNON 1978-c.

    Tl:Rhiannon:A paper for women in Wales

    Caerdydd;Newport, Gwent

    Quarterly;1978(?)-c.(?)

L:F (n°5, 1979 only)

A4 printed magazine publishing articles in English and Welsh.
Different groups of women take turns in producing the newsletter.
Local and national news wide-ranging features: Women's Aid, the
mass media, contraception, etc., plus photos, cartoons.

589. UNION WOMAN 1978-c.
     Tl:Union woman
     Pub. Organized Working Women
     Don Mills, Ontario, Canada
     Bi-monthly;5 per year;1978(?)-c.
     C:item 458
     L:not found
Not seen. Listed in item 294 (v.7,n°4, 1978, p.53). Coordinator
Deirdre Gallagher. Latest mention found occurs in item 612 (v.10,
n°4, December 1981/January 1982, p.46).

590. WOMEN AND THE NEW DEMOCRATIC PARTY 1978-?
     Tl:Women and the New Democratic Party
     Ottawa, Ontario, Canada
     Bi-monthly;1978(?)-?
     L:not found
Not seen. Only mention occurs in item 294 (v.7,n°4, 1978, p.53).

591. WOMEN AND THE VISUAL ARTS NEWSLETTER 1978-?
     Tl:Women and the visual arts newsletter
     York
     Quarterly;1978(?)-?
     L:not found
Not seen. Only trace found occurs in item 297 (n°71, June 1978,
p.24). Contents of issue 1 in preparation are given: personal
accounts by women artists, information on events and exhibitions
and reading lists. Contact person: Katherine Hamer. Unable to say
if the newsletter was eventually produced.

592. WOMEN AND THERAPY 1978-1980
     Tl:Women and therapy
     Ed. and pub. Women's Counselling Referral and Education
     Centre (WCREC)
     Toronto, Ontario, Canada
     Irregular;1978(?)-1980(?)
     L:not found

Not seen. Earliest mention occurs in item 294 (v.7,n°4, 1978, p.54). Item 612 (v.10,n°4, December 1981/January 1982, p.47) announces the discontinuation of publication. Not to be confused with the later US journal of the same title.

593. WOMEN IN THE LABOUR FORCE   1978-?
     T1:Women in the labour force:facts and figures
     Pub. Women's Bureau, Conditions of Work, Labour Canada
     Ottawa, Ontario, Canada
     Annual;1978(?)-?
     C:item 332
     L:not found
Not seen. Only trace found occurs in item 294 (v.7,n°4, 1978, p.54).

594. WOMEN'S DEPARTMENT NEWS   1978-?
     T1:Women's Department News
     Pub. Australian Union of Students, Women's Department
     Carlton, Victoria, Australia
     10 issues in 1978;1978(?)-?
     L:not found
Not seen. Only mention occurs in item 539 (n°21, 1978). Apparently, mainly newsclippings.

595. WOMEN'S RIGHTS AND NURSERY CAMPAIGN NEWSLETTER   1978-1981
     T1:Women's Rights Standing Committee Newsletter
     T2:Women's Rights and Nursery Campaign Newsletter
     Pub. Inner London NATFHE, WRSC
     Irregular;1978(?)-n°5, July 1981 (n.i.c.)
     L:Flic (n°5 only)
Very slim A4 printed newsletter of the Women's Rights Standing Committee established in 1977. Issue 5 was put together by Jenny Bailey, Pamela Calder, Angela Conway, Connie Ostman.

596. BROADSIDE   1979-c.
     T1:Broadside:A feminist review
     Pub. Broadside Communications Limited
     Toronto, Ontario, Canada
     10 issues per year
     L:Flic (v.2,n°10, August/September 1981 only)
A newspaper/review produced by a Toronto-based collective. Not to be confused with Broadside, USA.

597. FRIENDS OF THE FEMINIST ARCHIVE NEWSLETTER   1979
     Tl:Friends of the Feminist Archive Newsletter
     Ed. and pub. Feminist Archive
     Shepton Mallet, Somerset
     Irregular
     L:Flic (n°2, June 1979 only)
Very slim newsletter on the running of the library. Publication
was interrupted when the Feminist Archive had to close for a few
years. See also items 617 and 645.

598. HEALTHSHARING   1979-c.
     Tl:Healthsharing:A Canadian Women's Health Quarterly
     Eds. Ann Ford, Jennifer Penny
     Toronto, Ontario, Canada
     Quarterly
     L:not found
Not seen. Described in Feminist Periodicals, USA, not listed (v.3,
n°4, 1983, p.VI) as providing "a critical analysis of women's
health issues from a feminist perspective".

599. LABRISH   1979
     Tl:Labrish:Black Women for Wages for Housework (UK)
     F.n.k.;1979-?
     L:F (n°2, 1979 only)
Very thin A4 newsletter brought out by black women of the Wages
for Housework Campaign in Britain. "Labrish" is a West Indian word
for gossip. Free to women.

600. LONDON CISSY NEWSLETTER   1979-1982
     Tl:London CISSY Newsletter
     Ed. and pub. Campaign to Impede Sex Stereotyping in the Young
     L:not found
Not seen. CISSY formed in 1973. The original group produced the
children's book issue of Shrew, October 1973 (item 244). The
group reformed in 1976 and published a list of Non sexist picture
books in 1979. Following this the group become two regional ones:
Southern CISSY based in Bournemouth (item 602) and London CISSY.
London Cissy group includes Frances Cotton. It gave talks, led
workshops on sexism in children's books and started a thin
newsletter.

175

601. NATIONAL WOMEN'S ADVISORY COUNCIL 1979-c.

    Tl:National Women's Advisory Council:Annual Report

    Ed. NWAC

    Pub. Australian Government Publishing Service

    Canberra, A.C.T., Australia

    Annual

    L:not found

Not seen. Listed in Ulrich's, 1982. Report presented to the
Commonwealth Government on the position and the special needs of
women in Australia and carrying the Council's recommendations to
bring about change. See also item 634.

602. SOUTHERN CISSY NEWSLETTER 1979-1980

    Tl:Southern CISSY Newsletter

    Ed. and pub. Campaign to Impede Sex Stereotyping in the Young

    Bournemouth

    L:not found

Newsletter campaigning against sexism in children's books, listing
and reviewing non-sexist books. See also item 600.

603. VIVE LA DIFFERENCE 1979-c.

    Tl:Vive La Difference:The voice of the Campaign for the

    Feminine Woman (C.F.W.)

    Ed. David W. Stayt

    Swindon, Wilts.

    Irregular (11 issues by February 1984)

    L:F (incomplete)

Very thin anti-feminist newsletter for the membership of the
C.F.W., "Britain's new and only organization to counter women's
lib. and to promote the value and validity of the different sex
roles - the responsible dominant masculine man and the submissive
feminine woman . . . The CFW wants to see an end to Women's Lib./
Unisex legislation, education, propaganda, and attitudes which
undermine these valuable things in society. The CFW viewpoint is
strongly based on biblical teachings." It claims a circulation of
5,000 copies.

604. WOMEN AND WRITING NEWSLETTER 1979-1981

    Tl:Women and literature

    T2:Women, literature and Criticism Newsletter

    T3:Women and writing newsletter

    Birmingham, Cleveland

F.n.k.;1979-1981(?)

L:BM;P 523/1655 (n°5), Flic (n°2)

Started as a result of the Women, Literature and Criticism
Conference by Janet Batsleer and Rebecca O'Rourke. It included
theoretical articles, discussion of courses, book reviews. The
issues were undated. Latest trace found occurs in Cadman et al,
1981.

605. WOMEN'S REFUGES MAGAZINE   1979-c.(?)

T1:Women's refuges magazine

Ed. Women's Liberation Halfway House Collective

Elsternwick, Victoria, Australia

L:Flic (n°1 only)

Issue 1 was an interesting and substantial magazine. The
collective described its aims as follows. "The contents of our
magazine have come out of our experiences as an action-based
group, our commitment critical re-evaluation of our actions
inside and outside the refuge, and our desire to stimulate the
thoughts and actions of other groups . . . We don't see the
magazine as a theoretical or academic journal, but nor do we see
it as just a newsletter, reporting events and exchanging
information about activities. We see it as being somewhere in
between, based on action, but being able to step back and
critically evaluate" (n°1, p.3). Articles are concerned with life
in the refuges themselves but also with what women running them
are up against - law, violence, housing, health services, etc..

606. YORK FEMINIST NEWS 1979-c.

T1:York feminist news

Ed. and pub. York Women's Centre

York

3 or 4 issues per year

Not seen. Local women only paper. The coming out of issue 12 is
announced in item 410 (n°101, 1980). Described in ISIS (n°16,
1980, p.36) as a mixture of personal writing, fiction,
theoretical articles and comment on topical issues. Still listed
in item 612 (v.10,n°4, December 1981/January 1982, p.57).

607. ANARCHIST-FEMINIST NEWSLETTER 1979-1980

T1:Anarcha-feminist newsletter

T2:Anarchist-feminist newsletter

London

F.n.k.;January 1979-n°8, October 1980 (n.i.c.)

L:Flic

Women only newsletter. Latest mentions occur in item 297 (n°101, December 1980, p.30) and in Cadman et al, 1981. Sisterwrite bookshop was their contact address.

608. CO-COUNSELLING WOMEN'S NEWSLETTER 1979-?

Tl:Co-counselling women's Newsletter

Bristol;Sevenoaks

Monthly?;January 1979-?

L:Flic (n°1 only)

A4 newsletter concerned with women's mental health and intended to help re-evaluation women's groups keep in touch. Contact persons: Rosie Brennan; then Sheila Rose.

609. FEMINIST REVIEW 1979-c.

Tl:Feminist review

3 issues per year;January 1979-c.

L:F, Flic (incomplete)

A theoretical journal with an academic approach published by an editorial collective of 15 to 19 women most of whom are involved in teaching women's studies courses or in other feminist research. The group has included among others: Michele Barrett, Lesley Caldwell, Victoria Greenwood, Cora Kaplan, Annette Kuhn, Karen Margolis, Mary McIntosh, Maxine Molyneux, Rebecca O'Rourke, Mandy Snell, Angela Weir, Elizabeth Wilson and Ann-Marie Wolpe. Distributed by Pluto Press, each issue has approximately a hundred pages and includes around six long articles plus book reviews, a notice board, letters and illustrations. Up to issue 11 though the women on the collective described themselves as feminists and socialists, Feminist Review welcomed contributions from any point of view within feminism, although presently they only accept contributions from a distinctively socialist feminist perspective. Moreover the declared editorial policy is to give priority to articles which "develop the theory of Women's Liberation and debate the political perspectives and strategy of the movement". The review is also intended "to be a forum for work in progress and current research and debate in Women's Studies". It is interdisciplinary in content, topics covered have included the family, the State, work, sexuality, the arts . . . . It tries to have an international approach. Each past issue has included one article at least on and by Third World women. The collective

handed over issue 17 to a guest editorial group of Black women who
have had full editorial responsibility. Each issue had an average
circulation of 2,700 copies in 1982.

610. MANUSHI 1979-c.

Tl:Manushi:A journal about women and society

New Delhi, India

Bi-monthly;January 1979-c.

L:Flic (incomplete)

The first and only Indian Women's Liberation magazine distributed
nationally produced both in Hindi and English and available in
both languages in Great Britain. The Hindi title means "women".
Collectively produced by nine women belonging to the organisation
"Samta", it has faced serious financial difficulties having to
fundraise for each issue. It is one of the few magazines produced
by women from a Third World country and offers a valuable insight
of women's life situations in India and of their struggles for
change. Manushi hopes to provide a medium for women to "speak
out". It "wants to bring women's organizations and activists in
touch with each other. Reach women everywhere . . . Counter the
distortion of the life-situation and image of women and the
trivialization of women's issues". It tackles a wide variety of
political and social issues concerning women e.g. the dowry
system, women in the media, women in factories, the land struggle.
Contents include news, features and interviews but also regular
sections such as letters, health news, law reports, book and film
reviews, short stories, poems, etc.. It is a useful source of a
wide variety of information about Indian women.

611. FAST NEWSLETTER 1979-c.

Tl:FAST Newsletter

Ed. and pub. Feminists Against Sexual Terrorism

Leeds;Manchester

Irregular (8 issues in January 1983);February 1979-c.

L:Flic (incomplete)

National A4 newsletter aimed at women interested in the fight
against male sexual violence in all its forms and available to
women only through subscription mainly. FAST was started after
the national Anti-Rape Conference held in Bristol on 19 November
1978, by women active in Rape Crisis Centres, anti-rape groups
and Women's Aid Groups. Each issue is produced by a different
group of women. Only subscriptions, distribution and finance are

centralised. These were handled in Leeds until 1982 when
Manchester Crisis Line took them over. Originally FAST was
intended to "generate a national network to facilitate a dialogue
among feminists working to eliminate male violence against
women . . ." (n°1). Early issues had letters and news from a
variety of groups, theoretical articles, discussions of practical
action, book reviews. Topics covered have included rape but also
sexual abuse of female children, incest, pornography,
clitoridectomy, etc.. Yet FAST has very quickly become dominated
by contributions from women working in Rape Crisis groups. Hence
much of the contents is of most relevance to them. Now rape is
only one form of male violence. Moreover Rape Crisis groups are
overworked. Since 1981 there have been long gaps between each
issue. That makes it difficult for groups to swap information,
experiences, theories with each other and to coordinate national
actions through the newsletter. Many women think FAST should be
wider than a newsletter for Rape Crisis Centres and continue to
be a forum for all groups of women fighting against male sexual
violence against women.

612. RESOURCES FOR FEMINIST RESEARCH   1979-c.
    Tl:Resources for Feminist Research/Documentation sur la
    Recherche Feministe
    Pub. Department of Sociology, O.I.S.E.
    Editorial Board:Mary O'Brien, Jennifer L. Newton, Margaret
    Andersen, Jeri Wine, Marylee Stephenson, Carol Zavitz,
    Lynda Yanz
    Toronto, Ontario, Canada
    Quarterly;February 1979-c.
    C:item 294
    L:F
Improved and enlarged continuation of item 294. Aimed at feminist
scholars, the journal provides an essential source of updated
interdisciplinary and international information concerning
on-going research on women and sex roles. Contents include book
reviews, review essays, bibliographies, a periodicals and
resources guide, a list of new courses in women's studies,
abstracts of conference papers, work in progress and Canadian
theses. Text in English and French. Circulation: 1,200 copies per
issue (Ulrich's, 1982).

180

613. EVERYTHING   1979-c.
      Tl:Everything
      Pub. Sydney University
      Sydney, New South Wales, Australia
      F.n.k.;March 1979(?)-c.
      L:Flic (March 1979 issue only)
Anarcha-feminist magazine. Listed in item 697 (n°12, August/
September 1983, p.29).

614. LESBIAN EXPRESS   1979
      Tl:Lesbian Express
      Manchester
      F.n.k.;April 1979-September/October 1979 (n.i.c.)
      C:item 513?
      L:Flic (2 issues only)
Thin A4 printed newsletter. Thinking "almost all the Lesbian
publications" were "serious and heavily political" the publishing
group aimed to produce a newsletter reflecting some aspects of
lesbians' lives, thoughts, humour, art, feelings and politics.
(April 1979.)

615. CASSOE NEWSLETTER   1979-c.
      Tl:CASSOE newsletter
      Ed. and pub. Campaign Against Sexism and Sexual Oppression
      in Education
      Bi-monthly;May 1979-c.
      L:F, Flic (both incomplete)
Valuable informative newsletter. Contents self-explanatory.

616. NESSIE   1979-1981
      Tl:Nessie
      Edinburgh
      Monthly(?);May(?) 1979-1981 (n.i.c.)
      L:not found
Not seen. Item 297 (n°84, July 1979, p.25) announces the
publication of issue 2 in June 1979 describing it as a Scottish
radical and revolutionary newsletter for women only. Latest trace
found occurs in Cadman et al, 1981.

617. FEMINIST ARCHIVE SUBSCRIBERS' BULLETIN 1979
    Tl:Feminist Archive Subscribers' Bulletin
    Shepton Mallet, Somerset
    Irregular;June 1979-n°2, December 1979 (n.i.c.)
    L:F (2 issues), Flic (1 issue)
Thin bulletin of accessions of the Feminist Archive established in
1978. The collection includes books and research material but
also ephemera such as newsletters, pamphlets, posters, badges,
etc.. See also items 597 and 643.

618. FOWAAD 1979-1980
    Tl:FOWAAD:newsletter of the organization of women of Asian
    and African Descent (OWAAD)
    Ed. Newsletter Committee
    Pub. OWAAD
    Bi-monthly;July 1979-n°7, November 1980 (n.i.c.)
    L:Flic (incomplete)
National newsletter of OWAAD, an organization set up in February
1978. It printed news and analyses of current campaigns and events
of concern to Asian and Black women and workers in Britain. It
campaigned against education cuts, the anti-abortion Corrie Bill,
the Tory immigration and nationality laws, the Police Bill.
Together with features, it included a review section, letters and
contact addresses. It folded due to financial difficulties and
lack of woman power. OWAAD itself became defunct in 1982.

619. YOUNG WIMMIN 1979
    Tl:This magazine is for, about and by Young Wimmin
    Monthly(?);August 1979-?
    L:Flic (n°1 only)
Thin A4 duplicated newsletter produced by a group of young women
who "felt a real need for young wimmin to have somewhere to share
experiences and to help each other become more aware of the
daily oppressive/exploitative situations" (n°1). Only other trace
found was an announcement in item 297 (n°88, November 1979, p.29)
asking for contributions towards more issues.

620. AIMS NEWSLETTER 1979-1982
    Tl:AIMS Newsletter
    Ed. and pub. Association for Improvements in Maternity
    Services
    Hove;London

Quarterly;Autumn 1979(?)-1982(?)

C BY:item 887?

L:Flic (a few issues only)

National newsletter carrying reports on bad hospital/doctor treatment in childbirth, accounts of informative alternative experiences, details of research in progress and book reviews.

621. MERSEYSIDE WOMEN'S LIBERATION NEWSLETTER 1979-c.

Tl:Merseyside Women's Liberation Newsletter

Ed. and pub. Merseyside Women's Centre

Liverpool

Monthly;October 1979-c.

C:item 417?

L:not found

Thin local duplicated newsletter available to women only. It keeps women informed on what is going on locally and especially at the Women's Centre. Together with news, contents include letters, reports, on conferences, articles mostly written from a radical lesbian stand. Issue 1 had a circulation of 40 copies. In 1983 the newsletter had a current circulation of 70 copies per issue. Not to be confused with item 490.

622. WOMEN AT WORK 1979-c.

Tl:Women at work

Ed. and pub. ACTU Working Women's Centre

Melbourne, Victoria, Australia

Bi-monthly?;October/November 1979-c.

L:Flic (incomplete)

Multilingual tabloid collectively produced and focusing on working women. Features information about trade unions, occupational health, equal opportunities, child care facilities, etc.. Not to be confused with item 332.

623. WARPATH 1979-?

Tl:Warpath:Women Against Rape news sheet

Quarterly?;Winter 1979/1980(?)-?

L:F (1 issue only:Winter 1979/1980)

Slim A4 bulletin produced by the different WAR groups across the country.

624. ANTI-SEXIST MEN'S NEWSLETTER 1979-c.

Tl:Anti-sexist men's newsletter

London

Irregular;monthly;1979(?)-c.(?)

L:not found

Not seen. Earliest mention found in item 297 (n°88, November 1979, p.35). Latest one occurs in item 297 (n°111, October 1981, p.34). Brought out by men who consider themselves to be struggling against sexism. Each issue is produced by a different men's group. It also welcomes contributions from feminists commenting on their actions, etc.. Contact person: Misha Wolf. See also items 882, 883 and 884.

625. BLACK/BROWN WOMEN'S LIBERATION NEWSLETTER   1979-?

Tl:Black/Brown Women's Liberation newsletter

Bootham, York

Quarterly;1979(?)-?

L:not found

The publishing group introduced itself in 1978 in item 297 (n°72, July 1978, p.23) and in item 451 (n°8, August 1978), as women "committed to attacking the white-supremacist attitudes and ignorance of white sisters, as well as asserting their existence inside and outside the Women's Liberation Movement". It invited contributions for the forthcoming newsletter from brown and black sisters only (Asian, African, West Indian, Latin American, Oriental). The newsletter was advertised throughout 1979 in item 297. Distributed on a national level, it was available to all women only.

626. BUSWOMAN   1979

Tl:The Buswoman newsletter

Ed. and pub. Buswomen's Association

Beckenham, Kent

F.n.k.;1979(?)-?

L:not found

Not seen. Mentioned in item 297 (n°88, November 1979, p.54). Seems to have some feminist leanings.

627. DRASTIC MEASURES   1979-1980

Tl:Drastic measures - Rock Against Sexism Bulletin

Pub. Rock Against Sexism

Irregular;1979(?)-n°3, 1980 (n.i.c.)

L:Flic (n°3 only, undated)

Thin A4 printed bulletin produced by Rock Against Sexism. Item

297 (n°94, May 1980, p.30) announced the publication of issue 3.
No trace of further issues. R.A.S. is "an organisation of women
and men with the following aims: (1) to fight sexism in rock
music . . . (2) to challenge the stereotype images of women and
men . . . (3) to attack the exploitation of women in advertising
in the press and on the stage; (4) to assert the right of everyone
to determine their own sexuality . . .". The bulletin carried
news of the various regional groups, short articles, song lyrics,
letters. Contributors included Lucy Toothpaste.

628. EQUAL PAY AND OPPORTUNITY CAMPAIGN NEWSLETTER 1979-c.
     Tl:Equal Pay and Opportunity Campaign newsletter
     Ed. Susanne Lawrence, Nickie Fonda
     Monthly;quarterly;1979(?)-c.
     L:F (incomplete)
Very slim A4 newsletter representing "a group of men and women
from both sides of industry committed to the achievement of equal
opportunities in employment" (November 1979).

629. HULL WOMEN'S COLLECTIVE NEWSLETTER 1979-1981
     Tl:Hull Women's Collective newsletter
     Hull
     Irregular;1979(?)-August 1981
     C:item 351?
     L:F (2 undated issues)
A4 local newsletter some twenty pages long, publishing listings
but also features of interest to all women. Available to women
only.

630. IRISH COUNTRYWOMAN 1979-1980
     Tl:Irish Countrywoman
     Ed. and pub. Irish Countrywoman's Association
     Dublin
     Monthly;1979(?)-1980(?)
     C BY:item 757
     L:not found
Not seen. Listed in item 294 (v.9,n°4, December 1980/January 1981,
p.44).

631. NORTH PADDINGTON WOMEN'S CENTRE 1979-?
     Tl:North Paddington Women's Centre Annual Report
     F.n.k.;1979/80(?)-?

L:Flic (1 issue only)
Self-explanatory. See also item 811.

632. RESPONSE   1979-c.

    Tl:Response
    Ed. National Women's Advisory Council
    1983 convener:Quentin Bryce
    Pub. Australian Government Publishing Service
    Canberra City, A.C.T., Australia
    Irregular (n°6, August 1983);1979(?)-c.
    L:F, Flic (both incomplete)

Thin A4 printed bulletin publishing information about the
activities of the NEAC, an official body advising the Commonwealth
government on women's issues. See also item 601.

633. SAINT ANDREWS LESBIAN FEMINIST NEWSLETTER   1979

    Tl:Saint Andrews Lesbian Feminist Newsletter
    Saint Andrews
    F.n.k.;1979(?)
    L:not found

Not seen. Undated issue mentioned on Feminist Archive's list of
holdings dated December 1979.

634. SHEFFIELD WOMEN'S PAPER   1979-c.

    Tl:Sheffield Women's Paper
    Sheffield
    Irregular;1979(?)-c.
    L:not found

Not seen. Listed in item 297 (n°89, December 1979, p.30) and in
Spare Rib diaries from 1981 onwards. Paper on public sale not to
be confused with item 407.

635. SOUTH WEST WOMEN COMMUNICATE   1979

    Tl:South West women communicate
    Tiverton, Devon
    Quarterly;1979(?)
    L:not found

Not seen. Local newsletter announced as forthcoming in item 297
(n°81, April 1979, p.25). Production was to rotate among the
groups in the region. The first issue put together in Tiverton
was to feature women and health. Contact person: Chinks Grylls.

636. WINNZ 1979-c.

    Tl:WINNZ

    Whangarei, New Zealand

    Bi-monthly;1979(?)-c.

    L:Flic (a few issues only)

WINNZ stands for Women's Information Network of New Zealand. It is
an A4 duplicated newsletter started after the 1979 United Women's
Convention in Hamilton, as a communication link between women in
the New Zealand Women's Movement. In particular WINNZ supports
women's right to control their own fertility and to define their
own sexuality, their right to paid work and to twenty-four hour
child care, the abolition of sex role stereotyping and the
elimination of racism. The 1981 publishing collective included:
Anne Sharpe, Sue Lawrence, Karoline Patrick, Penny Otto and
Sylvia Jennings.

637. WOMEN AND MUSIC NEWSLETTER 1979-?

    Tl:Women and music newsletter

    F.n.k.;1979(?)-?

    L:not found

Not seen. Advertised as forthcoming in item 297 (n°71, June 1978,
p.24; n°72, July 1978, p.22 and n°78, January 1979, p.25). Listed
in item 613 (v.9,n°4, December 1980/January 1981, p.43 and v.10,
n°4, December 1981/January 1982, p.56). The first issue was to
include articles on guitar picking, feminist folk, women and
classical music, working in a women's band, etc..

638. WOMEN'S OWN 1979-c.

    Tl:Women's own:Bath feminist newsletter

    Bath

    Monthly;1979(?)-c.

    F:Flic

Local, women only newsletter printing contact addresses, news,
views and poetry.

639. AFFIRM NEWSLETTER 1980-1981

    Tl:AFFIRM newsletter

    Ed. and pub. Alliance For Fair Images and Representation in
    the Media

    Bi-monthly

    C BY:item 701

L:not found

Newsletter of AFFIRM, a collective of women campaigning against
sexist images of women which has existed since 1977. They "are
concerned about the belittling and trivialising of women - how
women are shown as sex objects in the media, especially in
advertising; the gender-role stereotyping of women and how
language reinforces assumptions that 'male' is the norm" (item
409, n°112, 1981, p.11). Their newsletter carries articles,
letters of complaints and reports on current campaigns.

640. CHANGE 1980-c.
    Tl:Change international reports:women and society
    Founding ed. Georgina Ashworth (of the Minority Rights Group
    until 1980)
    Pub. International Development Centre
    Irregular
    L:not found

Not seen. Change is an educational charitable trust "founded to
research and publish reports on the condition and status of
women all over the world", written whenever possible by authors
indigenous to the country concerned. Change's aims are among
others: "to educate and alert public opinion to the inequalities"
imposed on women . . .; "to advance the recognition of the
inalienable human rights and human dignity of women . . .".
Reports have been published so far on women in Singapore,
Thailand, USSR, Chile, Peru, Israel, Phillipines.

641. CRYSTAL CRONE 1980
    Tl:Crystal crone
    L:not found

Not seen. The only mentions found occur in item 297 (n°91,
February 1980, p.29 and n°102, January 1981, p.29). "The first
issue of this magazine of women's science fiction/fantasy contains
short stories and poems, drawings and beautiful photographs. May
have been a one-off issue.

642. DANGER:YOUNG WOMEN AT WORK 1980-?
    Tl:Danger:young women at work
    L:not found

Not seen. Listed in item 297 (n°99, October 1980, p.39). "A
feminist magazine written and produced by young women from
Starcross School".

643. FEMINIST ARCHIVE INFORMATION SHEET 1980
     Tl:Feminist Archive Information Sheet
     Bath
     F.n.k.;1980-?
     L:not found
Not seen. Issue 1 dated 1980 is mentioned in Cadman et al, 1981,
p.108. See also items 597 and 617.

644. GIRLS NEWSLETTER 1980
     Tl:Girls newsletter
     Pub. Camden Girls Centre Project
     F.n.k.;1980-?
     L:not found
Not seen. Listed in item 409 (n°101, 1980). Women only newsletter.

645. GIRLS TALK 1980
     Tl:Girls talk
     F.n.k.;1980-?
     L:not found
Not seen. Described in item 297 (n°99, October 1980, p.39) as "a
magazine written and produced by three girls (aged 10-12) from
Caxton House Youth Club".

646. HYSTERIA 1980-c.
     Tl:Hysteria:A feminist magazine by women in
     Kitchener-Waterloo
     Ed. Hysteria Magazine Collective including Catherine Edwards,
     Kae Elgie, et al
     Pub. Little Red Media Corporation
     Kitchener-Waterloo, Ontario, Canada
     Quarterly
     L:Flic (v.1,n°2, Summer/Autumn 1980 only)
Magazine featuring thematic, social and political issues of
interest to women, printing history articles and providing wide
coverage of feminist culture and art. Contents include articles,
news, film and book reviews and creative feminist work (fiction,
poetry, graphics).

647. LANCASTER WOMEN'S LIBERATION NEWSLETTER 1980-c.
     Tl:Lancaster Women's Liberation newsletter
     Lancaster
     Monthly;irregular;1980-March 1983;1984-c.

```
        C:item 503
        L:Flic (incomplete)
Straightforward continuation of item 503. Local women only
newsletter mainly carrying news of events and groups in the area.
Publication was interrupted from March 1983 onwards for about a
year and a half. Item 297 (n°147, October 1984, p.17) says the
newsletter was resurrected in mid 1984.
```

648. LEEDS BIRTH CENTRE NEWSLETTER 1980-c.(?)
        Tl:Leeds Birth Centre Newsletter
        Leeds
        L:not found
Not seen. Item 297 (n°96, July 1980, p.30) describes the centre
and the contents of issue 1 of the newsletter. "The Birth Centre
is a self-help group set up to support people who seek an
alternative to the ever-increasing mechanisation of birth".
Contact person: Angela Holt.

649. LESBIAN SWITCHBOARD NEWSLETTER 1980
        Tl:Lesbian Switchboard newsletter
        Nottingham;London
        L:not found
Not seen. Issue 1 available from Nottingham Women's Centre was
advertised in item 297 (n°91, February 1980, p.30). The
publication of issue 2, produced by London Lesbian Line was
announced in item 363 (May 1980, p.8). No further trace found.

650. NEWS LETTER 1980-c.
        Tl:News letter:Research Unit on Women's Studies
        Ed. and pub. Smt. Laj S. Deshmukh on behalf of the Research
        Unit on Women's Studies, SNDT Women's University
        Bombay, India
        Quarterly
        L:Flic (incomplete)
Research journal published in English and focusing on women's
education.

651. OXFORD WOMEN'S PAPER 1980-1981
        Tl:Oxford women's paper
        Oxford
        F.n.k.;1980-1981(?)
        C BY:item 824

        L:not found
Not seen. Issue 1 is described in item 297 (n°95, June 1980, p.30)
as "a broadly-based women's paper to increase communication and
discussion between women who live and/or study in Oxford".

652. WOMEN IN ACTION 1980-1981
        T1:Women in Action:A paper for action in the unions on
        women's rights
        Bi-monthly;1980-1981 (n.i.c.)
        L:F, Flic (both incomplete)
Women in Action is an A4 bulletin set up to fill a gap between
journals coming from the Women's Liberation Movement and the
publications of political organisations. It is "an open paper",
committed to "campaigning for women's equality and independence
with the support of the trade union and labour movements" (Spring
1980, p.2). "Women in Action promotes positive action to counter
discrimination against women. Formal equality alone does not
tackle the roots of discrimination" (New Year issue, p.2). It
includes a "guide to action". It supports "the demands embodied
in the TUC's Aims for Women at Work; the Working Women's Charter;
the TUC Charter for Women in the Unions; the TUC Equal
Opportunities Clause and the demands of the Women's Liberation
Movement". Some of the issues covered are women's right to work,
collective bargaining, low pay, sexual harassment at work,
abortion. The editorial collective included, among others: Val
Coultas, Denny Fitzpatrick, Sue Landau, Sheila Prophet and Yvonne
Taylor.

653. WOMEN IN MEDIA NEWSLETTER 1980-c.
        T1:Women in Media newsletter
        L:F (n°2, April(?) 1980 only)
Very thin A4 newsletter produced by WIM (Women in Media), a group
working towards accurate portrayal of women in the media and for
equality of opportunity for women working in the media.
Coordinators have included Suzie Hayman, Helen Franks, Caroline
Richmond. Not to be confused with item 701.

654. I.C.A.S.C. 1980-1982
        T1:I.C.A.S.C. Bulletin
        T2:I.C.A.S.C. News
        T3:I.C.A.S.C. Newsletter
        Ed. and pub. International Contraception, Abortion and

191

Sterilisation Campaign

3 issues per year;January 1980-n°8, 1982 (n.i.c.)

L:F, Flic (both incomplete)

I.C.A.S.C. was formed in 1978 to build an international campaign and solidarity network to exchange information and to fight for women's right to control their own fertility. The bulletin of the organisation is produced in English, French and Spanish. Its production is rotated among countries. Contents include news of campaigns and women's struggles against repressive laws, the Church, the medical profession internationally, requests for help and articles on fertility.

655. VOICE OF WOMEN 1980-c.

Tl:Voice of women:A Sri Lanka journal for women's emancipation known as Kantha Handa in Sinhala, and Pennin Kural in Tamil

Colombo, Sri Lanka

Irregular;January 1980-c.

L:Flic (incomplete)

Substantial magazine with a strong socialist feminist standpoint. Produced by a women's group of the same names started in September 1978, it is published in three different editions: in English, Sinhala and Tamil. The publishing group is committed "to the emancipation of women, and to the full participation of women in the economic, political and social life of the country" (n°1, p.1). "In this class society, men and women alike are subject to oppression and exploitation regardless of their sex . . . A number of biological and historial factors have been the root cause of male supremacy within the existing social order and have brought about the subjugation of women by men . . . (Their) struggle therefore, is one waged by one oppressed social group in a society that is based on principles of oppression and exploitation and not a struggle waged by women against men" (n°2, p.1). The magazine highlights "the oppressive structures that keep women in a subordinate position" (n°1, p.1) and focuses on the oppression and exploitation of women in Sri Lanka and other Third World countries. It discusses wide ranging issues: the dowry system, wife beating, women working in agriculture and industry, women in media, etc..

656. SPINSTER 1980-1982

Tl:Spinster:A quarterly magazine of feminist creative work

Irregular;January(?) 1980-n°3, 1982 (n.i.c.)
     L:F, Flic (both incomplete)
Feminist literary magazine put together by Spinster Collective
and featuring theory, short stories, poems, reviews, drawings and
photographs with an emphasis on the work of lesbians. Contributors
have included: Lynn Alderson, Mary Dorcey, Caroline Gruffin, Kay
Stirling, et al.

657. WOMEN'S VIEW   1980-1982
     Tl:Women's view
     Ed. and pub. National Women's Committee of Sinn Fein, The
     Workers' Party
     Dublin
     Quarterly;8 March 1980-n°8, Spring 1982 (n.i.c.)
     L:F, Flic (both incomplete)
Professional looking A4 magazine launched on International Women's
Day by the Women's Committee of (Official) Sinn Fein. It carries
news shorts, book and film reviews and a guide to women's groups.
It covers issues concerning women in Ireland such as health,
transport, Armagh prison, childcare, from a socialist-feminist
standpoint. It also publishes articles on women's lives
throughout the world. For instance, the experiences of women in
Palestine, in Nicaragua, in South Africa have been recorded. Some
criticism of Provisional Sinn Fein.

658. INSIST   1980-c.
     Tl:Insist:Birmingham Women's Paper
     Birmingham;printed in Nottingham
     Bi-monthly;April(?) 1980-1981;May 1982-c.
     C:item 406
     L:F (1 issue only), Flic (a few issues)
Neatly produced in a newspaper format by different collectives of
women. Members of the 1982 collective included Madeleine Fowler,
Parvaneh Mehdian, Mo White, Rhonda Wilson, Julia Wright, et al.
The publication was interrupted for about a year. Aimed at all
women "not solely women representative of the Women's Liberation
Movement" (n°9, September 1982, p.2), it has a national
circulation and attempts to spread feminism "in an accessible and
unacademic way" (ibid.). Each issue is centred on a theme: A
Women's Right to Choose (n°1), women in the media (n°9), sexuality
(n°10). It includes wide ranging features, plus local and national
news, letters, events and contact lists, cartoons, etc..

193

659. SOURCREAM   1981-1982
     Tl:Sourcream
     Pub. Sourcream Comic Collective
     Irregular;May/June 1980-n°3, 1982 (n.i.c.)
     L:not found
Thin collection of feminist cartoons published in variable
format. The publication of issue 3 was publicised in item 297
(n°123, October 1982, p.47). Contributors to issues 1 and 2 were:
Cari Ackroyd, Anne Marie Blatchford, Lucy Byatt, Ingrid Emsden,
Janis Goodman, Viv Quillin, Lesley Ruda, Fiona Scott, Rosalind
Scott, Catriona Sinclair, Susanna Smith, Fanny Tribble and Jo
Wreford. Not, apparently, identical with the series of books of
the same name.

660. PRESTON POLY WOMEN'S GROUP   1980
     Tl:Preston Poly Women's Group
     Pub. Preston Poly Students' Union
     Preston
     Irregular;Summer 1980-n°2, Winter 1980 (n.i.c.)
     L:Flic
The Preston Poly Women's Group began to meet in 1978 and was not
exclusively composed of students. The contents of its A4
newsletter were varied and interesting and reflected the group's
activities.

661. BITCHES, WITCHES AND DYKES   1980-c.
     Tl:Bitches, witches and dykes:A Women's Liberation newspaper
     Pub. Feminist Publication Collective
     Newton, Auckland, Wellington, New Zealand
     2 issues per year;August 1980-c.
     L:Flic (incomplete)
Substantial and valuable tabloid dealing primarily with New
Zealand Women's Liberation Movement and directed towards women
who already consider themselves feminists. The original editorial
collective included Alison Jones, Annabel Fagan, Carole Stewart,
Elizabeth Dowling, Nancy Peterson, Pilar Alba, Rebecca Evans. In
their own words, their "political stance is a revolutionary
rather than a reformist one". They believe that "the root of
women's oppression is power - male class power - men have power
over women . . . Equality with men inside the established society
will not change patriarchal, capitalist, heterosexist white
supremacist culture . . . (their) goal is a feminist revolutionary

process that changes the social order" (August 1980, p.1). Their
newspaper explored the theory and practice of the WLM and
includes a Black Forum.

662. WOMENERGY 1980
    Tl:Womenergy
    1 issue only;September(?) 1980
    C BY:item 727
    L:not found
Not seen. A women only newsletter that evolved out of the
Feminists Against Nuclear Power conference in 1980. A newsletter
group was formed at the conference but disbanded and so Womenergy
was delayed and finally put together by mainly one woman. Its
publication was publicised in item 297 (n°99, October 1980).

663. ELEKTRA 1980-?
    Tl:Elektra
    Ed. Mary Jane O'Brien
    Dublin
    Monthly?;1 November 1980-?
    L:F (n°1 only)
Twenty page A4 magazine with strongly feminist contents though the
publishing group included men. Issue 1 had features on
contraception, childcare, sex education, Armagh prison, lesbians
in the Irish Feminist Movement, etc.. Only one issue seems to have
been published.

664. NEWSHEET 1980-c.
    Tl:Newsheet:Office of Women's Affairs
    T2:Newsheet:Office of the Status of Women
    Pub. Department of Home Affairs and Environment;then
    Department of the Prime Minister and Cabinet
    Canberra, New South Wales, Australia
    Bi-monthly;1 November 1980-c.
    L:F
National newsheet of 20 pages or so in 1984, produced as a service
to women's non-government organisations and aiming to "keep (them)
informed of Commonwealth Government developments and international
progress specifically relating to women" (n°1). Reports on
Government policy to achieve equal status and equal opportunity
for women.

665. SHOCKING PINK 1980-1982

     Tl:Shocking Pink:The alternative young women's magazine

     Pub. Young Women's Magazine Group

     Irregular;November 1980-n°3, April(?) 1982

     L:F, Flic (both incomplete)

The idea for a magazine by and for young women came out of the
national Young Women's Conference in December 1979. It was
produced by a London-based group of women aged from 12 to 22. It
aimed to offer an alternative to Jackie, Oh Boy, My Guy, etc. and
an anti-sexist, non stereotyped view of the lives of teenage
women. The group stood against any protective social laws, such
as the age of consent, entertainment and licensing laws,
employment regulations, etc.. Shocking Pink looked at the problems
of sex, race and class discrimination both at school and work. It
discussed fashion, relationship with boys, contraception,
abortion but also controversial issues. For instance, it carried a
photo story about a young woman coming out of school as a lesbian,
an article about the age of consent law and one on masturbation.
It has lots of visuals. The collective disbanded in 1983 (see item
703, November/December 1982, n°12). The first issue had a print
run of 3,000 copies.

666. WOMEN IN DURHAM 1980-1982

     Tl:Women in Durham

     Durham

     Monthly;November(?) 1980-n°17, June 1982 (n.i.c.)

     L:F (incomplete), Flic

Local A4 duplicated newsletter. It includes a calendar of events,
lists of groups, news from the North East, letters but also
features of more general interest.

667. WOMEN AND TRAINING NEWS 1980-c.

     Tl:Women and Training News:The Newsletter of the Inter-Board
     Liaison Group on Training Opportunities for Women

     Ed. Ann Cooke (Gloucester)

     Pub. Manpower Services Commission

     London;Sheffield

     Quarterly;Winter 1980-c.

     L:F, Flic (both incomplete)

Newsletter set up to be "a vehicle for the exchange of information,
experience and views" to improve training opportunities for women
and thus to increase their contribution to the economy. Features,

book reviews and listings.

668. BEANSAOR 1980-?
    Tl:Beansaor
    Ed. Women Against Imperialism
    Pub. Beansaor Resource Centre
    Belfast, Northern Ireland
    F.n.k.;1980(?)-?
    L:not found
Not seen. Earliest mention found occurs in ISIS (n°16, 1980,
p.37): "The newsletter focuses on the struggle of the Northern
Irish Women Against Imperialism. It covers the sexual oppression
of women, and particularly women political prisoners by the
state . . . Information on contraception, how to handle assault,
militant poems, etc.". Beansaor is Irish for "free woman".

669. GLASTONBURY THORN 1980-c.
    Tl:Glastonbury Thorn
    Glastonbury
    F.n.k.;1980(?)-c.
    L:not found
Not seen. Listed in item 409 (n°101, 1980) and in Cadman et al,
1981. Local women only newsletter.

670. HARINGEY WOMEN'S CENTRE NEWSLETTER 1980-c.(?)
    Tl:Haringey Women's Centre Newsletter
    Bi-monthly;1980(?)-c.(?)
    C BY:item 725?
    L:Flic
Thin A4 duplicated newsletter for women only. It mainly carries
detailed reports on the centre's activities and a calendar of
events and activities of interest to local women, plus one or two
short articles.

671. M.O.W. NEWSLETTER 1980-c.
    Tl:M.O.W. newsletter
    Ed. and pub. Movement for the Ordination of Women
    Quarterly (13 issues by June 1984);1980(?)-c.
    L:F (incomplete)
Thin newsletter internal to the movement campaigning for the
opening of the ordained ministry to women in the Church of
England. The Moderator of the Movement was Stanley Booth-Clibborn

for three years, then Monica Furlong.

672. PLYMOUTH WOMEN'S CENTRE NEWSLETTER 1980-c.
      T1:Plymouth Newsletter
      T2:Plymouth Women's Centre Newsletter
      Pub. Women's Centre
      Plymouth
      Irregular;1980(?)-c.
      L:not found
Not seen. Listed in item 409 (n°101, 1980) and in Cadman et al,
1981. Local women only newsletter. Same as item 618?

673. PRESTON AND BLACKPOOL GAY WOMEN'S NEWSLETTER 1980
      T1:Preston and Blackpool Gay Women's Newsletter
      Preston
      F.n.k.;1980(?)
      L:Flic (1 issue only)
Self-explanatory. The only issue seen was an undated A4 newsletter
12 pages long.

674. PRESTON WOMEN'S INFO SHEET 1980
      T1:Preston Women's Info Sheet
      Preston
      F.n.k.;1980(?)
      L:Flic (1 issue only)
Four-page A4 news sheet mainly carrying listings.

675. SCOTTISH WOMEN'S AID NEWSLETTER 1980-c.
      T1:Scottish Women's Aid Newsletter
      Edinburgh
      F.n.k.;1980(?)-c.
      L:not found
Not seen. Listed in item 410 (n°101, 1980) and in item 297 (n°136,
November 1983, p.25). Women only newsletter distributed
nationally. See also items 518, 803 and 853.

676. VOICE OF WOMEN 1980-c.
      T1:Voice of women
      Ed. and pub. African National Congress, South Africa, Women's
      Section
      Lusaka, Zambia
      Quarterly;1980(?)-c.

```
C:item 429?
L:not found
```

Not seen. Latest mention appears in item 874 (n°2, Spring 1984, p.19). Valuable as being one of the few publications coming from black South African women about their situation and their struggle against apartheid and sexism. Available in London.

677. WIPLASH 1980-c.
```
Tl:Wiplash
Ed. and pub. Women in Publishing
London;Surbiton
Monthly;1980(?)-c.
L:not found
```
Not seen. Women in Publishing is a membership based group, set up by a few women who had attended a conference on Women and Writing. It is open to all women in the book trade. "It aims to increase women's contribution to publishing, to facilitate the exchange of information, to provide mutual support and to improve the status of women in the profession" (Isis, n°16, 1980, p.37). It provides a network and a forum for discussion, a centre for information and training and is also a pressure group. It works closely with the Women Monitoring Network and Women's Media Action Group (see items 700 and 704). Wiplash, the organisation's newsletter is put together by one of the three WIP sub-groups. It carries reports on talks and discussions held in the monthly meetings and highlights sexism in the media. Contributors have included Farrell Burnett, Jane Gregory, Anne McDermid. See also item 423.

678. WOMAN 1980-c.
```
Tl:Woman
F.n.k.;1980(?)-c.
L:not found
```
Not seen. Mentioned in item 612 (v.9,n°4, December 1980/January 1981, p.43 and v.10,n°4, December 1981/January 1982, p.55). "Newsletter of an organization fighting the unjust income tax system in Britain". Contact attn. Lynn Faulds Wood.

679. WOMAN SPEAK! 1980-c.
```
Tl:Woman speak!
Pub. Women and Development Unit, University of the West
Indies
```

Barbados

Quarterly;1980(?)-c.

L:Flic (n°9, December/January 1982/1983 only)

Newsletter about Caribbean women, co-sponsored by WAND Unit.
Listed in item 612 (v.9,n°4, December 1980/January 1981,
pp.61-2). Not to be confused with item 395.

680. WOMEN ON WHEELS 1980-c.

　　　T1:Women on wheels

　　　T2?:Women bikers newsletter

　　　T3:Women on wheels

　　　Ed. and pub. W.O.W.

　　　London and Nottingham

　　　F.n.k.;1980(?)-c.

　　　L:not found

Not seen. Mainly London-based feminist motorcycle club but a few
contacts in all areas of the country. The earliest mention seen of
the newsletter occurs in item 297 (n°91, February 1980, p.30). It
is a national women only newsletter entitled <u>Women Bikers
Newsletter</u> in Cadman et al, 1981. It aims to help women get
together for rides and meetings, exchange or sell spares, maintain
their motorbikes. The latest trace of the group occurred in item
703 (n°12, November/December 1982, p.5).

681. WOMEN'S AIM NEWSLETTER 1980-1982

　　　T1:Women's Aim newsletter

　　　Dublin

　　　Quarterly;1980(?)-n°11, autumn 1982 (n.i.c.)

　　　L:not found

Not seen. Listed in <u>Isis</u> (n°16, 1980, p.21). "A newsletter
produced by the Women's Aims Group, which was formed in 1972, to
campaign for law reform in areas related to women and the family.
Carries information on legal issues affecting women, articles
about women in Ireland as well as internationally, health,
education and politics". Last mention found occurs in item 548
(n°28, November/December 1982, p.62).

682. WOMEN'S FIGHTBACK 1980-c.

　　　T1:Women's Fightback:Monthly paper of the women's campaign
　　　Labour Movement Fightback for women's Rights

　　　T2:Paper of the women's campaign Fightback for Women's Rights

　　　T3:Women's Fightback:Paper of the women's campaign Labour

200

Movement Fightback for Women's Rights

Monthly;bi-monthly (24 issues by January/February 1983); 1980(?)-c.

L:F, Flic (both incomplete)

Women's Fightback is an autonomous women's campaign. It organises women in the trade unions and the Labour Party and struggles against the sexist atmosphere, men's control and the undemocratic structures. It fights for the implementation of the TUC Charter for women in the Unions. Its tabloid publication started as a four-page paper and has now about 12 pages. It reports on the many campaigns on women's rights in which Women's Fightback groups are involved, such as the right of women to control their own fertility, the right to health and childcare facilities, the right to a paid job. Contributors have included Ann Evans, Jenny Fisher, Rachel Lever, Brigid McConville, Linda Semple and Jo Thwaites.

683. WOMEN'S VOICE 1980-c.(?)

Tl:Women's Voice

Ed. and pub. The National Organization of Women (N.O.W.)

Bridgetown, Barbados

F.n.k.;1980(?)-c.(?)

L:not found

Not seen. Listed in item 612 (v.9,n°4, December 1980/January 1981) as a newspaper planned for 1980/81. Not to be confused with items 268 and 290.

684. YORKSHIREWOMEN 1980-?

Tl:Yorkshirewomen

Leeds

F.n.k.;1980(?)-?

L:not found

Not seen. Mentioned on a list published by item 409 (n°101, 1980) "Communist Party District Women's Newsletter".

685. CAWIS NEWS 1981-c.

Tl:CAWIS news

Ed. and pub. Canadian Association for Women in Science, including Shelly Beauchamp

Toronto, Ontario, Canada

L:not found

Not seen. Listed in item 612 (v.10,n°4, December 1981/January

1982, p.40).

686. CCCA   1981-c.
    Tl:CCCA Newsletter
    Ed. and pub. Concerned Citizens for Choice on Abortion
    Bi-monthly
    L:not found
Not seen. Listed in item 612 (v.10,n°4, December 1981/January
1982, p.40).

687. EQUAL OPPORTUNITIES INTERNATIONAL   1981-c.
    Tl:Equal Opportunities International
    Pub. Barmarick Publications
    Ed. Nancy Wise (London)
    Hull
    Quarterly
    L:F, Flic (both incomplete)
Articles, news, reviews. Contents focus on women in the labour
force and on equal opportunity legislation and practice.

688. FEMINIST FORUM   1981-c.
    Tl:Feminist forum
    Pub. Pergamon Press
    Oxford
    Bi-monthly
    L:F
Thin newsletter supplied as a news supplement to subscribers of
item 551. News of conferences, feminist resources and groups,
abstracts, book reviews. Not to be confused with item 748.

689. GIRL'S OWN   1981-c.
    Tl:Girl's own:Sydney Feminist Newspaper
    Sydney, New South Wales, Australia
    Bi-monthly
    L:Flic (2 issues)
A substantial tabloid supporting "the struggle of Aboriginal women
against the white invaders". Its declared aim is "to be
anti-sexist, anti-racist and anti-classist" (n°12, August/
September 1983, p.2). It carries news, articles, poetry, graphics.

690. GYNERATE   1981-c.
    Tl:Gynerate

Shelton;Stoke-on-Trent;Lancaster
Irregular
L:not found
Not seen. Listed in item 409 (n°109, 1981, p.12) and in item 297
(n°119, June 1982, p.36). A magazine of women's creative writing
produced by a collective. The original members met at a W.E.A.
summer school on "women and writing" at Wedgewood College,
Barlaston and were from all parts of Great Britain. The
publication is called <u>Gynerate</u> because it tries "to make
connections between mothers and daughters, sisters and ansisters -
generations". The two issues produced in 1981 consisted of a
collection of poems, stories and drawings.

691. L.E.G.   1981
        Tl:L.E.G.:Lesbian Exchange Grapevine newsletter
        Manchester;Sheffield
        Irregular (5 issues by 1984)
        L:Flic
Women only national newsletter of the National newsletters of the
National Lesbian Network produced by the LEG collectives in
variable formats. It grew out of the Durham Gayfest in 1981. It
carries information about events and campaigns of interest to
lesbians nationally, articles, letters, poems, reviews, cartoons,
etc. sent by readers. Production was interrupted for a while,
then LEG moved to Sheffield and resumed publication. Issue 4 was
only released in early 1984.

692. MAGDALENE   1981-1982
        Tl:Magdalene
        Epping, Australia
        Quarterly?;1981-v.2,n°4, December 1982 (n.i.c.)
        L:Flic (incomplete)
A sixteen-page women's liberation newsletter. Earliest issue seen:
n°2, June 1981.

693. MATRIARCHY RESEARCH AND RECLAIM NETWORK NEWSLETTER   1981-c.
        Tl:Matriarchy Research and Reclaim Network newsletter
        Monthly
        L:not found
Not seen. Item 409 (n°124, January 1982) advertises the
publication of issue 3. "It is more of an information sheet than
anything else but we're also planning a journal to appear at the

equinoxes and solstices". The news sheet is also mentioned in item
869 (n°7, March/April 1984). In both cases, the contact address is
A Woman's Place.

694. MSSCRIPT 1981-?
    Tl:MsScript
    Leicester
    L:not found
Not seen. Free magazine from the New Leicester Women's Writer
Group. Mentioned in item 297 (n°106, May 1981, p.30). "It contains
some enjoyable lurid sci-fi prose . . ., poetry . . . expressing
anger with men, concern for women, loneliness, hope". Contact
person: Pat Simpson. No other trace found.

695. NATIONAL WOMEN AND COMPUTING NEWSLETTER 1981-c.
    Tl:Women and Computing Newsletter
    T2:National Women and Computing Newsletter
    Quarterly
    L:Flic (incomplete)
Duplicated A4 women only newsletter of about ten pages. It is
produced by the Women and Computing Newsletter group now composed
of women from the collectives of the Women's Computer Centre and
of Microsyster. It was set up following a workshop on women and
computing at the Women and Science Conference in February 1981. It
aims to demystify computing and it discusses the impact of new
technology on women's lives and jobs.

696. RADICAL NURSES' NEWSLETTER 1981-c.
    Tl:Radical Nurses' Newsletter
    Sheffield
    L:not found
Not seen. Listed in item 297 (n°102, January 1981, p.29 and n°139,
February 1984, p.32). Produced by nurses "dissatisfied, not just
with their pay and conditions, but with the nature of their role
as (they) and other people see it".

697. SEXISM IN THE MEDIA 1981-c.
    Tl:Sexism in the Media
    Pub. Women's Monitoring Network
    F.n.k.;1981-c.
    L:not found
A series of thematic reports compiled by the Women's Monitoring

Network. The latter consists of groups and individual women around the country, who, on a national basis, are having a blitz day on the way women are portrayed by the commercial press. As Ronder Rotton states in the first report: "The portrayal of women as sex objects trivialises, degrades and dehumanises us. This affects the way we are viewed by men, the way we view ourselves. The male-controlled media industry uses women's bodies or parts of them for titillation and to sell products and publications". The material monitored includes national and local newspapers, magazines, teenage papers and comic, trade journals. The reports only carry press cuttings. Reports published so far have covered: n°1, women as sex objects, n°2 violence against women, n°3, stereotypes of women, n°4, sugar and spice: sex role stereotyping of children, n°5 ageism, n°6, women and food.

698. SISTERS   1981-c.
    Tl:Sisters:the journal of the National Assembly of Women
    Eds. Angelina Cobbina, Barbara McDermot, Celia Pomeroy
    Quarterly;monthly
    C:item 467?
    L:F (1 issue only), Flic (2 issues only)
Thin printed A4 newsletter which carries news on the work of the NAW. The aim of the organisation founded in 1952 is: "the full, social, economic, legal, political and cultural independence and equality for all women". It also supports "all women in the struggle against racism, fascism and imperialism", nuclear weapons, throughout the world. (See February 1982.) The journal features national and international information on women focusing on working women and women from ethnic minority groups.

699. WOMEN WITH CHILDREN   1981-c.
    Tl:Women With Children Group newsletter
    Sanderstead;Worcester Park;Thornton Heath, Surrey
    Irregular?;1981-c.(?)
    L:Flic (n°2, November 1981 only)
Issue 2 featured the medicalisation of childbirth, the feelings after pregnancy, state schooling, paid childcare, etc.. The publishing group has included Sylvia Newman, Jennie Fairweather, Gina Menon and Jill Servian.

700. WOMEN'S EXCHANGE   1981
    Tl:Women's exchange

Edinburgh;Glasgow

F.n.k.;1981-?

L:not found

Not seen. Announced in item 297 (n°101, December 1980, p.14 and n°103, February 1981, p.30) as a monthly magazine to be launched via Scottish supermarkets by Edinburgh women in media.

701. WOMEN'S MEDIA ACTION BULLETIN   1981-c.

Tl:Women's Media Action bulletin

Pub. WMAG

Bi-monthly

C:item 639

L:not found

Women's Media Action Group used to be AFFIRM. It aims "to eliminate sexism and stereotyping of women in the media". This includes abolishing the idea that heterosexuality is the only normal and acceptable mode of behaviour. WMAG is concerned "to fight for positive and balanced images of women in all aspects of (women's) lives; to inspire, encourage and support women to refuse to be passive recipients of media sexism". Their A4 newsletter is the straight continuation of item 639. It carries news of groups, accounts of current events in the media and current campaigns such as campaigns against sexist advertising, against pornography. It also includes book, film and television reviews.

702. NO-NAME NEWSLETTER   1981-c.

Tl:The No-Name newsletter

Ed. and pub. Resources for Feminist Research, Dept of Sociology, Ontario Institute for Studies in Education Toronto, Ontario, Canada

Irregular;January 1981-c.

L:F, Flic

A4 occasional newsletter produced by the staff of item 612 sent to subscribers of the latter. It contains an update on activities, opportunity to publish, requests for information, calls for papers, notices of forthcoming conferences, publications, awards, jobs, contacts.

703. WORKING WITH GIRLS NEWSLETTER   1981-c.

Tl:Working with girls newsletter

Pub. National Association of Youth Clubs, Girls Work

Leicester

    Bi-monthly;January 1981-c.

    L:F, Flic (both incomplete)

Interesting A4 magazine available by subscription only. It aims to "keep those working with or involved with young women, in touch with current developments and debates in the area of work with girls and young women" (item 866, n°1, p.16). Each issue includes an A3 pull-out centrefold poster; subscribers also receive free 4-page supplements describing clubs, projects and other on-going work in specific regions. The newsletter offers support, advice and information. It tackles racism, sexism and heterosexism. It tries to reassess girls' activities and has printed articles on football, motorcycling. Articles have discussed issues such as sex education, young women and violence. Contents also include news, reviews, letters, resource lists and report backs. Contributors have included, among others, Val Carpenter and Trisha McCabe.

704. CREW REPORTS 1981-c.

    T1:CREW reports:A regular factsheet on Community measures affecting women

    T2:CREW reports:news bulletin

    Ed. in 1984:R. Franceskides and An Independent Women's Cooperative

    Pub. Centre for Research on European Women

    Brussels, Belgium

    Monthly;February 1981-c.

    L:F, Flic (almost complete)

Thin factsheet on European Economic Community measures affecting women, also covering news in the Member States and other international organisations. From v.1,n°8, October 1981, printed in French and in English.

705. LONDON LESBIAN NEWSLETTER 1981-c.

    T1:London Lesbian Newsletter

    Every 6-8 weeks approx.;February/March 1981-c.

    L:Flic (incomplete)

Well produced duplicated A4 newsletter, 10 to 12 pages long. Put together by Gay's the Word Lesbian Group, it aimed at lesbians in London, new to London or just visiting. Though all the members of the collective are feminists, they try to reach all lesbians and not only lesbian feminists. They stated in item 409 (n°109, 1981, p.12), "We try to make (the newsletter) as feminist orientated as

possible although we do recognise that not all Lesbians identify
as feminist and include general information as well as feminist
info". Contents attempt to counteract feelings of isolation by
printing a diary of events, lists of groups and of places to go,
news of the London lesbian scene. They also gave space for lesbian
writing and include general articles, interviews, short stories,
poems and book reviews. Collective members have included: Sheril
Berkovitch, Elizabeth Draper, Jacki Heppard, Lesley Jones and
Amanda Russell. In 1982, the newsletter had an average circulation
of 300 copies per issue.

706. GAINING GROUND   1981-c.
     Tl:Gaining ground
     Belfast, Northern Ireland
     Monthly;February(?) 1981-c.
     L:Flic (2 issues only)
A very thin printed bulletin "produced independently by Anarcha
Feminists" and "sold with Outta Control". Very short articles,
letters, book reviews concerning mainly women in Ireland.

707. BARN MERCHED   1981-c.
     Tl:Barn Merched:Women's View
     Ed. and pub. Welsh Women's Aid
     Cardiff
     Quarterly;Spring 1981-c.(?)
     L:F (nº1 only)
Very thin printed newsletter published in English. It carries
"information on social and legal issues affecting women in Wales;
news from Welsh Women's Aid groups; news of events, conferences
and campaigns concerning women; book reviews" (nº1, p.1). See also
item 796.

708. GIRLSLINE   1981-c.
     Tl:Girlsline:A newsletter for girls and young women
     Quarterly;Spring 1981-c.(?)
     L:Flic (Spring 1981 only)
Sixteen-page duplicated A4 newsletter produced by two Youth
Opportunities Programme workers employed at the Islington and
Camden Girls and Young Women Projects. No trace of further issues.

709. FOCUS   1981-1982
     Tl:Focus:Labour women's bulletin

    Ed. Joyce Gould

    F.n.k.;March 1981-n°5, July 1982 (n.i.c.)

    L:F

A4 printed bulletin campaigning to get more women into office at
every level of the Labour Party and struggling for positive
discrimination in favour of women to compensate for years of
discrimination. It provides a "means for women in the party to
express their views on training methods, on policy matters and on
the activities within their own areas" (n°1, p.2). Features
concentrate on a women's right to work and on equal opportunities
in employment and training and support the demands of the Women's
Liberation Movement.

710. STATUS 1981-c.

    Tl:Status

    Ed. Marian Finucane;then Pat Brennan

    Pub. Status Publications

    Dublin

    Monthly;March 1981-c.

    L:F, Flic (both incomplete)

A professional-looking magazine of over 62 pages. It covers
wide-ranging issues concentrating on Irish women but including
some articles on Third World women. Issues regularly feature
women's health, sexuality, education and discuss the role of the
Church. Though the magazine shows some feminist leanings, it
remains very Catholic and closer to traditional women's magazines
than to women's liberation publications.

711. BOOM 1981-c.

    Tl:Boom

    Eds. included in 1981, Nicola Scott, Clare Calder-Marshall
    and Catherine Bennett

    F.n.k.;April 1981-c.(?)

    L:Flic (1 issue only)

Thin tabloid reporting the activities of the Women's Broadcasting
and Film Lobby born in September 1979. The members of the steering
committee include Helen Baehr and Eleanor Stephens.

712. WILPOWER 1981-c.

    Tl:Women in Libraries newsletter

    T2:WILPOWER

    Irregular (14 issues by 1984);May/June 1981-c.

L:F, Flic (incomplete)
Well produced A4 newsletter sent to the membership of Women in
Libraries, a pressure group on the role of women library workers
and trying to get more feminist books into libraries. The
newsletter reports on the group's activities across the country,
on the annual national conferences and includes book reviews.
Contact person in 1982: Sherry Jespersen.

713. WOMEN IN STRUGGLE   1981-c.
     Tl:Women in Struggle
     Stoke-on-Trent
     F.n.k.;June 1981-c,(?)
     L:Flic (June 1981 only)
A4 local newsletter produced by five women who want to keep alive
the local links between women and build "a strong unified voice"
in North Staffordshire. No trace of later issues.

714. CAMBRIDGE W.O.N.T.   1981-c.
     Tl:Cambridge W.O.N.T. newsletter
     F.n.k.;July 1981-c.(?)
     L:not found
Not seen. Mentioned in item 726 (December 1981, p.3). It reports
on conferences and announces forthcoming events. W.O.N.T. = Women
Oppose the Nuclear Threat.

715. CSW NEWSLETTER   1981-c.
     Tl:CSW newsletter:official publication of the Council for the
     Status of Women
     Ed. The Newsletter Committee
     Dublin
     Irregular;July 1981-c.
     L:F (n°6, April 1983 only)
Eight-page A4 printed newsletter focusing on the CSW activities
and sent to the membership. The Council "represents all the major
women's National Organisations; is the voice of the Women's
Movement in Ireland . . .". One of its declared aims is "to
provide liaison between Government Departments and Women's
Organisations". The Council is concerned with legal rights and
equal opportunities for women. The newsletter carries reports on
the group's conferences, workshops and research projects.

716. GAMMA   1981-c.

   Tl:GAMMA:Girls and Mathematics Association
   Pub. Girls and Mathematics Unit, University of London,
   Institute of Education
   Irregular (5 issues by May 1984);September 1981-c.
   L:Flic (incomplete)
A4 national newsletter of the association encouraging girls'
participation in mathematics.

717. WOMEN'S TAPEOVER   1981-c.

   Tl:Women's Tapeover
   Monthly;September 1981-c.
   L:Not found
Not seen. A feminist taped magazine of some 12,000 words produced
by blind/partially sighted women among whom are Sue Hancock, and
Kirsten Hearne with the help of sighted readers. Its aim is "to
make feminist printed magazines accessible for blind and partially
sighted women and to campaign for more feminist literature on
tape" (item 825, n°19, November 1983, p.11). Contents are articles
extracted from feminist publications. The editorial group has
succeeded in getting some women's magazines to tape themselves
(items 297, 556, 567, 825, 836).

718. WOMEN-RITE   1981-c.

   Tl:Women-rite:A newsletter of the Women's Movement in
   Northern Ireland
   Belfast
   Monthly;September(?) 1981-c.
   L:Flic (incomplete)
A4 duplicated newsletter of about 10 pages.

719. THREE HUNDRED GROUP:THE NEWS   1981-c.

   Tl:Three Hundred Group:the news
   Burford, Henley-on-Thames
   Quarterly;Autumn(?) 1981-c.
   L:F, Flic (both incomplete)
Newsletter of the Three Hundred Group, a national movement for
women in politics. The Group, formed on 18 September 1984, is
non-party-political and aims to get more women into British
Parliament. The name shows that the target might be some 300

women MPs out of the full House of 635. The Group informs women, helps them to develop the relevant skills, encourages them to stand for local Council for the Party of their choice. The national contacts have been Lesley Abdela and Molly Sawbridge. Issue 2 claimed a circulation of 2,000 copies, issue 3 of 3,000.

720. MATRIARCHY NEWS 1981-1982
    Tl:Matriarchy news:quarterly newsletter of the Matriarchy Study Group
    Quarterly (3 issues only);October 1981-July 1982
    L:Flic
A4 duplicated newsletter available to women only. It was the organ of the Matriarchy Study Group. The editorial collective included Mary Coghill. The publications of the issues coincided with the quarter days - festivals linked to the Celtic calendar. The group aimed to speak to the Women's Liberation Movement and to matriarchists, occultists, scientists, etc.. It had an average circulation of 100 copies per issue.

721. WRITING WOMEN 1981-c.
    Tl:Writing women
    Eds. Eileen Aird, Linda Anderson, Gay Clifford, Sheila Whitaker
    3 issues per year approx.;October 1981-c.
    L:Flic
Printed substantial journal established particularly in response to "the continued resistance to women writers, (which) combined with the small number of journals in the UK publishing poetry, short stories and essays" results in contemporary women writers finding it difficult to get into print. Dedicated to publishing creative writing by women, it also includes critical and theoretical articles and book reviews.

722. WOMEN & WORK 1981-c.
    Tl:Women & Work:Changing Times
    Ed. Women's Office Within the Employment Opportunity Programs Branch
    Pub. Ministry of Labour
    Burnaby, British Columbia, Canada
    Bi-monthly;November 1981-c.
    L:not found
Not seen. Listed in item 612 (v.10,n°4, December 1981/January

1982, p.46). Not to be confused with item 501.

723. WOMEN'S STUDIES ASSOCIATION 1981-c.
    Tl:Women's Studies Association Newsletter
    Auckland, New Zealand
    3 issues per year;November 1981-c.
    L:not found
Not seen. Mentioned in items 584 (n°19, December 1981, p.10) and
612 (v.10,n°4, December 1981/January 1982, p.64). Newsletter of
the association "formed to promote radical social change through
the medium of women's studies". It carries organisational news,
articles, abstracts, news items, reports of work in progress.

724. ANTI-APARTHEID MOVEMENT WOMEN'S COMMITTEE NEWSLETTER 1981-c.
    Tl:Anti-Apartheid Movement Women's Committee Newsletter
    Irregular to n°5, November 1982;then bi-monthly;November/
    December 1981-c.
    L:Flic
A4 printed newsletter of 6 to 10 pages, published by the
Anti-Apartheid Movement Women's Committee set up in 1980 to focus
attention on the role of women in the fight for freedom in South
Africa, Namibia, etc., and on the impact of apartheid on women who
are the worst off. Very much a single campaign periodical about
Anti-Apartheid movements to try to reach more women in Britain
and get their support.

725. DIRTY DISHES 1981-c.
    Tl:Dirty dishes
    Monthly;bi-monthly;December 1981-n°4, April 1982 (n.i.c.)
    C:item 670?
    L:Flic (incomplete)
A4 local newsletter of about 30 pages and available to women only.
Published by Haringey women, it concentrates on the facilities
for women in this area such as Women's Aid or the Rape Crisis
Centre. Yet it also includes opinions, news, interviews, poems and
general articles (sexism in education, Kathe Kollwitz, nuclear
weapons, etc.). The group stated a circulation of 400 copies per
issue in April 1982.

726. WIMMIN 1981-c.
    Tl:Wimmin
    Editorial collective:Caroline Butler, Fiona Casey, Mary

Flanagan, Grainne Healy, Veronica Quinn, et al
Dublin
Irregular?;December 1981-c.
C:item 559
L:F, Flic (both incomplete)
Magazine printed in variable format, produced by an independent
Women's Collective with backing from Trinity College, Dublin,
Students' Union. Coming from various ideological and occupational
backgrounds, its members are concerned with social change to put
an end to women's oppression and see themselves as part of the
women's movement. They publish news items, articles, reviews,
fiction and poetry from a strongly feminist standpoint. Topics
regularly covered: women and work, sexism in education,
self-defence, A Women's Right to Choose campaign, etc..

727. WONT NEWSLETTER   1981-?
    Tl:Women Oppose the Nuclear Threat Newsletter
    Nottingham (national contact)
    F.n.k.;December 1981-?
    C:item 662
    L:Flic (1 issue only)
WONT is a network of autonomous women's groups campaigning
throughout Britain for nuclear disarmament. It was set up after
the Nottingham Conference on Women and the Military, partly in
reaction against men's domination of the disarmament movement even
in CND but the women of WONT also saw the nuclear threat as a
specially feminist issue. The newsletter of the network came
partly out of item 662 and partly out of the WONT conference in
Leeds on 7, 8 June 1981. The Hackney/Islington group produced the
first issue. "The recommendation of the conference was that if it
worked . . . (the newsletter) could become an ongoing newsletter
passing from group to group. Otherwise it would be a one-off
issue" (December 1981). As no trace of issue 2 was found, may
have been a one-off publication. The newsletter produced discussed
the relationship between feminism and nuclear technology,
strategies, women and militarism, the feminist theories of science.
It carried news and feedback from local groups, reviews, poems and
cartoons. Contributors included among others Lucy Whitman,
Gillian Allnutt, Kay Stirling.

728. WHIM 1981-c.
    Tl:WHIM:Women in Medicine Newsletter

Monthly?;December(?) 1981-c.

L:Flic (n°2, January 1982 only)

A4 duplicated newsletter. Issue 2 produced by the South London
Group was eight pages long.

729. ABOUT WOMEN   1981-c.

Tl:About women

Ed. and pub. Women's Bureau, Manitoba Department of Labour
and Manpower

Winnipeg, Manitoba, Canada

Bi-monthly;1981(?)-c.

L:not found

Not seen. Free newsletter listed in item 612 (v.10,n°4, December
1981/January 1982, p.39). Not to be confused with item 491.

730. APWA PROFILE   1981-c.

Tl:APWA profile:quarterly newsletter of the All Pakistan
Women's Association

Karachi, Pakistan

Quarterly;1981(?)-c.

L:not found

Not seen. Listed in item 612 (v.10,n°4, December 1981/January
1982, p.50).

731. AUCKLAND FEMINIST TEACHERS' NEWSLETTER   1981-c.

Tl:Auckland feminist teachers' newsletter

Auckland, New Zealand

F.n.k.;1981(?)-c.

L:not found

Not seen. Mention in item 462 (n°33, August/September 1981).

732. AWAZ NEWSLETTER   1981-?

Tl:AWAZ Newsletter

Southall, Middlesex

F.n.k.;1981(?)-?

L:not found

Not seen. Listed in item 612 (v.9,n°4, December 1980/January
1981). Newsletter of AWAZ, an autonomous Asian women group set up
in 1978. It campaigns against racism, sexism and general State
oppression (e.g. the immigration laws, the Nationality Bill,
police intimidation, etc.). The publishing group included Ms
Chowdar.

733. BREAKING THE SILENCE   1981-c.
     Tl:Breaking the silence:A newsletter on feminism in social
     welfare research, action, policy and practice
     Pub. Feminist Caucus, School of Social Work, Carelton
     University
     Ottawa, Ontario, Canada
     F.n.k.;1981(?)-c.
     L:not found
Not seen. Listed in item 612 (v.10,n°4, December 1981/January
1982).

734. CANADIAN ABORTION RIGHTS ACTION LEAGUE NEWSLETTER   1981-c.
     Tl:Canadian Abortion Rights Action League Newsletter
     Toronto, Ontario, Canada
     F.n.k.;1981(?)-c.
     L:not found
Not seen. Mentioned in item 612 (v.10,n°4, December 1981/January
1982, p.39).

735. CANADIAN ASSOCIATION OF SEXUAL ASSAULT CENTRES:THE NEWSLETTER
     1981-c.
     Tl:Canadian Association of Sexual Assault Centres:the
     newsletter - Association Canadienne des Centres Contre le
     Viol:le bulletin
     Terrace, British Columbia, Canada
     3 issues per year;1981(?)-c.
     L:not found
Not seen. Listed in item 612 (v.10,n°4, December 1981/January
1982, p.40). Apparently a substantial newsletter. Two
English-Language and one French-Language issues per year.

736. CANADIAN CATHOLICS FOR WOMEN'S ORDINATION   1981-c.
     Tl:Canadian Catholics for Women's Ordination
     Toronto, Ontario, Canada
     F.n.k.;1981(?)-c.
     L:not found
Not seen. Listed in item 612 (v.10,n°4, December 1981/January
1982, p.40).

737. CANADIAN COMMITTEE ON WOMEN'S HISTORY   1981-c.
     Tl:Canadian Committee on Women's History
     Co-ordinator M. L. McDougall

        Pub. Dept of History, Simon Fraser University

        Burnaby, Ontario, Canada

        Twice-yearly;1981(?)-c.

        C:item 573?

        L:not found

Not seen. Listed in item 612 (v.10,n°4, December 1981/January
1982, p.40).

738. CANADIAN WOMEN AND RELIGION NEWSLETTER   1981-c.

        Tl:Canadian women and religion newsletter

        Saskatoon, Saskatchewan, Canada

        F.n.k.;1981(?)-c.(?)

        L:not found

Not seen. Mentioned in item 612 (v.10,n°4, December 1981/January
1982, p.40). "An ecumenical Christian feminist publication".

739. CFUW-FCFDU JOURNAL   1981-c.

        Tl:CFUW-FCFDU journal

        c/o M. Louise McArthur (Clarence Creek, Ontario)

        Pub. Canadian Federation of University Women, University of
        Montreal

        Montreal, Quebec, Canada

        F.n.k.;1981(?)-c.

        L:not found

Not seen. Mentioned in item 612 (v.10,n°4, December 1981/January
1982, p.40). Partially bilingual.

740. CLARION   1981-1982

        Tl:Clarion:The voice of Women's Ecology Group

        Quarterly?;1981(?)-n°5, Autumn 1982 (n.i.c.)

        L:F (n°5 only)

A4 printed newsletter of about twelve pages, campaigning for
ecology and against vivisection and cruelty to animals in general.
Not very obtrusive feminism.

741. CONGRESS OF CANADIAN WOMEN NEWSLETTER   1981-c.

        Tl:Congress of Canadian Women newsletter

        Toronto, Ontario, Canada

        F.n.k.;1981(?)-c.

        L:not found

Not seen. Earliest mention found in item 612 (v.10.n°4, December
1981/January 1982, p.41). "Canadian affiliate of the Women's

International Democratic Federation".

742. CRIAW NEWSLETTER/BULLETIN 1981-c.
    Tl:CRIAW newsletter/bulletin:Canadian Research Institute for
    the Advancement of Women Newsletter/Bulletin de l'Institut
    Canadien de Recherchez pit l'Avancement de la Femme (CRIAW/
    ICRAF)
    Ottawa, Ontario, Canada
    Monthly;1981(?)-c.(?)
    L:not found
Not seen. Listed in item 612 (v.10,n°4, December 1981/January
1982, p.40). The Institute was mentioned in item 294 (v.7,n°4,
1978, p.48).

743. DECADE NETWORK NEWSLETTER 1981-c.
    Tl:Decade Network Newsletter
    Pub. Change
    F.n.k.;1981(?)-c.
    L:not found
Not seen. Listed in item 612 (v.10,n°4, December 1981/January
1982, p.53). The Decade Network was "set up to provide a forum
for discussion and coordination among non-governmental
organisations and others prior to the 1985 Decade for Women
Conference". See also item 640.

744. ELIZABETH FRY SOCIETY NEWSLETTER 1981-c.
    Tl:Elizabeth Fry Society Newsletter
    Toronto, Ontario, Canada
    F.n.k.;1981(?)-c.
    L:not found
Not seen. Only mention occurs in item 612 (v.10,n°4, December
1981/January 1982, p.41). A newsletter for members concerned with
women and the criminal justice system.

745. EQUAL TIMES 1981-c.
    Tl:Equal times:A Publication of the Federal NDP Women's
    Organizer
    Ed. Mary Humphrey
    Ottawa, Ontario, Canada
    Irregular;1981(?)-c.(?)
    L:not found
Not seen. Listed in item 612 (v.10,n°4, December 1981/January

1982, p.42). A free publication from the office of the New
Democratic Party.

746. EX AEQUO   1981-c.
    Tl:Ex aequo
    Ed. and pub. New Brunswick Advisory Council on the Status of
    Women
    Moncton, New Brunswick, Canada
    Quarterly;1981(?)-c.
    L:not found
Not seen. Mentioned in item 612 (v.10,n°4, December 1981/January
1982, p.42). "Articles on research results, news about N.B.
women's activities, council activities and general women's
interest articles. Bilingual".

747. F/ARTS   1981-c.
    Tl:F/ARTS:A Womyn's Arts Newsletter
    Lillyfield, Australia
    Bi-monthly;1981(?)-c.
    L:not found
Not seen. A newsletter for "isolated women arts-workers in all
creative areas". Publicised in item 661 (November 1981, p.31) as a
communication network to "help in the organisation and publicity
of women's arts events". It publishes women's arts news and
women's criticism of women's art.

748. FEMINIST FORUM   1981-c.
    Tl:The feminist forum
    Ed. Association of Women Teaching at Queen's
    Pub. Queen's Women's Centre, Queen's University
    Kingston, Ontario, Canada
    F.n.k.;1981(?)-c.
    L:not found
Not seen. Earliest mention found in item 612 (v.10,n°4, December
1981/January 1982, p.42). Not to be confused with item 688.

749. FEMINIST NETWORK NEWSLETTER   1981-c.
    Tl:Feminist Network newsletter
    Bombay, India
    F.n.k.;1981(?)-c.
    L:not found
Not seen. Listed in Gallagher, 1981, p.180.

750. FEMINIST PARTY OF CANADA:NEWS 1981-c.

    Tl:Feminist Party of Canada:news - Parti Feministe du Canada:
    Nouvelles
    Toronto, Ontario, Canada
    F.n.k.;1981(?)-c.
    L:not found
Not seen. Mentioned in item 612 (v.10,n°4, December 1981/January
1982, p.42). The FPC was formed in June 1979.

751. FREE WOMAN 1981-?

    Tl:Free Woman
    Ed. and pub. Belfast Women Against Imperialism
    Belfast, Northern Ireland
    F.n.k.;1981(?)-?
    L:not found
Not seen. Listed in Spare Rib Diary 1981. "Magazine on public
sale". Contact person: Anne Marie Loughran.

752. GRAPEVINE 1981-c.

    Tl:Grapevine:The newsletter of the Lesbian Mothers' Defense
    Fund
    Toronto, Ontario, Canada
    F.n.k.;1981(?)-c.(?)
    L:not found
Not seen. Mentioned in item 612 (v.10,n°4, December 1981/January
1982, p.42). "For mothers who are fighting for child custody".
Interviews, information on legal rights, short personal
experiences, etc..

753. HERIZONS 1981-c.

    Tl:Herizons:the Manitoba women's newspaper
    Winnipeg, Manitoba, Canada
    F.n.k.;1981(?)-c.
    L:not found
Not seen. Earliest mention found occurs in item 612 (v.10,n°4,
December 1981/January 1982, p.42), latest one in ISIS (n°27, June
1982, p.8).

754. ICA NEWSLETTER 1981-c.

    Tl:Irish Countrywomen's Association Newsletter
    Ed. and pub. Irish Countrywomen's Association
    Dublin

Quarterly;1981(?)-c.
    C:item 630
    L:not found
Not seen. Mentioned in item 612 (v.10,n°4, December 1981/January
1982, p.37).

755. INNER LONDON NATFHE   1981-c.
    Tl:Inner London Natfhe:Women's Rights and Nursery Campaign
    newsletter
    Pub. NATFHE (National Association of Teachers in Further and
    Higher Education)
    F.n.k.;1981(?)-c.(?)
    L:F (n°5, 1981 only)
Women's newsletter of the union.

756. INTERNATIONAL FEMINIST VIDEO NEWSLETTER   1981-c.
    Tl:International feminist video newsletter
    International locations
    F.n.k.;1981(?)-c.(?)
    L:not found
Not seen. Women in SynC, a London group born in December 1980, was
responsible for the production of the first issue. The newsletter
evolved out of the First International Feminist Film and Video
Conference in Amsterdam and was aimed "to set up some kind of
international communication network for women video workers";
(see item 409, n°121, 1981, p.10). Each country was to contribute
and "compile a list of women's video groups and feminists working
in video; access to equipment and a list of feminist videotapes".

757. INTERNATIONAL WOMEN'S DAY COMMITTEE NEWSLETTER   1981-c.
    Tl:International Women's Day Committee Newsletter
    Toronto, Ontario, Canada
    F.n.k.;1981(?)-c.
    L:not found
Not seen. Listed in item 612 (v.10,n°4, December 1981/January
1982, p.43).

758. ISSUE   1981-c.
    Tl:Issue
    Ed. and pub. Ontario Association of Midwives
    Guelph, Ontario, Canada
    Quarterly;1981(?)-c.

L:not found

Not seen. For further information see item 612 (v.10, n°4,
December 1981/January 1982, p.44).

759. KENT WOMEN'S NEWSLETTER 1981-c.
    Tl:Kent Women's Newsletter
    Dartford
    F.n.k.;1981(?)-c.(?)
    L:not found

Not seen. Local Women's Liberation newsletter produced by Dartford
women's group. Mention in item 297 (n°112, November 1981, p.35).
News, views, lists of groups.

760. LESBIAN ACTION NEWSLETTER 1981-c.
    Tl:Lesbian Action Newsletter
    West Melbourne, Victoria, Australia
    F.n.k.;1981(?)-c.
    L:not found

Not seen. Listed in item 612 (v.10, n°4, December 1981/January
1982, p.62).

761. LESBIAN FEMINIST CIRCLE 1981-c.
    Tl:Lesbian Feminist Circle
    Wellington, New Zealand
    Quarterly approx.;1981(?)-c.
    L:not found

Not seen. Mentioned in item 661 (May 1981, p.23). Same as item
316?

762. LESBIAN/LESBIENNE 1981-c.
    Tl:Lesbian/Lesbienne
    Toronto, Ontario, Canada
    F.n.k.;1981(?)-c.
    L:not found

Not seen. Mentioned in item 612 (v.10,n°4, December 1981/January
1982 and v.11,n°3, November 1982). A publication by, for and about
lesbians put together by a Toronto collective aiming to be first
a "news" letter though it prints articles, reviews, poetry.

763. LESBIAN NEWSLETTER 1981-c.
    Tl:Lesbian Newsletter
    North Carlton, Australia

Bi-monthly;1981(?)-c.(?)

    L:not found

Not seen. Listed in item 612 (v.10,n°4, December 1981/January
1982, p.62). "Articles, reviews, discussion and information about
lesbian/feminist events".

764. LIVERPOOL CRECHES AGAINST SEXISM NEWSLETTER 1981-c.

    Tl:Liverpool Creches Against Sexism Newsletter

    Liverpool

    Monthly?;1981(?)-c.(?)

    L:not found

Not seen. N°12, September 1982 was mentioned in item 826 (n°8,
October 1982). Very thin, men against sexism newsletter.

765. MAMMA 1981-c.

    Tl:MAMMA:Modern Activities for Mothers' Mental Awareness

    Willowdale, Ontario, Canada

    Bi-monthly (plus 1 major issue);1981(?)-c.

    L:not found

Not seen. Mentioned in item 612 (v.10,n°4, December 1981/January
1982, p.43). Not to be confused with item 483.

766. MATCH 1981-c.

    Tl:MATCH:Mothers Apart from Their Children newsletter

    Ed. Anne Hooper

    Quarterly;1981(?)-c.(?)

    L:Flic (incomplete)

National printed A4 newsletter. Its main aim is to help women keep
in touch and "gain a sense of support and self-esteem" from others
in similar situations. It mainly contains organisational news,
contact lists, letters and articles of the personal experience
type. The feminist line seems rather moderate. Latest issue seen
n°5, April 1982. Not to be confused with item 529.

767. MATRIX 1981-c.

    Tl:Matrix

    Ed. and pub. London Status of Women Action Group

    London, Ontario, Canada

    Bi-monthly;1981(?)-c.

    L:not found

Not seen. Mentioned in item 612 (v.10,n°4, December 1981/January
1982, p.43).

768. MONTHLY   1981-c.

    Tl:The Monthly

    Ed. and pub. Women's Health Education Network (WHEN)

    Truro, Nova Scotia, Canada

    Quarterly;1981(?)-c.

    L:not found

Not seen. For further information see item 612 (v.10,n°4, December 1981/January 1982, p.47).

769. NAC MEMO   1981-c.(?)

    Tl:NAC Memo

    Pub. National Action Committee on the Status of Women

    Toronto, Ontario, Canada

    F.n.k.;1981(?)-c.(?)

    L:not found

Not seen. Mentioned in item 612 (v.10,n°4, December 1981/January 1982, p.43). See also item 325.

770. NATIONAL CHILDCARE CAMPAIGN - LONDON NEWS-SHEET   1981-c.

    Tl:National Childcare Campaign - London News-sheet

    F.n.k.;1981(?)-c.(?)

    L:Flic (1 undated issue)

Self-explanatory. See items 771 and 833.

771. NATIONAL CHILDCARE CAMPAIGN NEWSLETTER   1981-c.

    Tl:National Childcare Campaign Newsletter

    Pub. National Childcare Campaign

    Bi-monthly?;1981(?)-c.

    L:Flic (incomplete)

A4 printed newsletter of about twenty pages. It carries news on childcare and nursery campaigns nationally and internationally, articles on childcare and men, childcare and racism, etc.. See also items 770 and 833.

772. NATIONAL WOMEN'S ORGANIZATION NEWSLETTER   1981-c.

    Tl:National Women's Organization Newsletter

    Jamaica

    F.n.k.;1981(?)-c.(?)

    L:Flic (1 issue only)

Eight page newspaper.

773. NAWL NEWSLETTER 1981-c.
     Tl:NAWL Newsletter:Bulletin de l'A.N.F.D.
     Pub. National Association of Women and the Law
     Ottawa, Ontario, Canada
     F.n.k.;1981(?)-c.
     L:not found
Not seen. Listed in item 612 (v.10,n°4, December 1981/January
1982, p.43).

774. NEWFOUNDLAND STATUS OF WOMEN COUNCIL NEWSLETTER 1981-c.
     Tl:Newfoundland Status of Women Council newsletter
     Saint John's, Newfoundland, Canada
     F.n.k.;1981(?)-c.
     L:not found
Not seen. Only trace found occurs in item 612 (v.10,n°4, December
1981/January 1982, p.44).

775. NEWSLINK 1981-c.
     Tl:Newslink
     Ed. and pub. Centre for Women's Studies and Development
     Lucknow, India
     Twice-yearly;1981(?)-c.
     L:not found
Not seen. Listed in item 612 (v.10,n°4, December 1981/January
1982, p.51).

776. NORTH SHORE WOMEN 1981-c.
     Tl:North Shore women:newsletter of the North Shore Women's
     Centre
     North Vancouver, British Columbia, Canada
     F.n.k.;1981(?)-c.(?)
     L:not found
Not seen. Mentioned in item 612 (v.10,n°4, December 1981/January
1982, p.44).

777. NORTHERN IRELAND WOMEN'S AID NEWSLETTER 1981-c.
     Tl:Northern Ireland Women's Aid Newsletter
     Derry
     F.n.k.;1981(?)-c.
     L:not found

Not seen. Listed in Cadman et al, 1981. Circulates within the Womens' Aid Federation. See also item 537.

778. NOTTINGHAM WOMEN'S DIARY   1981-?
     Tl:Nottingham women's diary
     Nottingham
     F.n.k.;1981(?)-?
     L:Flic (March 1981 only)
A women's liberation newsletter.

779. OAWE EXCHANGE   1981-c.
     Tl:OAWE exchange
     Ed. and pub. Ontario Association for Women and Education
     Toronto, Ontario, Canada
     F.n.k.;1981(?)-c.
     L:not found
Not seen. For further information see item 612 (v.10,n°4, December 1981/January 1982, p.44).

780. ONTARIO NATIVE WOMEN'S ASSOCIATION NEWSLETTER   1981-c.
     Tl:Ontario Native Women's Association newsletter
     Thunder Bay, Ontario, Canada
     F.n.k.;1981(?)-c.
     L:not found
Not seen. Listed in item 612 (v.10,n°4, December 1981/January 1982, p.44).

781. RADICAL REVIEWER   1981-c.
     Tl:The radical reviewer
     Founding eds. Barbara Herringer and Cy-Thea Sand
     Vancouver, British Columbia, Canada
     3 issues per year;1981(?)-c.
     L:not found
Not seen. Earliest mention found in Feminist Bookstores Newsletter, not listed (v.5,n°1, June 1981). A lesbian feminist literary journal.

782. ROUGE   1981-c.
     Tl:Rouge
     Pub. National Newspaper Collective
     Lyncham;Canberra;Sydney, Australia
     Bi-monthly;1981(?)-c.

L:not found
Not seen. Listed in item 612 (v.10,n°4, December 1981/January 1982, p.63).

783. SCOTTISH WOMEN'S NEWSLETTER 1981-c.
    Tl:Scottish Women's Newsletter
    St Andrews
    F.n.k.;1981(?)-c.(?)
    L:not found
Not seen. Listed in item 612 (v.10,n°4, December 1981/January 1982, p.50).

784. SISTERHOOD 1981-c.
    Tl:Sisterhood
    Ed. and pub. Women's Rights Committee, BC Federation of Labour
    Burnaby, British Columbia, Canada
    Quarterly;1981(?)-c.(?)
    L:not found
Not seen. Mentioned in item 612 (v.10.n°4, December 1981/January 1982, p.45). "A newsletter for union women".

785. SORWUC 1981-c.
    Tl:SORWUC news
    Vancouver, British Columbia, Canada
    F.n.k.;1981(?)-c.
    L:not found
Not seen. Listed in item 612 (v.10,n°4, December 1981/January 1982, p.45). "Newsletter of the union which is actively organizing women bank and service workers, and which has an espoused feminist position".

786. SPEAK OUT 1981-c.
    Tl:Speak out
    Irregular;1981(?)-c.(?)
    L:Flic (1 issue only)
A4 printed magazine of Brixton Black Women's Group. National and international news focusing on racism (e.g. immigration laws, police brutality, "Sus" laws, etc.) and national liberation struggles, book, and film reviews, poems. Publications seems to have ceased with issue 4 in 1981 and to have been resumed in December 1983.

787. SPIRALE 1981-c.

    Tl:Spirale:A women's art and culture quarterly

    Pub. Womanspirit Art Research and Resource Centre

    London, Ontario, Canada

    F.n.k.;1981(?)-c.

    L:not found

Not seen. Listed in item 612 (v.10,n°4, December 1981/January 1982, p.45).

788. STATUS 1981-c.

    Tl:Status

    Pub. Ontario Status of Women Council

    Toronto, Ontario, Canada

    F.n.k.;1981(?)-c.

    L:not found

Not seen. Listed in item 612 (v.10,n°4, December 1981/January 1982, p.44).

789. SUDBURY WOMEN'S CENTRE NEWSLETTER 1981-c.

    Tl:Sudbury Women's Centre Newsletter

    Sudbury, Ontario, Canada

    F.n.k.;1981(?)-c.

    L:not found

Not seen. Mentioned in item 612 (v.10,n°4, December 1981/January 1982, p.45). Bilingual.

790. S/W NEWSLETTER 1981-c.

    Tl:S/W newsletter

    Ed. and pub. Status of Women Programme, British Columbia Teachers' Federation

    British Columbia, Canada

    Bi-monthly;1981(?)-c.

    L:not found

Not seen. For further information see item 612 (v.10,n°4, December 1981/January 1982, p.45).

791. SWAP NEWSLETTER 1981-c.

    Tl:SWAP Newsletter

    Ed. Anita Myers

    Pub. Section on Women and Psychology, Dept of Psychology, University of Guelph

    Guelph, Ontario, Canada

3 issues per year;1981(?)-c.(?)

    C:item 577

    L:not found

Not seen. Mentioned in item 612 (v.10,n°4, December 1981/January 1982, p.45).

792. TAMARACK 1981-c.

    T1:Tamarack

    Ed. and pub. Terrace Women's Centre

    Terrace, British Columbia, Canada

    F.n.k.;1981(?)-c.

    L:not found

Not seen. Only mention occurs in item 612 (v.10,n°4, December 1981/January 1982, p.45).

793. TRADE UNION WOMEN'S FORUM 1981-c.

    T1:Trade Union Women's Forum

    Dublin

    F.n.k.;1981(?)-c.(?)

    L:not found

Not seen. Listed in item 612 (v.10,n°4, December 1981/January 1982, p.57).

794. U OF T WOMEN'S NEWSMAGAZINE 1981-c.

    T1:The U[nion] of T[eachers] women's newsmagazine

    Toronto, Ontario, Canada

    6 issues during the school year;1981(?)-c.

    L:not found

Not seen. Mentioned in item 612 (v.10,n°4, December 1981/January 1982, p.46).

795. VOW 1981-c.

    T1:VOW:Ontario newsletter

    Ed. and pub. Ontario Voice of Women

    Toronto, Ontario, Canada

    F.n.k.;1981(?)-c.

    L:not found

Not seen. Listed in item 612 (v.10,n°4, December 1981/January 1982, p.46). "Covers the organization's activities locally and nationallly around the issues of disarmament, nuclear power, peace".

796. WELSH WOMEN'S AID NEWSLETTER 1981-c.

    Tl:Welsh Women's Aid Newsletter

    Cardiff

    F.n.k.;1981(?)-c.

    L:not found

Not seen. Listed in Cadman et al, 1981. Circulates within the
Women's Aid Federation. See also items 709 and 538.

797. WIT NEWS 1981-c.

    Tl:WIT News

    Ed. and pub. Women In Trades

    Edgeley, Saskatchewan, Canada

    F.n.k.;1981(?)-c.

    L:not found

Not seen. Mentioned in item 612 (v.10,n°4, December 1981/January
1982, p.46).

798. WOMEN AND MEDICAL PRACTICE 1981-c.

    Tl:Women and medikill practice newsletter

    T2:Women and medical practice newsletter

    Leicester;Nottingham

    Irregular;1981(?)-c.(?)

    L:not found

Not seen. Newsletter of WAMP group featuring how the things
doctors do, can damage women's health (item 297,n°139, February
1984, p.32).

799. WOMEN FOR POLITICAL ACTION NEWSLETTER 1981-c.

    Tl:Women for Political Action Newsletter

    Toronto, Ontario, Canada

    F.n.k.;1981(?)-c.

    L:not found

Not seen. For further information, see item 612 (v.10,n°4,
December 1981/January 1982, p.46).

800. WOMEN IN ENTERTAINMENT NEWSLETTER 1981-c.

    Tl:Women in Entertainment newsletter

    Co-ordinator Paul Brown

    F.n.k.;1981(?)-c.

    L:F, Flic (both issue 3, September 1981 only)

Very thin A4 printed newsletter produced by Women in Entertainment,
a national pressure group, co-ordinator of Women Live May 1982. It

aims "to challenge the position of women working in the
entertainment industry". It is concerned with the status (sexual
stereotyping in the work place and the type of material women are
expected to perform) and the working conditions (childcare
facilities, etc.) of all women throughout the entertainment
industry (i.e. performers, directors, writers, etc. and all behind
the scene workers in film, TV, theatre, radio, music etc.).

801. WOMEN IN TELECOM   1981-c.
    Tl:Women in Telecom
    Ed. Marcella Fitzgerald
    F.n.k.;1981(?)-c.
    L:Flic
A printed magazine produced by a group of women organising through
their own unions for real sexual equality within British Telecom,
with the aid of a grant from the Equal Opportunities Commission.
It reports on equal rights and opportunities in telecommunications
in Great Britain and abroad but also in other sectors. It suggests
positive action programmes to end discriminations. Contributions
from men are welcomed (see issue 2).

802. WOMEN IN TRADES ASSOCIATION NEWSLETTER   1981-c.
    Tl:Women in Trades Association newsletter
    Winnipeg, Manitoba, Canada
    Bi-monthly;1981(?)-c.
    L:not found
Not seen. Mentioned in item 612 (v.10,n°4, December 1981/January
1982, p.46). News of the membership and information on women
working in non-traditional occupations.

803. WOMEN MATTER   1981-c.
    Tl:Women matter
    Kerse Lane, Falkirk
    F.n.k.;1981(?)-c.
    L:not found
Not seen. Listed in Cadman et al, 1981. Central Scottish Women's
Aid newsletter. See also items 515, 675, 846 and 853.

804. WOMEN WORKING WITH IMMIGRANT WOMEN   1981-c.
    Tl:Women Working with Immigrant Women
    Pub. WWIW Labour Committee
    Toronto, Ontario, Canada

F.n.k.;1981(?)-c.

L:not found

Not seen. Listed in item 612 (v.10,n°4, December 1981/January 1982, p.46).

805. WOMEN'S CENTRE OF HAMILTON-WENTWORTH NEWSLETTER 1981-c.

   Tl:Women's Centre of Hamilton-Wentworth Newsletter

   Hamilton, Ontario, Canada

   8 issues per year;1981(?)-c.(?)

   L:not found

Not seen. Listed in item 612 (v.10,n°4, December 1981/January 1982, p.47). "Centre news, announcements, short articles".

806. WOMEN'S CONCERNS NEWSLETTER 1981-c.

   Tl:Women's concerns newsletter

   Toronto, Ontario, Canada

   Bi-monthly;1981(?)-c.

   L:not found

Not seen. Listed in item 612 (v.10,n°4, December 1981/January 1982, p.47). Free of charge. Contact person: Marion Longan, Division of Mission, United Church of Canada.

807. WOMEN'S FORUM 1981-c.

   Tl:Women's Forum

   Maharashtra, India

   Quarterly;1981(?)-c.

   L:not found

Not seen. Only mention found occurs in item 612 (v.10,n°4, December 1981/January 1982, p.51). "Magazine devoted to women's rights and to publicize and support United Nations Program on Women's Decade".

808. WOMEN'S HEALTH NETWORK NEWSLETTER 1981-c.

   Tl:Women's Health Network Newsletter

   Hamilton, New Zealand

   Bi-monthly;1981(?)-c.

   L:not found

Not seen. Only mention occurs in item 612 (v.10,n°4, December 1981/January 1982, p.64).

809. WOMEN'S INTER-CHURCH COUNCIL OF CANADA NEWSLETTER 1981-c.

   Tl:Women's Inter-Church Council of Canada Newsletter

Toronto, Ontario, Canada

F.n.k.;1981(?)-c.

L:not found

Not seen. Only mention found occurs in item 612 (v.10,n°4, December 1981/January 1982, p.47).

810. WOMEN'S NETWORK 1981-c.

Tl:Women's network

Belleville, Ontario, Canada

Monthly;1981(?)-c.(?)

L:not found

Not seen. Mentioned in item 612 (v.10,n°4, December 1981/January 1982, p.47). Local. "Information about meetings, reports, creative work".

811. WOMEN'S RIGHTING 1981

Tl:Women's Righting:North Paddington Women's Centre newsletter

F.n.k.;1981(?)-August 1981 (n.i.c.)

L:Flic (2 issues only)

A4 duplicated newsletter of 12 pages. Short articles, reviews, poems. See also item 633.

812. WOMEN'S SOCIOLOGICAL BULLETIN 1981-c.

Tl:Women's Sociological Bulletin

Pub. Department of Sociology, La Trobe University

Bundoora, Victoria, Australia

3 issues per year;1981(?)-c.(?)

L:not found

Not seen. Listed in item 612 (v.10,n°4, December 1981/January 1982, p.63). "A forum for the publication of research and theory addressing a feminist problematic within the social sciences".

813. WOMEN'S STUDIES NEWSLETTER 1981-c.

Tl:Women's Studies Newsletter

Pub. Women's Studies Resource Centre

Adelaide, South Australia, Australia

3 issues per year;1981(?)-c.(?)

L:not found

Not seen. Listed in item 612 (v.10,n°4, December 1981/January 1982, p.63).

814. YORK WOMEN'S CENTRE NEWSLETTER   1981-c.

    T1:York Women's Centre Newsletter

    Pub. York University

    Downsview, Ontario, Canada

    F.n.k.;1981(?)-c.

    L:not found

Not seen. Listed in item 612 (v.10,n°4, December 1981/January 1982, p.47).

815. YORK WOMEN'S LIBERATION NEWSLETTER   1981-c.

    T1:York Women's Liberation Newsletter

    York

    F.n.k.;1981(?)-c.

    C:item 347?

    L:not found

Local women only newsletter listed in Cadman et al, 1981. No other trace found.

816. GREENHAM WOMEN'S PEACE CAMP NEWS   1982-c.

    T1:Greenham Common Women's Peace Camp News-sheet

    T2:Greenham Women's Peace Camp News

    Pub. Greenham Women's Peace Camp and the South Oxfordshire Peace Camp

    Wallingford, Oxon.

    Irregular

    L:F (n°3, 25 January 1983 only)

Thin A4 printed newsletter on the peace movement and the camps' activities.

817. IRREGULAR PERIODS   1982-c.

    T1:Irregular Periods:Bradford women's newsletter

    Shipley, Bradford

    About every six weeks

    C:item 572?

    L:Flic (incomplete)

A substantial and well produced A5 printed newsletter put together by a collective of women for women only. Contents include letters, a noticeboard of local events, news of groups and general articles, e.g. violence against women, sexist advertisements, anti-semitism, health, etc..

818. OLDER FEMINISTS NETWORK NEWSLETTER 1982-c.
    Tl:Older feminists network newsletter
    Twickenham;Osterley;London
    Bi-monthly
    L:not found
Not seen. The network began to form in 1981. The newsletter is
mentioned in item 297 (n°126, January 1983, p.34 and n°137,
December 1983, p.30) and in item 688 (v.7,n°2, 1984, p.x). Contact
persons: Judith Pritchard, Moyra Peralta, Pat Jennings.

819. SINISTER WOMEN 1982-1983
    Tl:Sinister women
    Ed. Jude Brigley
    Cheltenham
    L:not found
Not seen. Advertised in item 297 (n°122, January 1983, to n°125,
April 1983) as a periodical carrying short stories, poetry and
reviews.

820. SISTERHOOD 1982-c.
    Tl:Cleveland Women's Centre Newsletter
    T2:Sisterhood
    Middlesborough
    Quarterly
    L:Flic (incomplete)
Interesting A4 newsletter of some 30 pages, available to women
only. It deals with issues affecting local women but also with
matters of general feminine concern such as health, peace,
domestic violence. It published book reviews and fiction as well.

821. CONTRA-DICTION 1982
    Tl:Contra-diction
    Ed. and Pub. Women's Music Organisers
    Moseley, Birmingham
    Irregular;January(?) 1982-n°3, 1982 (n.i.c.)
    L:Flic (n°1, January(?) 1982 and n°2, July 1982)
Printed women's music paper published by a collective of five
young women. It is designed to provide a feminist view of music
through interviews, articles and reviews. It especially provides
space for and promotes women musicians and bands but it also

covers other issues relevant to young women such as rape,
pornography, Y.O.P.S., photography. It claims a national
distribution of 1,500 copies per issue. Last mention found n°3,
1982 in item 297 (n°125, December 1982, p.29).

822. BROXA   1982-c
    Tl:Broxa
    Ed. Greengate Women's Group (N.E.L.P.)
    3 issues per year approx.;February 1982-c.
    L:F
Substantial A4 printed newsletter produced by women's art students
"to provide an alternative, collective and critical approach to
viewing each other's work" (n°2, p.2). Cartoons, drawings, poems,
etc..

823. NAPPIES   1982-c.
    Tl:It's not all nappies . . . A lesbian and feminist
    newsletter on children and childcare
    Irregular?;February(?) 1982-c.(?)
    L:Flic (February 1982 only)
Duplicated A4 multi-coloured newsletter collated by a collective
of mothers. It came out of both the 1981 National Lesbian
Conference and the Edinburgh Lesbian Feminist Conference on
child-rearing. It is for "women with, wanting and/or involved
with, and caring for children" (see item 409, n°111, p.12). Topics
covered: motherhood, boy children, shared childcare, etc..

824. LILITH   1982-c.
    Tl:Lilith:Oxford Women's Paper
    Oxford
    Monthly to n°11, January 1983;then bi-monthly;1 March 1982-c.
    C:item 651?
    L:F, Flic (both incomplete)
Interesting A4 printed publication produced by an open collective
of women. "Set out to reach as wide a range of women as possible –
not just those committed to feminism" (issue 12, February/March
1983, p.3). It has printed letters by men. It claims a circulation
of 500 copies, half of them being sold through local newsagents.
Contents include news, articles, a calendar of events, poetry,
film and book reviews, etc.. Features have covered wide-ranging
issues such as foot-binding in China, racism, the Women's
Liberation Movement, etc.. Not to be confused with item 337.

825. OUTWRITE   1982-c.

    Tl:Outwrite

    Pub. Feminist Newspaper Group

    Monthly;10 issues per year;8 March 1982-c.

    L:F, Flic

Substantial tabloid launched on International Women's Day.
Produced by a radically mixed collective, it is the only national
women's liberation newspaper. It was GLC funded in 1984. It has
a print run of 10,000 copies and a current distribution of 7,000
copies. Unsold ones are given away. Outwrite has a strong
anti-classist, anti-racist and anti-imperialist stand. It includes
more news than features and regularly covers women's rights, work
inside and outside the home, health, sexuality, violence against
women, lesbian pride. It not only provides news from within the
Women's Liberation Movement but also tries to offer a pro-woman
perspective on world news and an international information
service. It focuses on "the lives and struggles of women all over
the world, especially Black and Third World women, so as to
promote and serve the interest of a truly internationalist
movement for the liberation of women" (publicity leaflet). It also
carries reviews, poetry, cartoons, graphics, photographs.

826. A.S.A.P.   1982-c.

    Tl:Anti-sexism, Anti-patriarchy news sheet

    T2:A.S.A.P.:Against sexism, against patriarchy newsletter
    (n°4, June 1982)

    Eds. have included Graham Dale, David Michael

    Monthly;bi-monthly;March 1982-n°13, March/April 1983 (n.i.c.)

    L:F, Flic (both incomplete)

"A pro-feminist newsletter for people in London", a printed
publication produced by men struggling against sexism and
patriarchy and society. Welcomes contributions from women.
Contents feature creches against sexism, men and childcare,
pornography, etc.. N°12 claims a circulation of 220 copies.

827. SOUTHAMPTON WOMEN'S LIBERATION NEWSLETTER   1982-c.(?)

    Tl:Southampton Women's Liberation newsletter

    Southampton

    Monthly?;March 1982-c.(?)

    L:not found

Not seen. Only mention found occurs in item 297 (n°121, August
1982, p.29).

828. TUC WOMEN WORKERS' BULLETIN   1982-1983
      Tl:TUC women workers' bulletin
      Irregular;March 1982-n°3, 1983 (n.i.c.)
      L:Flic
A4 printed bulletin "reporting on the work of the TUC Women's
Advisory Committee and TUC policies for women workers" (n°1).

829. WOMEN'S REPORT   1982-c.
      Tl:The women's report:A federal perspective
      Ed. Pauline Jewett, MP
      Ottawa, Ontario, Canada
      Monthly?;March 1982-c.
      L:not found
Not seen. Listed in item 612 (v.10,n°4, December 1981/January
1982, p.47). Focuses on the New Democratic Party position on
women's issues,

830. INCEST SURVIVORS' CAMPAIGN NEWSLETTER   1982-c.
      Tl:Incest Survivors' Campaign Newsletter
      Bi-monthly (approx.)?;March(?) 1982-c.
      L:Flic (March 1982 to Winter 1983)
A4 women only publication. News from the campaign and the support
network, extensive space devoted to media contents analysis.

831. GLC WOMEN'S COMMITTEE BULLETIN   1982-c.
      Tl:Bulletin on the GLC Women's Committee
      T2:GLC Women's Committee Bulletin
      Pub. Women's Committee Support Unit (originally headed by
      Louise Pankhurst)
      Bi-monthly;monthly;May/June(?) 1982-c.
      L:F, Flic (both incomplete)
Well produced and substantial A4 printed bulletin providing
information about the work and aims of the Women's Committee as
well as other information for the use of women in London, news,
facilities, services, campaigns, contacts. It has featured racism
(issue 13), lesbianism (issue 17), etc..

832. NOWME   1982-c.
      Tl:NOWME:National Organisation for Women's Management
      Education
      Beaconsfield
      Quarterly;Summer 1982-c.

        L:F
Four-page A4 printed newsletter of the organisation which was set
up in 1981 to help women get into and be more successful in all
levels of management. The newsletter contains organisational news,
information on courses, conferences, and a contact list intended
"for women keen to develop a career in management". Otherwise,
contents are not perceptibly feminist.

833. BLACK WORKING PARTY NEWSLETTER 1982-c.(?)
        T1:Black Working Party newsletter
        T2:Black Working Party newsletter:national childcare campaign
        F.n.k.;September(?) 1982-c.(?)
        L:Flic (2 issues)
Thin A4 printed newsletter produced by a group of women of African
and Caribbean descent "who have come together to achieve good
quality childcare for black children". It questions the Women's
Liberation Movement's demand for more nurseries. Most of the
latter do not value the culture of ethnic minorities "producing
black children with an inferior white identity" (September 1982).
See items 770 and 771.

834. PANAKAEIA 1982-c.
        T1:Panakaeia:A journal of feminist psychics and alternative
        healing
        Ed. and pub. Marlene Packwood
        Twice yearly;Hallowe'en 1982-c.
        L:Flic (incomplete)
A4 printed journal of some thirty pages available to women only.
It is produced by Marlene Packwood, a tarot reader, writers and
psychic. Articles on the various facets of women's spirituality
and psychic awareness - clairvoyance, magic, mysticism, astrology,
witchcraft, alchemy, matriarchy, etc.. Large space is also devoted
to alternative healing - acupuncture, herbalism, homeopathy,
naturopathy, hypnosis, etc..

835. SAD NEWSLETTER 1982-c.
        T1:SAD newsletter
        Pub. Sisters Against Disablement
        Quarterly;October(?) 1982-c.
        L:not found
Not seen. Mentioned in items 297, 825 and 831. Produced by a
collective of feminist and lesbian feminist women who described

themselves as follows. "We are concerned with taking the position of disablement out of the understanding of 'disability as individual tragedy' and show it for what it really is, political . . . We are disabled by society not by ourselves or our 'disabilities'" (item 297,n°124, November 1982, p.42). Available on tape.

836. LYSISTRATA 1982-c.
     T1:Lysistrata:A women and peace magazine
     T2:Lysistrata:A wimmin's peace magazine
     T3:Lysistrata:fighting for freedom from oppression for all
     women
     Brighton
     Irregular;Winter 1982-c.
     L:F, Flic (both incomplete)
A4 magazine that came out of the Brighton Women's Peace Group. It is put together by a mixed collective in class and race and is available in print and on tape. Issue 1 was only 22 pages long and focused on women's actions for peace in the Brighton area and on Greenham Common Peace Camp. Topics broadened with the following issues and the number of pages grew to 48 in 1984. Lysistrata "Wants to cover wimmin's peace action from all over this country and the world" (n°3, Spring 1983, p.11). It gathers contact addresses, news and articles from women's peace groups nationally and internationally. Yet for the collective the struggle for peace must not be restricted to fighting against the nuclear threat. As they stated in their editorials, some women are struggling for peace from the daily threats that are racism, anti-lesbianism, anti-semitism, physical ability prejudices, classism. Lysistrata has included articles on imperialism, Third World liberation struggles in Namibia, in El Salvador, in Turkey, for instance, on all forms of male violence against women (nuclear war but also rape, pornography) and also on oppressed minorities (black women, Jewish women, women with disabilities). It carries letters, drawings, photographs, poems, and book reviews too.

837. WOMEN FOR LIFE ON EARTH 1982-c.
     T1:Women for life on earth
     Glastonbury
     Quarterly;Winter 1982(?)-c.
     L:F, Flic (both incomplete)
A4 newsletter of Women For Life On Earth, "a unifying network for

feminism and ecology". It aims to keep the various groups across
the country informed on each other's activities and to give
support. Production of the newsletter is rotated among the groups.
The national contact since 1982 has been Stephanie Leland.
Features focus on nuclear, peace and ecological issues. Contents
also include a listing of groups, poems and drawings. Not to be
confused with item 401.

838. CWDS BULLETIN 1982-c.
    Tl:CWDS bulletin:Centre For Women's Development Studies
    bulletin
    Ed. Dr Vina Mazumdar
    New Delhi, India
    Twice yearly (April-October);December 1982-c.
    L:Flic (1 issue only)
Sixteen-page printed newsletter produced by an editorial committee
of academics "to forge links between researchers and activists
so that they can learn from each other's experience". See item
856.

839. WOMEN FOR SOCIAL DEMOCRACY 1982-c.
    Tl:Women for Social Democracy
    Quarterly;December(?) 1982-c.
    L:F (incomplete)
Thin A4 newsletter of the women's section of the Social Democratic
Party. The production team has included Robbi Robson, Colleen
Saunders, Kate Tayler and a man, Brian Whitt. Contents have
featured the 300 group, the Fawcett Society, women at work, etc..

840. BALLYMENA 1982
    Tl:Ballymena
    F.n.k.;1982(?)-?
    L:not found
Not seen. Only mention occurs in item 297 (n°122, September 1982,
p.36). A magazine by Ballymena Women's group, Antrim.

841. CWIRES NEWSLETTER 1982-c.
    Tl:CWIRES newsletter
    Pub. CWIRES
    Oxford
    Quarterly;1982(?)-c.
    L:F, Flic

The Christian Women's Information and Resource Service was
started in 1979 as an umbrella organisation linking together all
the Christian groups working for change in the position of women
in the churches. Since 1982 the service has had its own
publication. Its A4 very slim newsletter carries articles from
within the British Christian feminist network, dates of events,
book reviews and library holdings.

842. FEMTECH 1982-c.
    Tl:Femtech:new newsletter on feminist perspectives on new
    technology
    Eds. Wendy Faulkner (S.P.R.U. Univ. of Sussex), Anne Lloyd
    Brighton and Richmond
    F.n.k.;1982(?)-c.
    L:not found
Not seen. The first issue was described in item 698 (n°6, July
1982) as "the newsletter for the DELFT group - an international
group of women developing a feminist perspective on new
technology". It aimed to demystify new technology for women. It
had articles on what's happening in Denmark and Sweden, on the
Brighton Women and Technology group at the Science Policy Research
unit and on the Leeds Conference, plus a literature list.

843. KENRIC NEWSLETTER 1982-c.
    Tl:Kenric newsletter
    F.n.k.;1982(?)-c.
    L:not found
Not seen. Kenric is a purely social organisation for lesbians of
all ages which is "non political" and "non militant". It arranges
social activities (music meetings, coffee evenings, walks, etc.).
The London group runs a newsletter mainly aimed at members outside
London area. Though the organisation has existed since 1974, the
earliest trace found of the newsletter occurs in Sequel Week End
Guide 1983, p.11. The publication is also mentioned in item 831
(June 1984, p.41).

844. MAITREYI 1982-c.
    Tl:Maitreyi
    Pub. Feminist Resource Centre
    Bombay, India
    Monthly;bi-monthly;1982(?)-c.
    L:Flic (incomplete)

This newsletter is "an attempt to bring together scattered news
items on women from regional and English dailies, and information
about women's groups, struggles, books, etc.". Earliest issue seen
dated June/July 1982.

845. NATIVE WOMEN'S ASSOCIATION OF CANADA NEWSLETTER   1982-c.
      Tl:Native Women's Association of Canada Newsletter
      Ottawa, Ontario, Canada
      F.n.k.;1982(?)-c.
      L:not found
Not seen. Listed in item 612 (v.11,n°3, November 1982).
Organisational paper of a group lobbying for aboriginal and
women's rights.

846. SCOTTISH WOMEN'S AID NEWSLETTER   1982-c.
      Tl:Scottish Women's Aid Newsletter
      Dundee
      F.n.k.;1982(?)-c.
      L:not found
Not seen. Christmas 1982 issue is mentioned in item 297 (n°128,
March 1983, p.28). The publication of issue 5, October 1983 is
publicised in item 297 (n°138, January 1984, p.24). See also items
518, 675, 803 and 853.

847. WOMEN'S CAMPAIGN FOR JOBS   1982-c.(?)
      Tl:Women's Campaign for Jobs
      Bi-monthly?;1982(?)-c.(?)
      L:Flic (n°3, February/March 1983 only)
Self-explanatory.

848. WOMEN'S ELECTORAL LOBBY NEWSLETTER   1982-c.
      Tl:Women's Electoral Lobby newsletter
      Invercargill, New Zealand
      F.n.k.;1982(?)-c.
      L:not found
Not seen.

849. WOMEN'S STUDIES NEWSLETTER   1982-c.
      Tl:Women's studies newsletter
      Toronto, Ontario, Canada
      F.n.k.;1982(?)-c.
      L:not found

Not seen. Listed in item 612 (v.11,n°3, November 1982). Published
by the University of Toronto, the newsletter carries notices of
lectures, conferences, workshops, new books and journals, etc..

850. YOUNG WOMEN MAGAZINE   1982-c.
    Tl:Young women magazine
    Ed. and pub. Madeley Young women's Writing and Designing
    Group
    Madeley, Telford, Salop.
    F.n.k.;1982(?)-c.(?)
    L:not found
Not seen. Only mention occurs in item 563 (n°6, p.28). Interviews
and extensive use of photography. With the help of Telford
Community Arts, the group has printed colour photos.

851. ARACHNE   1983-c.
    Tl:Arachne:A magazine of wimmin's spirituality
    Ed. and pub. Matriarchy Research and Reclaim Network
    C:item 722?
    L:F, Flic (both incomplete)
Self-explanatory.

852. COMMITTEE ON SOUTH ASIAN WOMEN NEWSLETTER   1983
    Tl:Committee on South Asian Women newsletter
    Keele?
    L:not found
Not seen. Mentioned in item 825 (n°14, May 1983, p.5). No further
detail. Any link with the South Asia Women's Workshop co-ordinated
by Ursula Sharma, Department of Sociology, University of Keele,
listed in item 612 (v.10,n°4, December 1981/January 1982, p.55)?

853. DUNDEE WOMEN'S AID   1983-c.
    Tl:Dundee Women's Aid
    Dundee
    L:not found
Not seen. The summer 1983 issue is listed in item 297(n°136,
November 1983, p.25). "Articles on disability, class, incest and
more".

854. LESBIAN NURSES NEWSLETTER   1983-c.
    Tl:Lesbian nurses newsletter
    L:not found

Not seen. Only trace found occurs in item 297 (n°132, July 1983, p.40).

855. NORWICH WOMEN'S CENTRE NEWSLETTER 1983-c.
    Tl:Norwich Women's Centre Newsletter
    Norwich
    Bi-monthly
    L:not found
Local A4 printed newsletter for women only. Number 4 April/May
1984 was the only issue seen. Its 24 pages included a calendar of
events, information about the activities of the local Women's
Liberation Movement and local issues but also some more general
features (i.e. women and advertising), poems, etc..

856. SAMYA SHAKTI 1983-c.
    Tl:Samya Shakti
    Pub. Centre for Women's Developments Studies
    New Delhi, India
    Yearly
    L:not found
Not seen. Mentioned in item 838.

857. SISTERMATIC 1983-1984
    Tl:Sistermatic:Wolverhampton women's paper
    Wolverhampton
    Bi-monthly?;January(?) 1983-n°9, June 1984
    L:F (incomplete)
Well produced A4 magazine of some twenty pages. "Sponsored by
Wolverhampton Trades Council as a part of a Community Enterprise
Programme to create . . . employment opportunities and experience
for women . . ." (n°7, p.2), it carried contact lists, issues and
events of interest to local women. Yet it also included national
news, general features such as sexual harassment at work, rape,
breast cancer, the police bill, Asian women and book reviews.

858. WOMEN'S PEACE CAMP NEWSLETTER 1983
    Tl:Women's Peace Camp Newsletter
    F.n.k.;February 1983
    L:not found
A4 newsletter collectively produced and focusing on Greenham
Common and non-violence. Apparently a one-off publication.

859. PANKHURST FRIENDS   1983-c.

   Tl:Pankhurst Friends:newsletter
   Ed. the "steering committee" including Jennifer Barraclough,
   Deirdre Candlin, Lorna Hempstead, Sue Jackson, Gerry Morris,
   Charlotte Sing
   Handforth, Wilmslow
   Twice yearly;Spring 1983-c.
   L:F
Slim A4 printed newsletter reporting on the activities of the
Pankhurst House Appeal Committee.

860. STUDIES ON WOMEN ABSTRACTS   1983-c.

   Tl:Studies on Women Abstracts
   Ed. Rosemary Dean (Faculty of Educational Studies, The Open
   University, Milton Keynes)
   Pub. Carfax Publishing Company
   Abingdon Oxfordshire
   Quarterly;bi-monthly (from January 1985);March 1983-c.
   L:F
Each issue contains between 150 and 200 abstracts prepared by an
international team of experts and is of much use to librarians
and researchers. Abstracts range from articles in international
journals to books and pamphlets and include both theoretical and
empirical materials. The major focus is "on education, employment,
women in the family and community, medicine and health, female sex
and gender role socialisation, social policy, the social
psychology and women, female culture, media treatment of women,
and historical studies".

861. W.E.P.G.   1983-c.

   Tl:W.E.P.G.:Women's Employment Projects Group newsletter
   Liverpool
   Every month approx.;March(?) 1983-c.
   L:Flic
Thin A4 printed national newsletter for women only produced by a
national group of women including Jean Proctor. Information about
employment, courses, training projects, funding campaigns. News
items, cartoons, photographs.

862. WOMEN IN BOOKTRADES NEWSLETTER   1983-c.

   Tl:Women in Booktrades newsletter
   Manchester

Quarterly;April 1983-c.

L:Flic

A5 duplicated newsletter for women only that grew out of the
women in Booktrades conference held in Nottingham in February
1983. The first issues have been put together by a group of women
in London but responsibility will rotate. The group has included:
Rosemary Illet (Housmans Bookshop), Roz Parr (Compendium
Bookshop), Alison Read (Sheba Feminist Publishers) and Jenny Walsh
(Bush Books). Aimed at women working in all areas of the
booktrade bookshops, libraries, publishing, etc. - it features
how women are seen in the printed word but also their status and
working conditions in the booktrade. It circulates information on
feminist and anti-racist material available.

863. NANNY 1983-c.

Tl:Nanny:quarterly newsletter of the Bureau of Women's
Affairs
Ed. and pub. Bureau of Women's Affairs
Kingston, Jamaica
Quarterly;May 1983-c.
C:item 552
L:F (n°1 only)

Thin governmental publication mainly carrying information about
the activities of the Bureau.

864. WEDG NEWSLETTER 1983

Tl:WedG newsletter
Ed. Women's Education Group
Pub. Women's Education Resource Centre
2 issues only:n°1 May 1983, n°2 October 1983
C BY:item 874
L:not found

Not seen. Short-lived newsletter collectively produced and
circulated within the ILEA and the GLC. It was "a forum for news,
activities and practical action currently undertaken within
schools and the wide community" (item 874, n°1, Autumn 1983). It
promoted the work of anti-sexist, equal opportunities working
parties and projects and kept teachers informed of conferences,
school initiatives, new teaching materials, etc.. It was merged
with item 874 "to break down the artificial divisions between
theory and practical action inherent in the two publications"
(ibid.).

865. PLANNING AND WOMEN 1983-c.

    Tl:Planning and women:A quarterly bulletin

    Quarterly;June 1983-c.

    L:Flic (n°1 June 1983 only)

Bulletin that came out of the Women and the Planned Environment
Conference held in November 1982. The publishing group based at
the Planning Unit, School of the Environment, Polytechnic of
Central London, includes Lynda Addison, Judy Less, Lynne Davies,
Camilla Wickens, Lynn Hefferman, Nelica La Gro, Janice Morphet and
Beverly Taylor. The first issue covered disability, mugging,
bureaucracy, etc.. Articles on employment, housing, retailing,
transport, new technology, etc. were planned.

866. MUKTI 1983-c.

    Tl:Mukti:Asian women's magazine

    Quarterly;June/August 1983-c.

    L:F, Flic (both incomplete)

A4 printed magazine produced by a collective of ten Asian women
from Birmingham and London. Sponsored by the GLC, EOC and Women's
International Solidarity Fund, it is published in six separate
language editions: Hindi, Punjabi, Gujerati, Bengali, Urdu and
English. For the first issue over 1,500 copies were printed in
English and 600 copies in each other language. The group wants to
write about Asian women's own experiences, share their own
struggles and triumphs and create their own images. "The need for
Mukti has arisen in part from having no access or control of the
white male dominated media which usually ignores (them) or
distorts (their) views and experiences". It blamed "the exploited
as the cause of unemployment, bad housing, poor education, etc.
. . . Token attempts have been made within white feminist writing
to interpret the experiences of Asian women" (item 825, n°12,
March 1983, p.2). "Mukti" means "freedom". The issues covered are
the media, health, education, employment, welfare rights,
immigration and nationality laws, news from the Women's Movement
in Britain and in India. The magazine also carries a directory of
Asian women's groups in Britain, plus poetry, short stories,
cartoons, book and film reviews.

867. ARTEMIS 1983-c.

    Tl:Artemis

    Bi-monthly;then monthly?;June(?) 1983-c.

    C:item 556?

L:not found

Not seen. Mentioned in items 825 (n°16, July 1983, p.19), 297
(n°136, November 1983, pp.36-8), 829 (June 1984, p.24). "The
magazine for lesbians and all women who love women"
(advertisement). It contains news, articles, short stories,
pictures, a penfriend/contact list for out of London lesbians.
Successor to item 556?

868. CAMDEN WOMEN'S COMMITTEE NEWSLETTER 1983-c.
     Tl:Camden Women's Committee Newsletter
     Ed. Camden Women's Unit
     Monthly;June(?) 1983-c.
     L:Flic (1 issue only:June 1983)
Local A4 printed newsletter of about twenty pages. Contains
newshorts and reports on the Working Group's activities.

869. COMMUNICAT 1983-c.
     Tl:Communicat
     Eds. Jo Abbot, Shan Jayran and Chris Bolton
     Pub. Tabbies
     Every six weeks (7 issues by March/April 1984);June(?) 1983-
     c.
     L:Flic (1 issue only)
Thin A4 printed newsletter for women only. List of groups, diary
of events, advertisements from Tabbies' customers, poems,
cartoons.

870. LONDON W.A.M.T. NEWSLETTER 1983-c.
     Tl:London W.A.M.T. Newsletter
     Ed. and pub. London Women and Manual Trades Group
     Monthly;July 1983-c.
     L:Flic
A4 printed newsletter of interest to women working in manual
trades and to those planning to take up some sort of course.
Mainly practical and informative it essentially carries
information on courses and skill centres, job advertisements,
conference announcements, and very short articles.

871. NETWORK 1983-c.
     Tl:Network:news from the English Collective of Prostitutes
     Ed. Nina Lopez-Jones
     F.n.k. (issue 2/3 dated June 1984);July 1983-c.

L:F, Flic

Very slim A4 printed bulletin reporting on E.C.P. activities. The group campaigns for "the abolition of all laws against prostitutes", the increase of all Social Security benefits and women's wages, and payment for housework, so that no woman is forced into prostitution by lack of money. Their slogan is "No bad women, just bad laws".

872. 52% 1983-c.
     Tl:Southwark women's equality news
     T2:Women are 52% of Southwark's community
     Ed. and pub. Southwark Women's Equality Unit:Nathalie
     Hadjifotiou, Rita Stallard, Tanya Whitty
     Bi-monthly;August 1983-c.
     L:Flic (incomplete)

A4 newsletter aiming to let local women know what is going on for them and reporting on the activities of the Unit "to promote the achievement of equality of opportunity for women and improvements in the status, living conditions and environment of women in the borough" (n°1). Plus stories, drawings, poems, cartoons.

873. EQUALITY NOW! 1983-c.
     Tl:Equality now!
     Ed. Catherine Cairncross
     Pub. Equal Opportunities Commission
     Manchester
     Quarterly;Autumn 1983-c.
     C:item 553
     L:F, Flic

20-page A4 magazine. Distributed free, it claims a circulation of 60,000 copies per issue. It publicises the EOC's actions to help eliminate sexual discrimination, and retraces the progress or setbacks of women's fight for equality.

874. GEN 1983-c.
     Tl:Gen:An anti-sexist educational journal
     T2:Gen:An anti-sexist education magazine
     Ed. Women's Education Group
     Pub. Women's Education Resource Centre
     3 issues per year;Autumn 1983-c.
     C:item 864
     L:F, Flic

A4 printed magazine also available on tape produced by an
editorial collective. Funded by the GLC Women's Committee and the
Inner London Education Authority, it wants to be a space for girls
and women to share their experiences of the educational process.
It changed its format with number 2 when it merged with item 864
and incorporated some of its elements. Number 2 was a 64 page
magazine. Unlike item 864, GEN has a national circulation. It
aims to promote feminist, anti-sexist and non-racist education
and now includes not only long articles on theoretical issues of
anti-sexist schooling but also stories, letters, graphics, reviews
of new resources, lesson plans and visual aids.

875. WHIC 1983-c.
    Tl:WHIC:Women's Health Information Centre Newsletter
    Ed. WHIC Collective Newsletter Sub Group
    Quarterly;Autumn 1983-c.
    L:Flic
A4 printed magazine. Features Depo Provera, women's health in
Britain and internationally. Book reviews.

876. ALTERNATIVE SEX 1983-c.(?)
    Tl:Alternative sex
    F.n.k.;October 1982-c.(?)
    L:Flic (n°l, October 1983 only)
A women only magazine collectively produced by anarcha and
feminist women aged 18-23. The first issue features: "Is there
life without men?", "Debbie remembers how she got into punk", etc.
and poetry.

877. OUTDOOR WOMEN 1983-c.
    Tl:Outdoor women
    Bi-monthly;October 1983-c.
    L:Flic
Thin A4 duplicated newsletter for women only. It provides
information on the facilities for outdoor activities (climbing,
hiking, etc.) available to women through the network. It gives
details on holiday centres, access to transport, trips, equipment
needs, childcare facilities, etc..

878. ROUND-UPS 1982-c.
    Tl:What's On:Round-Up:Women's News
    T2:Round-Ups

251

Ed. and pub. Dublin Women's Centre Newsletter Group
Dublin, Eire
Monthly;October 1983-c.
L:F, Flic (both incomplete)
Local, thin newsletter mainly providing "information about groups,
meetings and facilities based at the Women's Centre".

879. TROUBLE AND STRIFE   1983-c.
Tl:Trouble and strife:A radical feminist magazine
Editorial collective including:Lynn Alderson, Jalna Hanmer,
Sophie Laws, Diana Leonard, Sheila Saunders, Ruth Wallsgrove
Leeds;printed Manchester
3 issues per year;Winter 1983-c.
L:F,Flic
Substantial, well produced magazine, also available on tape. It
aims to provide a forum for radical feminism. As is stated on the
inside front cover: "Trouble and Strife is cockney rhyming slang
for wife. We chose this name because it acknowledges the reality
between women and men. As radical feminists, our politics come
directly from this tension between men's power and women's
resistance". Moreover the collective wants to fill the gap between
the internal, local Women's Liberation newsletters and the
academic reviews. Trouble and Strife is "a place where live issues
in the movement can be discussed at greater length and depth than
is possible in our newsletters, and where long term questions of
the theory and practice of feminism can be addressed more
adventurously and concretely than in academic journals"
(advertisement). However, as several members of the collective
work in academic spheres, some articles tend to be difficult for
non-academic readers. Trouble and Strife features wide-ranging
national and international issues: Greenham Common, Thatcherism,
NAC split, Wires, lesbians in France, etc.. It aims to explore the
history of women's liberation in recent years through interviews
of the women involved. Finally it includes reports of feminist
conferences and reviews.

880. AMNESTY FOR WOMEN   1983-c.
Tl:Amnesty for women:action sheet
Ed. and pub. Amnesty International, British Section
Quarterly?;December 1983-c.
L:Flic
A very slim duplicated newsletter "detailing cases of women

political prisoners of concern to Amnesty International".

881. WIPAROUND   1983-c.
     Tl:Wiparound:The newsletter of Women In Publishing
     Dublin
     F.n.k.;1983/4-c.
     L:F (n°1, 1983/4 only)
Very slim A4 newsletter "for all women in the booktrade: editors,
designers, publishers, printers, writers, booksellers,
typesetters, reps and freelancers", reporting on WIP activities
(n°1).

882. ANTI-SEXIST MEN'S NEWSLETTER   1983-c.
     Tl:Anti-Sexist Men's Newsletter
     Cardiff
     F.n.k.;1983(?)-c.(?)
     L:not found
Not seen. Mentioned in item 826 (n°13, March/April 1983, p.8).
See also item 626.

883. ANTI-SEXIST MEN'S NEWSLETTER   1983-c.
     Tl:Anti-Sexist Men's Newsletter
     Leeds
     F.n.k.;1983(?)-c.(?)
     L:not found
Not seen. Mentioned in item 826 (n°13, March/April 1983, p.8).
See also item 626.

884. ANTI-SEXIST MEN'S NEWSLETTER   1983-c.
     Tl:Anti-Sexist Men's Newsletter
     Manchester
     F.n.k.;1983(?)-c.(?)
     L:not found
Not seen. Mentioned in item 826 (n°13, March/April 1983, p.8).
See also item 626.

885. CWIRES   FACTSHEET   1983-c.
     Tl:CWIRES factsheet
     Ed. and pub. Christian Women's Information and Resource
     Service
     Oxford
     Monthly?;1983(?)-c.

L:F (n°2, February 1983 only)

Two-page sheet aiming to help women "track down books and other organisations producing material on women in the churches and Christian feminism" (n°2). See also item 841.

886. JEWISH FEMINIST GROUP NEWSLETTER   1983-c.

   Tl:Jewish Feminist Group newsletter

   Every six weeks;1983(?)-c.

   L:not found

Not seen. Mentioned in item 831 (January/February 1984, p.12, June 1984, p.35). For Jewish women only.

887. MATERNITY SERVICES   1983-c.

   Tl:Maternity services

   Eds. E. Key, G. Green Barn, M. Hoole

   Pub. Association for Improvements in the Maternity Services

   Preston

   Quarterly;1983(?)-c.

   C:item 620?

   L:not found

Not seen. Mentioned in item 297 (n°136, November 1983, p.25).

888. SPECULUM SPEAKES   1983-c.

   Tl:The speculum speakes

   Leichhardt, New South Wales, Australia

   F.n.k.;1983(?)-c.

   L:not found

Not seen. Only mention found occurs in item 297 (n°138, January 1984, p.24). A health newsletter.

889. SOUTHALL BLACK WOMEN'S CENTRE NEWSLETTER   1983-c.

   Tl:Southall Black Women's Centre newsletter

   Irregular;1983(?)-c.

   L:not found

Not seen. The centre opened in July 1983. Item 831 (January/February 1984, p.8) mentions the publication of issue 1.

890. TAKING LIBERTIES   1983-c.

   Tl:Taking liberties

   Pub. Women's Education Centre

   Shirley, Southampton

   F.n.k.;1983(?)-c.

L:not found

Not seen. Only trace found occurs in item 297 (n°136, November 1983, p.25). Collectively produced.

891. CHILD-CARE BULLETIN   1984-c.(?)
     T1:Child-care bulletin:creches for political meetings and
     events
     L:not found

Not a genuine periodical but rather a pamphlet produced by class-conscious anarchists on how to organise a creche for a political meeting and which, it was hoped, would be the first issue of a regular bulletin. A one-off publication? Other areas the group is concerned with: contraception, illegitimacy, housework, communes, etc..

892. LA PLUMA   1984-c.
     T1:La pluma
     L:not found

Not seen. Item 825 (n°29, September/October 1984, p.6) advertises the publication of the first issue. Described as a multi-lingual journal of women's writing carrying poetry, fiction, reviews, notes, photographs. Text in original and in translation.

893. LAVENDER LESBIAN LIST   1984-c.
     T1:Lavender lesbian list
     Ed. and pub. Lavender Menace Bookshop
     Edinburgh
     L:not found

Not seen. Mentioned in The Bimonthly (n°3, May/June 1984, not listed) and in item 297 (n°144, July 1984). "A lesbian books newsletter" featuring new and recommended books - lesbian and feminist, fiction and non-fiction. It contains short descriptions, longer reviews and events of interest to lesbians.

894. LESBIAN ARCHIVE NEWSLETTER   1984-c.
     T1:The Lesbian Archive Newsletter
     L:not found

Not seen. The Lesbian Archive was set up in 1984. It publishes a newsletter available in print and on tape detailing the Archive's activities and providing a list of what the Archive has acquired. For further information, see item 825 (n°32, January 1985, p.2).

895. MATRIARCHY RESEARCH AND RECLAIM NETWORK NEWSLETTER 1984-c.

    Tl:Matriarchy Research and Reclaim Network Newsletter

    Quarterly?;1984(?)-c.

    L:not found

The only issue seen dated Spring 1984 was an A4 publication ten
pages long. The contact address was Felicity, 1 Ravenstone Road.
Continuation of item 693?

896. OLDER LESBIAN NETWORK NEWSLETTER 1984-c.

    Tl:Older Lesbian Network Newsletter

    L:not found

Not seen. An advertisement in item 297 (n°147, October 1984, p.33)
publicises the publication of the first free issues. Financially
supported by the GLC. Also available on cassette.

897. BATTERSEA BLACK WOMEN'S GROUP NEWSLETTER 1984-c.

    Tl:Battersea Black Women's Group Newsletter

    Monthly;January 1984-c.

    L:not found

Not seen. Mentioned in item 831 (January/February 1984, p.11).
Aims "to fight racism and sexism at all levels".

898. WOMEN'S REPRODUCTIVE RIGHTS CAMPAIGN NEWSLETTER 1984-c.

    Tl:Women's Reproductive Rights Campaign newsletter

    Ed. London Women's Reproductive Rights Campaign Group

    Monthly;January 1984-c.

    L:F

A4 duplicated, multi-coloured newsletter funded by the GLC Women's
Committee. Organisational news, features dealing exclusively with
campaign issues. Their main tenets are as follows: abortion is not
the central issue for all women; women's experiences of fertility
control and reproductive choice differ with age, race, class,
disability, sexuality and marital status. Topics covered:
reproductive technology, racism and health (Depo Provera, forced
sterilisation, etc.), lesbian mothers' rights, etc.. See also item
409.

899. FEMINIST LIBRARY 1984-c.

    Tl:Feminist Library and Information Centre newsletter

    Bi-monthly;January/February 1984-c.

    C:item 411

    L:F, Flic

Straight continuation of item 411 under a different title
following the name change of the Centre.

900. WEB QUARTERLY 1984-c.
     Tl:Web quarterly:newsletter of women in the built environment
     Eds. Nelica LaGro, Beverley Taylor, Barbara MacFarlane,
     Camilla Wickens and Michele Haniotis
     Quarterly;Spring 1984-c.
     L:Flic
Thin A4 printed newsletter produced both by women involved in item
865 and women from the Feminist Architects Network. It addresses
women working in "fields concerned with the built environment,
such as women planners, architects, surveyors, builders and women
involved in campaigns to change the environment to include the
needs of women" (n°1, p.1).

901. WILD WORDS 1984-c.
     Tl:Wild words
     Editorial collective:Julia Casterton, Dallas Sealy, Diane
     Biondo
     London;printed Manchester
     2 or 3 issues per year;Spring 1984-c.
     L:Flic
Substantial women's writing magazine funded by the GLC. Issue
number 1 was a well produced periodical carrying stories and
poems. Contributors included among others: Gillian Allnutt, Judy
Stevens, Lucy Whitman.

902. SIZE 8 1984-c.
     Tl:Size 8:A magazine for young women
     Manchester
     F.n.k.;Spring(?) 1984-c.
     L:not found
Not seen. Only mention occurs in item 874 (n°2, Spring 1984, p.9).
Apparently wide ranging contents covering not simply love and
teenage relationships but also racism, sexism, unemployment, YOPs,
etc..

903. BABY MILK ACTION COALITION NEWSLETTER 1984-c.
     Tl:Baby Milk Action Coalition newsletter
     Cambridge
     F.n.k.;March 1984-c.

L:Flic

Thin campaign newsletter supporting the boycott of the Nestle
Company, the largest distributor of infant formula in developing
countries.

904. WOMEN FOR PALESTINE NEWSLETTER   1984-c.
    Tl:Women for Palestine newsletter
    3 issues per year;March 1984-c.
    L:Flic

Thin A4 printed newsletter by Women for Palestine organised as an
autonomous women's group following the Israeli invasion of
Lebanon in 1982. They "campaign in support of the Palestinian and
Lebanese people in their fight against US/Iraeli aggression and
occupation", against Zionism which they see as "racist,
anti-semitic, and expansionist" (nº1, pp.1-2).

905. WOMEN'S NEWS   1984-c.
    Tl:Women's news
    Belfast
    Monthly;bi-monthly;March 1984-c.
    L:Flic

Thin A4 printed newsletter that "does not reflect the views of
any one group" but aims "to develop a forum for communication"
(nº1, p.1). It mainly addresses Irish women: current listings of
events, short articles on Armagh, for instance, and poems.

906. EDINBURGH WOMEN   1984-c.
    Tl:Edinburgh women
    Ed. and pub. Women's Centre Newsletter Group
    Edinburgh
    Monthly;March(?) 1984-c.
    L:not found

Not seen. Listed in item 297 (nº140, March 1984, p.32).

907. WOMAN SOUND   1984-c.
    Tl:Woman sound
    Bi-monthly?;April 1984-c.
    L:Flic

A magazine produced by a collective of four women and discussing
music, literature, theatre, drama and art from a feminist
standpoint. In the collective's own words, they aim for the most
part to write "about women in music and the arts and not as much

about men" (June 1984). <u>Woman Sound</u> is intended "to encourage
women in their creative endeavours". It includes news, long
articles, plus reviews, cartoons and a gig list.

908. BLACK WOMEN'S CO-OPERATIVE NEWSLETTER 1984-c.
     Tl:Black Women's Co-operative Newsletter
     Wolverhampton
     Monthly?;May 1984-c.
     L:Flic
Local A4 duplicated newsletter. Issue 1 was 20 pages long and
carried articles on sickle cell anaemia, Wolverhampton Social
Services, etc..

909. DAWN WORKERS NEWSLETTER 1984-c.
     Tl:DAWN workers newsletter:Drugs-Alcohol-Women-Nationality
     Eds. for issue 1:Betsy Ettors from the ARU, Fiona Richmond
     of the ARP, Sally Dix from the ACS, Jayne Murray and Lisa
     Power from London DAWN
     4 issues per year;June 1984-c.
     L:Flic
A4 newsletter funded by the GLC Women's Committee. Its stated aim
is "to coordinate a directory of information on services for
women", i.e. mainly information on women's group and alcohol and
drug agencies.

910. IRANIAN WOMEN'S SECTION NEWSLETTER 1984-c.
     Tl:Iranian Women's Section Newsletter
     Pub. Iranian Community Centre
     Monthly?;June 1984-c.
     L:Flic
Self-explanatory.

911. FOR THE LIKES OF US 1984-c.
     Tl:For the likes of us
     Ed. and pub. Julia Tant
     Irregular;June(?) 1984-c.
     L:Flic
A4 duplicated newsletter for women only. Advertised itself as a
working-class women's newsletter. Contents of issue 1 are
essentially poems and cartoons by Julia Tant.

912. FX 1984-c.

   Tl:FX:The women's film and video bulletin

   Quarterly;September 1984-c.

   L:Flic

Produced by a London-based collective of women involved in film
and video, it carries news of what's going on in colleges, groups,
TV and film companies. It spreads information on community cinema
and alternative distributors. It includes opinions, projects, film
and TV reviews, cartoons, etc..

913. BIRMINGHAM BLACK SISTERS NEWSLETTER 1984-c.

   Tl:Birmingham Black Sisters Newsletter

   Ed. and pub. Link Centre

   Birmingham

   F.n.k.;1984(?)-c.

   L:not found

Not seen. Only trace found occurs in Spare Rib Diary 1984.

914. CHESTER WOMEN'S CENTRE NEWSLETTER 1984-c.

   Tl:Chester Women's Centre Newsletter

   Chester

   F.n.k.;1984(?)-c.

   L:not found

Not seen. Local newsletter mentioned in item 297 (n°140, March
1984, p.33). Contact persons: Val Green, Brenda Lett.

915. HYSTERECTOMY SUPPORT GROUP NEWSLETTER 1984-c.

   Tl:Hysterectomy Support Group Newsletter

   F.n.k.;1984(?)-c.

   L:not found

Not seen. Only mention occurs in item 297 (n°139, February 1984,
p.33).

916. SHIFRA 1984-c.

   Tl:Shifra:A Jewish feminist magazine

   Ed. a collective of eleven Jewish feminists including:Bev
   Gold, Elizabeth Sarah, Linda Belloc, Sheila Saunders et al

   Leeds

   Quarterly;1984(?)-c.

   L:not found

Not seen. Mentioned in items 688 (v.7,n°2, 1984, p.XI) and 836
(n°9, 1984). A 48 page magazine for, by and about Jewish women.

Articles, stories, biographies, poems, pictures, etc..

917. SWANSEA WOMEN'S CENTRE NEWSLETTER 1984-c.
     Tl:Swansea Women's Centre Newsletter
     Swansea
     F.n.k.;1984(?)-c.
     L:not found
Not seen. Only mention found occurs in item 297 (n°147, October
1984, p.24).

918. VOICE OF WOMEN 1984-c.
     Tl:Voice of women:Kadinlarin Sesi
     Quarterly?;1984-c.
     L:F
Published by the Unions of Turkish Women in Britain. Deals mainly
with racism, immigration and nationality.

919. WALTHAM FOREST WOMEN'S CENTRE NEWSLETTER 1984-c.
     Tl:Waltham Forest Women's Centre Newsletter
     Waltham Forest
     Monthly;1984(?)-c.
     L:not found
A4 duplicated local newsletter funded by the GLC and available to
women only. June 1984 issue was eighteen pages long and carried
not only listings, a calendar of events and news on the women's
centre but also features on multifarious issues: the police bill,
women under apartheid, women in Ireland, images of women in public
transport, bicycle maintenance, etc..

920. WOMEN'S PEACE ALLIANCE NEWSLETTER 1984-c.
     Tl:Women's Peace Alliance newsletter
     Nottingham
     F.n.k.;1984(?)-c.
Not seen. Mentioned in item 869 (n°6, February 1984, p.6).

References and Additional Reading

AUBREY Crispin, LANDRY Charles and MORLEY Dave (1980), Here is the other news. London, Minority Press Group.

BAEHR Helen (1981), 'The impact of feminism on media studies' in Dale Spender, Men's studies modified. Oxford, Pergamon.

BARROW Margaret (1980), Women 1870-1928. London, Mansell.

BERRY Dave, COOPER Liz and LANDRY Charles (1980), Where is the other news? London, Minority Press Group.

BRADY Norman (1978), 'Shafts' and the quest for a new morality (M.A. thesis). Centre for Study of Social History, University of Warwick.

BUTLER Matilda and PAISLEY William (1980), Women and the mass media. New York, Human Sciences Press.

CAMPAIGN FOR PRESS FREEDOM (1979), Towards press freedom. London, Campaign for Press Freedom.

CADMAN Eileen, CHESTER Gail and PIVOT Agnes (1981), Rolling our own. London, Minority Press Group.

CEULEMANS Micke and FAUCONNIER Guido (1979), Mass media:the image, role and social conditions of women. Paris, UNESCO (Notes and Documents n°84).

COHEN Phil and GARDNER Carls (eds) (1982), It ain't half racist, mum. London, Comedia and Campaign Against Racism in the Media.

COLLINS Wendy, FRIEDMAN Ellen and PIVOT Agnes (1978), Women:the directory of social change. London, Wildwood.

COLWELL Molly (1979), Sexual politics in Britain during 1976 (Harvester primary social sources). Brighton, Harvester.

COOPER Liz, LANDRY Charles and BERRY Dave (1980), The other secret service. London, Minority Press Group and Campaign for Press Freedom.

DOWNING John (1980), The media machine. London, Pluto.

ELLSWORTH Edward W. (1979), Liberators of the female mind. Westport, Conn., Greenwood.

ENGLISHWOMAN'S REVIEW (1900), pp.217-19.

FELL Alison (1979), Hard feelings. London, Women's Press.

FREDEMAN William E. (1973), 'Emily Faithfull and the Victoria Press', The Library, June 1973, pp.139-64.

GALLAGHER Margaret (1979), The portrayal and participation of women in the media. Paris, UNESCO.

GALLAGHER Margaret (1981), Unequal opportunities. Paris, UNESCO.

GARDNER Carl (ed.) (1979), Media, politics and culture. London, Macmillan.

GOLDMAN Harold (1974), Emma Paterson. London, Lawrence and Wishart.

HARRIS Brenda (1978), Sexual politics in Britain during 1975 (Harvester primary social sources). Brighton, Harvester.

HARRISON Brian (1978), Separate spheres. London, Croom Helm.

HARRISON Royden et al (1977), The Warwick guide to British labour periodicals. Brighton, Harvester.

HECATE v.5,n°2, 'Australian feminist periodicals'.

HEMMINGS Susan (1982), Girls are powerful. London, Sheba.

HODGE C. Esther (1984), 'A women's international quarterly over 30 years', Women's Studies International Forum 1984, v.7,n°4, pp.265-73.

HUME Leslie Parker (1982), The National Union of Women's Suffrage Societies 1897-1914. New York, Garland.

INTERNATIONAL WOMEN'S TRIBUTE CENTRE NEWSLETTER Spring 1981. New York. [Special issue on women and the media.]

I.S.I.S. International Bulletin issues 2, 16, 18.

KANTER Hannah, LEFANU Sarah and SPEDDING Carole (eds) (1984), Sweeping statements. London, Women's Press.

KING Josephine and STOTT Mary (1977), Is this your life? London, Virago.

LABOUR RESEARCH v.70,n°4 (April 1981),

LEVENSON Leah (1983), With wooden sword. Dublin, Gill & Macmillan.

LEVENSON Leah and NATTERSTAD Jerry (1985), A biography of Hannah Sheehy Skeffington. Dublin, Arlen House.

LIDDERDALE Jane and NICHOLSON Mary (1970), Dear Miss Weaver. London, Faber.

LINKLATER Andro (1979), An unhusbanded life. London, Hutchinson.

LIPSCHITZ Susan (ed.) (1977), Sexual politics in Britain (Harvester primary social sources). Brighton, Harvester.

MAPPEN Eileen (1985), Helping women at work:the Women's Industrial Council 1889-1914. London, Hutchinson Education.

NATIONAL UNION OF JOURNALISTS EQUALITY WORKING PARTY (1977),
Images of women (2nd ed.). London, The Union.

NEWS FROM NEASDEN n°11 (Spring 1979).

NOYCE John Leonard (1979), The directory of British alternative
periodicals. Hassocks, Harvester.

OERTON Sarah (1981), The feminist press in Britain since 1970
(M.A. thesis). University of Swansea.

OLDFIELD Sybil (1984), Spinsters of this parish. London, Virago.

OWENS Rosemary Cullen (1984), Smashing times:a history of the
Irish women's suffrage movements. Dublin, Attic Press.

PARKES Bessie Rayner (1864), 'A review of the last six years'.
English Woman's Journal, February 1864, pp.361-8.

PETHICK LAWRENCE, Frederick (ca 1943), Fate has been kind. London,
Hutchinson.

RESOURCES FOR FEMINIST RESEARCH v.9,n°4 (December/January 1980/1),
v.10,n°4 (December/January 1981/2). Toronto, OISE.

ROGERS Mirabel (1956), The Black Sash. Johannesburg, Rotonews.

ROPER Esther (ed.) (1929), The collected poems of Eva Gore-Booth:
with a biographical sketch. London, Longmans, Green.

ROWE Marsha (ed.) (1982), Spare Rib reader. Harmondsworth,
Penguin.

SPENDER Dale (1980), Man made language. London, Routledge.

SPENDER Dale (1984), Time and tide wait for no man. London,
Pandora.

STANDARD PERIODICAL DIRECTORY (8th ed.) (1983-4). New York,
Oxbridge Communications.

STRACHEY Ray (1931), Millicent Garrett Fawcett. London, John
Murray.

SWANWICK Helena Maria (1935), I have been young. London, Gollancz.

THOMAS Mavis (ed.) (1981), Sexual politics in Britain during 1977
and 1978 (Harvester primary social sources). Brighton,
Harvester.

TUCKMAN Gaye, DANIELS Arlene K. and BENET James (eds) (1978),
Hearth and home. New York, O.U.P..

ULRICH'S INTERNATIONAL PERIODICALS DIRECTORY (22nd ed.) (1982).
New York, Bowker.

ULRICH'S IRREGULAR SERIALS AND ANNUALS (6th ed.) (1980). New York,
Bowker.

VANARSDEL Rosemary T. (1979), Mrs Florence Fenwick-Miller,
feminism and the Woman's Signal. Tacoma, Wa., University of

Paget Sound.

WHITAKER Brian (1981), <u>News limited</u>. London, Minority Press Group.
WOMEN'S STUDIES INTERNATIONAL QUARTERLY v.3,n°1 (1980).

Name and Title Index

NOTE: An underlined item number indicates a principal entry for a given title

Abbam, Kate, 265

Abbot, Jo, 869

Abdela, Lesley, 719

Aberconway, Lady, 125

Aberdeen Women's Liberation
  Newsletter, 367

Abortion Law Reform Action
  Group Newsletter, 368

Abortion Law Reform
  Association, 239, 368, 408,
  502

About Women (Manitoba), 729

About Women (Saskatchewan),
  491

Achilles Heel, 562

Ackroyd, Cari, 659

Action, 571

Action for Lesbian Parents,
  293

Adams, Parveen, 549

Adams, Shelley, 324

Addison, Lynda, 865

Ades, Rose, 297

Advisory Committee on Women's
  Affairs, 584

Advisory Council on the Status
  of Women, 370

A.E.U., see Amalgamated Union
  of Engineering Workers

A.F.F.I.R.M. Newsletter, 639

Africa Woman, 432

African National Congress,

429, 676

African Women, 222

Aheane, Dee, 567

A.I.M.S. Newsletter, 620

Aird, Eileen, 721

Alba, Pilar, 661

Alderson, Lynn, 656, 879

Aldridge, Sue, 490

Alexander, Sally, 284

Alexandra Magazine, 7

Allen, Sue, 546

Alliance for Fair Images and
  Representation in the Media,
  639

All-India Congress Committee,
  226

All-India Women's Conference, 200

Allnutt, Gillian, 727, 901

All Pakistan Women's Association,
  232, 730

A.L.R.A. Newsletter, 239

Alternative Sex, 876

Althusser, Louis, 549

Altruist, 121

Amalgamated Union of Engineering
  Workers, 216

Amnesty for Women, 880

Anarcha Feminist Newsletter, 504

Anarchist Feminist Newsletter,
  498, 607

Anarchist Women's Network, 504

Andersen, Margaret, 612

Bridges, _516_

Brighton and Hove Women's
Liberation Newsletter, _323_

Brighton Lesbian Group
Newsletter, _517_

Brighton Women's Rights Action
Group Newsletter, 444

Brigley, Jude, 819

Bristol Anti-Rape Group
Newsletter, _510_

Bristol Gay Women's Group
Newsletter, _363_

Bristol W.A.C.C. Newsletter,
_300_

Bristol Womens Abortion and
Contraception Campaign
Newsletter, _300_

Bristol Women's Charter, _402_

Bristol Women's Liberation
Group, 252, 354

Bristol Women's Liberation
Newsletter, _354_

Britannia, _128_

British Commonwealth League,
182, _234_

British, Continental and General Federation for the Abolition of State Regulation of
Vice, 40

British Federation for the Emancipation of Sweated Women, 117

British Federation of Business
and Professional Women, 194,
218

British Federation of Business
and Professional Women:News-
letter, _218_

British Pregnancy Advisory
Service Newsletter, _383_

British Sociological Association, 561

British Soroptimist, _175_

British Telecom, 801

British Women's Emigration
Association, 77

British Women's Temperance
Association, 35, 38, 42, 46,
56, 59, 60, 62, 69, 70

British Women's Temperance
Journal, _35_

British Workwoman, _5_

Brittain, Vera, 152, 194, 228

Brixton Black Women's Group, 786

Brixton Women's Centre
News-sheet, _335_

Broadsheet, _281_

Broadside, _596_

Broken Rib, _518_

Brothers, _328_

Brothers Against Sexism, _328_

Brown, Barbara, 489

Brown, Beverly, 549

Brown, Carolyn, 486

Brown, Paula, 800

Brown, Wilmette, 286

Browne, F. W. Stella, 119

Broxa, _822_

Bruegel, Irene, 549

Brum Women's Liberation
Newsletter, _303_

Brum Women's Paper, _406_

Brum Women's Press, _406_

Bryant and May, 39

Bulletin of the Council of Women
Civil Servants, _183_

Bulletin of the Indian Women's
Movement, _182_

Bulletin of the National Council
of Women in India, _176_

Bulletin of the W.I.S. Women's
Caucus, _256_

Bulletin, Women's Information
and Referral Centre, _385_

Bureau of Women's Affairs

Newsletter, 552

Burnett, Farrell, 677

Burton, Elaine, 174

Business and Professional
    Woman, 257

Business and Professional Woman
    (Canada), 369

Business Girl, 110

Buswoman, 626

Butcher, Linda, 286

Butler, Caroline, 726

Butler, Josephine Elizabeth,
    10, 11, 13, 37, 39, 40, 44,
    71

Butler, Joyce, 262

B.W.T.A., see British Women's
    Temperance Association

Byatt, Lucy, 659

Bystram, Yolanda, 688

C.A.C.S.W. Bulletin, 370

Cairncross, Catherine, 873

Calder, Pamela, 595

Calder-Marshall, Clare, 711

Caldwell, Lesley, 609

Calgary Women's Newspaper, 384

Call to Women, 233

Calling All Women, 215

Cambridge Anti-Discrimination
    Against Women Group, 350

Cambridge Scarlet Women, 478

Cambridge Women's Liberation
    Group, 273

Cambridge Women's Liberation
    Newsletter, 416

Cambridge W.O.N.T., 714

Camden Girls' Centre Project,
    644

Camden Women's Centre
    Newsletter, 495

Camden Women's Committee
    Newsletter, 868

Campaign Against Sexism and
    Sexual Oppression in
    Education, 615

Campaign for Nuclear Dis-
    armament, 217, 233

Campaign for the Feminine Woman,
    603

Campaign to Impede Sex Stereo-
    typing in the Young, 600, 602

Campbell, Beatrice, 284

Campbell, Fiona, 354

Canadian Abortion Rights Action
    League Newsletter, 734

Canadian Advisory Council on the
    Status of Women, 370, 433

Canadian Association for Women
    in Science, 685

Canadian Association of Sexual
    Assault Centres, 735

Canadian Catholics for Women's
    Ordination, 736

Canadian Committee on Learning
    Opportunities for Women, 540

Canadian Committee on Women's
    History, 737

Canadian Federation of Business
    and Professional Women's
    Clubs, 369

Canadian Federation of Univer-
    sity Women, 739

Canadian Housewives' Register
    Newsletter, 519

Canadian Newsletter of Research
    on Women, 294

Canadian Psychiatric Association
    Task Force on Women's Issues,
    520

Canadian Psychological Assoc-
    iation, 577

Canadian Research Institute for
    the Advancement of Women
    Newsletter, 742

270

Haslett, Dame Caroline, 194
Hayman, Suzie, 653
Haynes, Joanna, 564
Hays, Mary, 4
Heal, Sue, 502
Healthsharing, 598
Healy, Grainne, 726
Hearne, Kirsten, 717
Hecate, 393
Hefferman, Lynn, 865
Hemming, Alice, 199, 234
Hempstead, Lorna, 859
Henry, Sally, 499, 564
Heppard, Jacki, 705
Herizons, 753
Heroine, 554
Herringer, Barbara, 781
Herstory, 417
Hester, Marianne, 567
Hicks, Margaretta, 105
Hindess, Barry, 549
Hirst, Paul, 549
Hodge, C. Esther, 228
Hoffman, Edie, 566
Holden, Inez, 174
Holdsworth, Annie E., 60
Holland, Barbara, 489
Holmes, Liz, 559
Holmes, Marion, 101
Holt, Alix, 489
Holt, Angela, 648
Holtby, Winifred, 32, 152, 173
Home and Country, 146
Home and Politics, 154
Homes of the East, 36
Honourable Fraternity of
   Ancient Freemasons, 165
Hoole, M., 887
Hooper, Anne, 766
Hooper, Mrs, 67
Hornsey Women's Centre
   Newsletter, 524

Housewives in Dialogue, 496
Housman, Lawrence, 111
Houston, Helen, 110
How-Martyn, Edith, 96
Hubback, Eva, 151
Hubbard, Louisa Maria, 19, 22,
   28
Hueffer, Ford Maddox, 101
Hull Woman, 351
Hull Women's Collective
   Newsletter, 629
Humanity, 117
Humber College Centre for Women,
   362
Humphrey, Mary, 745
Hunkins Hallinan, Hazel, 204,
   228
Hunter-Henderson, M. A., 206
Hurcombe, Linda, 574
Hysterectomy Support Group
   Newsletter, 915
Hysteria (Kitchener-Waterloo),
   646
Hysteria (Reading University),
   418

I.C.A. Newsletter, 754
I.C.A.S.C., 654
I.F.L. Newsletter, 336
Illet, Rosemary, 862
Images, 457
Images of Women, 578
Images of Women Newsletter, 413
I.M.G., 248, 270
Imperial Colonist, 77
Imray, Linda, 561
Incest Survivors' Campaign
   Newsletter, 830
Independent Suffragette, 133
Independent Women's Social and
   Political Union, 133
Indian National

277

League of Nations, 132

League of the Church Militant, 137

Lee, Judy, 865

Leeds Birth Centre Newsletter, 648

Leeds Women's Conservative and Unionist Publications Ltd, 158

Leeds Women's Liberation Newsletter, 333

L.E.G., 691

Leicester Women's Liberation Newsletter, 493

Leigh, Blanche L., 158

Leigh Smith, Barbara, see Bodichon, Barbara Leigh Smith

Leland, Stephanie, 837

Leonard, Diana, 879

Lesbian Action Newsletter, 760

Lesbian Archive Newsletter, 894

Lesbian Exchange Grapevine, 691

Lesbian Express, 614

Lesbian Feminist Circle, 316, 761

Lesbian/Lesbienne, 762

Lesbian Mothers' Defense Fund, 752

Lesbian News-letter, 437

Lesbian Newsletter, 763

Lesbian Nurses Newsletter, 854

Lesbian Switchboard Newsletter, 649

Lesbians Come Together, 277

Lett, Brenda, 914

Lever, Rachel, 682

Lewis, Amelia, 16

Liaison Committee for Women's Peace Groups, 233

Liberaction, 308

Liberal Party, see Liberal Women's Suffrage Union;

Scottish Women's Liberal Federation; Women's Liberal Federation; National Women's Liberal Association

Liberal Woman (Australia), 78

Liberal Woman's News, 164

Liberal Women's Review, 125

Liberal Women's Suffrage Union, 125

Liberation, 282

Libertarian Women's Network Newsletter, 527

Libertarian Women's Network News-sheet, 292

Libido, 388

Liley, Sir William, 535

Lilith, 824

Lilith (Ireland), 337

Link 1888, 39

Link 1911-1913, 105

Link 1973-c., 324

LIP, 511

Lipschitz, Susan, 549

Liverpool Creches Against Sexism Newsletter, 764

Livewire, 445

Living as Women, 338

Lloyd, Anne, 842

Lloyd, Leonora, 270

Lockwood, Betty, 118

Lodl, Karen, 384

Logan, Marion, 806

London CISSY Newsletter, 600

London Communist Women's Bulletin, 497

London Homeworking Campaign Bulletin, 482

London Lesbian Newsletter, 705

London Nursery Campaign Newsletter, 466

London W.A.M.T. Newsletter, 870

London Women's Liberation

Murray, Jane, 909
Myers, Anita, 791

N.A.C., see National Abortion
   Campaign
N.A.C. Memo (National Action
   Committee), 769
Nanny, 863
Nathan, Ros, 292
National Abortion Campaign,
   354, 406, 408, 879
National Assembly of Women,
   467, 698
National Assembly of Women
   Newsletter, 467
National Association for the
   Defence of Personal Rights,
   29
National Association for the
   Promotion of Social Science,
   4
National Association for the
   Repeal of the Contagious
   Diseases Acts, 13
National Association of Teach-
   ers in Further and Higher
   Education, 595, 755
National Association of Women
   and the Law (Canada), 773
National Association of Women
   Citizens, see National Women
   Citizens' Association
National Association of Women
   Civil Servants, 156
National British Women's Temp-
   erance Association, see
   British Women's Temperance
   Association
National Childcare Campaign,
   770, 771
National Conference of Labour
   Women, 118

National Council for Civil
   Liberties, 446, 556
National Council of Women in
   India, 176
National Council of Women of
   Great Britain and Northern
   Ireland, 68, 141, 161, 179,
   298, 301
National Council of Women of
   South Africa, 184
National Federation of Business
   and Professional Women's Clubs
   of Great Britain and Northern
   Ireland, 257
National Federation of Women
   Teachers, 143
National Federation of Women
   Workers, 90
National Federation of Women's
   Institutes, 146
National Food and Fuel Reformer,
   16
National Housewives Register,
   238
National League for Opposing
   Woman Suffrage, 93
National League Journal, 20
National Lesbian Newsletter, 366
National Medical Association for
   the State Regulation of
   Prostitution, 21
National Newsletter, 238
National Newsletter of the
   Canadian Rape Crisis Centres,
   581
National Organisation for
   Women's Management Education,
   832
National Organisation of
   Lesbians, 546
National Society for Women's
   Suffrage, 12, 48

National Spinsters' Pensions
   Association, 188
National Union for Improving
   the Education of All Classes,
   15
National Union of Conservative
   and Constitutional Assoc-
   iations, 172
National Union of Societies for
   Equal Citizenship, 151
National Union of Teachers,
   143, 544
National Union of Townswomen's
   Guilds, 151, 180
National Union of Women
   Teachers, 143
National Union of Women Workers
   of Great Britain and Ireland,
   49, 68
National Union of Women's Suf-
   frage Societies, 79, 87, 88,
   94, 95, 115, 120
National Vigilance Association,
   29
National W., 582
National Women and Computing
   Newsletter, 695
National Women Citizens' Assoc-
   iation, 149, 208, 398
National Women's Advisory
   Council, 601, 632
National Women's Aid Federation
   Newsletter, 538
National Women's Labour League,
   see Women's Labour League
National Women's Organisation
   Newsletter, 772
National Women's Social and
   Political Union, see Women's
   Social and Political Union
Native Women's Association of
   Canada Newsletter, 845

N.A.W.L. Newsletter, 773
N.C.W. News, 161
N.C.W. News [South Africa], 184
Neilans, Alison, 13
Nemesis, 352
Nesbit, Edith, 39
Nessie, 616
Network, 871
Network of Saskatchewan Women,
   583
Nevinson, Margaret Wynn, 101
New Citizen, 149
New Democratic Party, 318, 590,
   745, 829
New Feminist, 246
New Freewoman, 119
New South Wales League of Women
   Voters, 227
New Women's Magazine Society,
   311
Newbould, Grace, 155, 164
Newfoundland Status of Women
   Council Newsletter, 774
Newman, Marion, 502
Newman, Sylvia, 699
News and Views of the Josephine
   Butler Society, 215
News from Women's Liberation,
   327
News Letter, 650
News Sheet (New Zealand), 584
Newsheet, 664
Newsletter for Women Working in
   Publishing, 423
Newsletter of the Women's Place,
   359
Newslink, 775
Newsome, Stella, 204
Newson, Vivienne, 196, 220
Newton, Jennifer L., 612
N.H.R., 238
Nicholls, Barbara, 502

Nicholls, Jill, 297, 350

Nigerian Organisation of Women, 280

Nightingale, Camilla, 295

Nirjhar, 339

No-Name Newsletter, 702

Non-Sexist Children's Books Newsletter, 295

N.O.O.L. News, 546

Norris, Jill, 331

North Paddington Women's C Centre, 631, 811

North Shore Women, 776

North Staffordshire Women's Action Group Newsletter, 509

Northern Ireland Women's Aid Newsletter, 777

Northern Woman Journal, 391

Norwich Women's Centre Newsletter, 373, 855

Norwich Women's Liberation Newsletter. 530

Norwich Women's Movement Newsletter, 374

Notting Hill Women's Paper, 468

Nottingham Socialist Women's Committee, 248

Nottingham Women's Diary, 778

Nottingham Women's Liberation Group, 271

Nottingham Women's Liberation Newsletter, 405

N.O.W., 280

Now-a-days, 11

N.O.W.M.E., 832

Nurses' Action Group, 314

Nursing Mirror, 81

Nursing Mirror, 80

O.A.W.E. Exchange, 779

Obaa Sima, 265

O'Brien, J., 248

O'Brien, Mary, 612, 663

Occasional Paper of the National Union of Women Workers, 68

Older Feminists Network Newsletter, 818

Older Lesbian Network Newsletter, 896

On Our Way, 376

Only Way, 100

Ontario Association for Women and Education, 779

Ontario Committee on the Status of Women Newsletter, 531

Ontario Institute for Studies in Education, 254, 294, 612, 702

Ontario Native Women's Association Newsletter, 780

Ontario Women and the Law Association, 533

Open Door, 173

Open Door International, 173

Opportunity, 156

Oppression of South Asian Women, 505

Optimist, 532

Options for Women, 376

Organisation of Women of Asian and African Descent, 619

Organised Working Women Toronto Association, 456

O'Rourke, Rebecca, 604, 609

Ostman, Connie, 595

O'Sullivan, Sue, 284

Other Half Lives, 326

Other Woman, 319

Otto, Penny, 636

Our Sisters, 67

Outdoor Women, 877

Outwrite, 825

Oversea Settler, 77

O.W.A.A.D., 619

Owens, Wendy, 490

Programme for the Reform of the
    Soliciting Laws, 507
Prophet, Sheila, 652
P.R.O.S. Bulletin, 507
Pyke, Margaret A., 193

Quarterly Bulletin of the
    Council of Women Civil
    Servants, 183
Quarterly Review of the Women's
    National Liberal Association,
    65
Quillin, Viv, 659
Quinn, Veronica, 726

Radford, Jean, 284
Radical Nurses' Newsletter, 696
Radical Reviewer, 781
Railway Women's Annual, 210
Ramirez, Judith, 455
Rathbone, Eleanor, 151, 163
Raverat, Gwendolen, 152
Ray, 165
Read, Alison, 862
Reading University Women's
    Group, 418
Reading Women's Group Magazine,
    424
Red Herring, 400
Red Rag, 284
Reddi, S. Muthulakshmi, 140
Redstocking, 350
Refractory Girl, 285
Regan, Carole, 544
Rendel, Margherita, 404
Renn, Margaret, 267
Report to women, 212
Research Committee on Sex Roles
    and Politics, 404
Research Unit on Women's
    Studies, 650
Resources for Feminist

Research, 612, 702
Response, 632
Revolting Women, 587
Revolutionary and Radical Femin-
    ist Newsletter, 567
Rhiannon, 588
Rhondda, Lady, 152
Richards, Elisina Grant, 95
Richmond, Caroline, 653
Richmond Community Centre, 380
Richmond, Fiona, 909
Rights for Women Unit
    Newsletter, 446
Rights of Women Bulletin, 514
Risbridger, Andrew, 207
Roberts, Michele, 297
Robins, Elizabeth, 152
Robinson, Margaret, 400
Robinson, Sheelagh, 574
Robson, Robbi, 839
Rock Against Sexism, 627
Rogozin, D., 150
Roman Catholic Feminists, 469
Room of One's Own, 403
Roper, Esther, 76
Rose, Joy, 331
Rose, Sheila, 608
Roshni, 200
Ross, Monica, 563
Rothman, Rona, 286
Rotton, Ronder, 697
Rouge, 782
Round-Ups, 878
Rover, Constance, 208
R.O.W. Bulletin, 514
Rowbotham, Sheila, 228, 284, 297
Rowe, Marsha, 297
Royal College of Nurses, 80
Royden, Agnes Maude, 94, 108,
    116, 129, 137, 162, 169, 177
Ruda, Lesley, 659
Russell, Amanda, 705

Rust, Tamara, 198
Rye, Maria S., 4
Ryrie, Sue, 490

Sacha-Savannah, 556
S.A.D. Newsletter, 835
Saint Andrews Lesbian Feminist
  Newsletter, 633
St Joan's, Australia, 213
St Joan's [International]
  [Social and Political] Alli-
  ance, 138, 143, 182, 213
St John, Christopher, 152
Sales, Mrs M. J., 53
Samta, 610
Samuel, Judy, 331
Samya Shakti, 856
Sand, Cy-Thea, 781
Sanders Comer, Lee, 295, 302
Sappho, 237, 293, 541
Sarah, Elizabeth, 916
Sash, 225
Saskatoon Women's Liberation
  Newsletter, 378
Saunders, Colleen, 839
Saunders, Sheila, 879, 916
Sawbridge, Molly, 719
Scarlet Women, 450
Scarlet Woman (Australia), 425
Scarlet Woman or Revolt, 450
Scarlet Woman (York), 272
Scarlet Women, 450
Scarlet Women (Australia), 470
Schoolmistress, 32
Schwartz, Margaret, 13, 275
Scope, 241
Scott, Alison, 499
Scott, Diana, 508
Scott, Fiona, 659
Scott, Nicola, 711
Scott, Rosalind, 659
Scott, Sue, 563

Scottish Convention of Women,
  479
Scottish Minorities Group
  Newsletter, 379
Scottish Women's Aid Newsletter,
  675, 803, 846
Scottish Women's Liberal Feder-
  ation Magazine, 73
Scottish Women's Liberation
  Journal, 499
Scottish Women's Liberation
  Newsletter, 340
Scottish Women's Liberation
  Workshop Newsletter, 426
Scottish Women's Newsletter, 783
Scottish Women's Temperance
  News, 70
Sealy, Dallas, 901
Sebestyen, Amanda, 297
Seed, 167
Seelers, Maggie, 366
SEMC Newsletter, 224
Semple, Linda, 682
Sempstress, 1
Sentinel, 30
Sequel, 556
Servian, Jill, 699
Sex Roles, 404
Sexism in the Media, 697
Sexual Liberation Action Group,
  320
Shafts, 57
Sharma, Ursula, 852
Sharpe, Anne, 636
Sharples, Eunice, 688
Shaw, George Bernard, 95
Sheba Feminist Publishers, 862
Sheehy Skeffington, Francis, 111
Sheehy Skeffington, Hannah, 111
Sheepshanks, Mary, 83
Sheffield Childbirth Group
  Newsletter, 471

Sheffield University Women's
Liberation Group, 388
Sheffield Women's Liberation
Newsletter, 407
Sheffield Women's Paper, 634
Shenfield, Bella, 579
Sheppard, Kate, 64
Sheridan, Geoff, 270
Shield, 13
Shifra, 916
Shilston, Miss, 59
Shipstone, Eva, 382
Shireff, Emily, 15
Shocking Pink, 665
Shrew, 244, 600
Sibthorpe, Margaret Shurmer, 57
Silvera, Makeda, 566
Sim, Barbara, 241
Simpson, Pat, 694
Sims, E., 220
Sinclair, Catriona, 659
Sing, Charlotte, 859
Singh, J. D., 317
Singha, Mrs Santosh, 382
Sinister Women, 819
Sinn Fein, 111
  (Official), 657
  (Provisional), 657
Sisterhood, 820
Sisterhood (Canada), 784
Sistermatic, 857
Sisters 1895-1898, 67
Sisters 1981-c., 698
Sisters Against Disablement,
  835
Six Point Group, 152, 182, 204
Six Point Group Newsletter, 204
Size 8, 902
Sjoo, Monica, 252, 363, 483
Skeffington, Francis/Hannah
  Sheehy, see Sheehy
  Skeffington, Francis/Hannah

Skinner, Beverley, 252, 483
Slag, 320
Smith, Annie, 567
Smith, Barbara Leigh, see
  Bodichon, Barbara Leigh Smith
Smith, Christine, 454
Smith, Elizabeth, 456
Smith, Linda, 270, 324
Smith, Stevie, 174
Smith, Sue, 504
Smith, Susanna, 659
Smyth, Donna, 410
Smyth, Geri, 564
Smythe, Roslyn, 483
Snell, Mandy, 609
Snowden, Ethel, 90
Snowden, Philip, 116, 154
Social Democratic Party, 839
Social Purity Alliance, 37
Socialist International Women
  Bulletin, 484
Socialist Woman, 248, 270
Socialist Workers' Party, 488,
  see also International
  Socialists
Society for Constructive Birth
  Control, 160
Society for the Equal Ministry
  of Men and Women in the
  Church, 224
Society for the Ministry of
  Women (Interdenominational)
  177
Society for the Ministry of
  Women in the Church, 224
Society for the Oversea Settle-
  ment of British Women, 77
Society for the Protection of
  the Unborn Child, 536
Society of Women Journalists,
  103
Somerset, Isabel (Lady Henry

Somerset), 46, 59, 60, 62

Somerville, Mary, 125

Soroptimist, 175

Soroptimist International, 175

S.O.R.W.U.C. Mews, 785

Source, 427

Sourcream, 659

South African Expansion
   Committee, 77

South Asia Women's Workshop,
   852

South London Women's Centre
   Newsletter, 472

South West Women Communicate,
   635

Southall Black Women's Centre
   Newsletter, 889

Southampton Women's Liberation
   Group, 309, 326

Southampton Women's Liberation
   Newsletter, 827

Southern CISSY Newsletter, 602

Southwark Women's Equality
   News, 872

Spare Rib, 297

Spark, Vicky, 489

Speak Out, 786

Speaking of women, 214

Speculum Speakes, 888

Spender, Dale, 551

Spiers, Sharon, 502

Spinster 1938, 188

Spinster 1980-82, 656

Spiral, 439

Spirale, 787

S.P.U.C. Newsletter, 535

Spunner, Suzanne, 511

Stallard, Rita, 872

Standing Committee on Women's
   Rights of the B.C. New
   Democratic Party, 318

Standing Conferences of Women's

Organisations, 240

Starcross School, 642

Status (Canada), 788

Status (Ireland), 710

Status of Women News, 325

Stayt, David W., 603

Stead, Ethel, 143

Stead, William Thomas, 39, 115

Stephens, Eleanor, 711

Stephenson, Dr Sue, 520

Stephenson, Marylee, 612

Stern, Jenny, 302

Stevens, Judy, 901

Stewart, Bill, 541

Stewart, Carole, 661

Stirling, Kay, 656, 727

Stocks, Baroness Mary Danvers,
   151

Stoke Women's Action Newsletter,
   558

Stone, Emma, 237

Stopes, Charlotte Carmichael,
   45, 57

Stopes, Marie Carmichael, 160

Storm-bell, 71

Stott, Mary, 145

Stout, Edwin H., 46

Stri-dharma, 140

Studies on Women Abstracts, 860

Sudbury Women's Centre
   Newsletter (Canada), 789

Suffragette, 114

Suffragette Fellowshop, 215

Suffragette News Sheet, 131

Suffragettes of the Women's
   Social and Political Union,
   131

Suffragist, 98

Suffragist's Vigilance League,
   98

Summerskill, Edith, 189, 191,
   192, 199

Wilson, Elizabeth, 284, 324, 609

Wilson, Rhonda, 658

Wimmin, 726

Wine, Jeri, 577, 612

Wings 1892-1925, 56

Wings 1976, 475

Winner, Dame Albertine, 476

W.I.N.N.Z., 636

Wiparound, 881

Wiplash, 677

W.I.R.E.S., 409

Wise, Nancy, 687

W.I.T. News, 797

Witch and the Cameleon, 361

Wittick, Helen, 240, 398

Witty, Frank, 112

Wivenhoe Women's Liberation Group, 255

W.L.F., see Women's Liberal Federation

Wolf, Misha, 624

Wolpe, Ann-Marie, 609

Wolstenhome, M. S., 63

Wolstenhome Elmy, Elizabeth C., 11, 29, 57

Wolverhampton Women's Paper, 857

Woman (Australia), 91

Woman (New Zealand), 287

Woman 1872, 14

Woman 1887, 38

Woman 1890-1910, 44

Woman 1980-c., 678

Woman Citizen, 87

Woman Citizen Publishing Company, 87

Woman Clerk, 147

Woman Councillor and Citizen, 208

Woman Engineer, 144

Woman Freemason, 165

Woman Journalist, 103

Woman of Today and Tomorrow, 172

Woman Sound, 907

Woman Speak!, 679

Woman Teacher, 143

Woman Today (Canada), 430

Woman Today 1936-1940, 185

Woman Today 1944-1959, 198

Woman Voter, 106

Woman Worker 1907-1921, 90

Woman Worker 1926-1927, 168

Womanhood, 72

Woman's Angle, 216

Woman's Charter, 142

Woman's Daily Newspaper, 190

Woman's Dreadnought, 124

Woman's Financial Letter, 568

Woman's Gazette, 19

Woman's Herald, 46

Woman's Leader, 151

Woman's National Newspaper, 189

Woman's Newspaper, 191

Woman's Opinion 1874, 16

Woman's Opinion 1915-1916, 127

Woman's Outlook, 145

Woman's Outlook (South Africa), 113

Woman's Place? (Brighton), 323

Woman's Place (London), 249, 492

Woman's Signal, 60

Woman's Signal Budget, 62

Woman's Times, 153

Woman's Tribune, 41

Woman's View, 166

Woman's Voice (Australia), 63

Woman's Voice 1916-1918, 130

Woman's Voice 1972-1976, 290

Woman's World, 9

Womanspeak, 395

Women Against

Occasional Paper, 101
Women's Freedom League Temporary News Sheet, 96
Women's Gas Council/Federation, 186, 194, 203, 241
Women's Gazette, 43
Women's Group on Public Welfare, 301
Women's Health Information Centre Newsletter, 875
Women's Health Network Newsletter, 808
Women's India Association of the United Kingdom, 317
Women's Indian Association, 140
Women's Industrial Council, 66
Women's Industrial News, 66
Women's Information Centre Newsletter, 431
Women's Information Network of New Zealand, 636
Women's Information Referral and Enquiry Service, 409, 879
Women's Institute, 57
Women's Institutes, see National Federation of Women's Institutes
Women's Inter-Church Council of Canada Newsletter, 809
Women's International Democratic Federation, 741
Women's International League for Peace and Freedom, 89, 111, 132, 182, 217
Women's Labour League, 104, 118
Women's Labour News, 76
Women's Land Army, 193, 201
Women's League of Health and Beauty, 189, 191
Women's League of Unity, 189, 191
Women's Legal Resource

Centre, 514
Women's Liberal Federation, 41, 42, 43, 46, 65, 73
Women's Liberal League of New South Wales, 78, 130
Women's Liberal Magazine, 148
Women's Liberation, 250, 486
Women's Liberation Campaign for Legal and Financial Independence Newsletter, 412
Women's Liberation Front, 250, 486
Women's Liberation Information Service Newsletter, 261
Women's Liberation Literature Collective, 295, 302
Women's Liberation Movement National Information Service, 409
Women's Liberation News, 327
Women's Liberation Review, 302
Women's Liberation Union Newsletter, 266
Women's Liberation Workshop Newsletter/Newsheet, 249
Women's Liberation Workshops, 244, 305
Women's Literature Collective, 302
Women's Lobby, 304
Women's Local Government News, 157
Women's Local Government Society, 157
Women's Media Action Group, 701
Women's Monitoring Network, 697
Women's Music Organisers, 821
Women's National Anti-Suffrage League, 93
Women's National Cancer Control Campaign, 262
Women's National Commission,

Subject Index

Abortion, 99, 181, 239, 299, 300, 324, 354, 368, 383, 396, 401, 408, 420, 434, 446, 499, 502, 535, 582, 618, 652, 654, 665, 686, 734, 898

Advertisements, 42, 255, 701, 817

Africa, 222, 236, 432

African women, 625

Afrikaans, 225

Age of consent, 665

Ageism, 697

Agriculture, 75, 193, 201

Air Raid Precautions, 191

Anarca-feminism, see Anarchism

Anarchism, 292, 498, 504, 506, 527, 543, 587, 607, 613, 706, 876, 891

Androgyny, 134

Animal liberation, 556

Anorexia, 351

Anti-feminism, 93, 207, 603

Anti-semitism, 817, 836, 904

Anti-suffragism, 93

Apartheid, 225, 724, 919

Architecture, 442, 900

Armagh women prisoners, 657, 663, 905

Artificial insemination, 293

Arts, 4, 439, 483, 511, 563, 591, 747, 787, 822, 907

Asian women, 505, 619, 625, 732, 852, 857, 866

Association of Radical Midwives

Newsletter, <u>557</u>

Astrology, 834

Australia, 52, 63, 78, 91, 106, 130, 139, 194, 213, 220, 227, 242, 264, 282, 285, 288, 308, 341, 345, 386, 389, 393, 395, 397, 414, 419, 425, 428, 441, 443, 462, 470, 501, 511, 525, 536, 539, 545, 580, 594, 601, 605, 613, 622, 632, 664, 689, 692, 747, 760, 763, 782, 813, 888

Bangladesh, 339

Barbados, 679, 683

Bee-keeping, 84

Bengali, 339

Birth control, see Contraception

Black women, 184, 269, 333, 335, 496, 609, 619, 661, 786, 825, 833, 836, 889, 897, 908, 913

Blind women, 717

British Railways, 210

Bus women, 269, 626

Business women, 194, 218, 257

Canada, 246, 247, 254, 294, 311, 312, 313, 318, 319, 322, 325, 332, 344, 346, 347, 353, 356, 359, 361, 362, 369, 370, 371, 372, 375-8, 384, 385, 391, 403, 410, 415, 421, 427, 430, 431, 433, 440, 442, 455, 456, 457, 464, 474, 477, 481, 491,

Chronological Index

44, 46, 47, 48, 49, 50, 51,
52, 53, 54, 55, 56, 57, 58
1893, 5, 8, 22, 23, 27, 28, 29,
31, 32, 34, 36, 37, 40, 44,
46, 47, 48, 49, 50, 51, 55,
56, 57, 58, 59
1894, 5, 8, 22, 23, 27, 29, 31,
32, 34, 36, 37, 40, 44, 47,
48, 49, 50, 51, 55, 56, 57,
58, 60, 61, 62, 63, 64
1895, 5, 8, 22, 23, 27, 29, 31,
32, 34, 36, 37, 40, 44, 47,
48, 49, 50, 51, 55, 56, 57,
58, 60, 62, 63, 65, 66, 67
1896, 5, 8, 22, 23, 27, 29, 31,
32, 34, 36, 37, 40, 44, 47,
48, 49, 50, 51, 56, 57, 58,
60, 63, 65, 66, 67, 68, 69
1897, 8, 13, 22, 23, 27, 29,
31, 32, 34, 36, 37, 44, 47,
48, 50, 51, 56, 57, 58, 60,
65, 66, 67, 68, 69, 70
1898, 8, 13, 22, 23, 27, 29,
31, 32, 34, 36, 37, 44, 47,
48, 50, 51, 56, 57, 58, 60,
65, 66, 67, 68, 69, 70, 71,
72
1899, 8, 13, 22, 23, 27, 29,
31, 32, 34, 36, 44, 47, 48,
50, 51, 56, 57, 58, 60, 65,
66, 68, 69, 70, 71, 72, 73
1900, 8, 13, 22, 23, 27, 29,
31, 32, 34, 36, 44, 47, 48,
50, 51, 56, 57, 58, 65, 66,
68, 69, 70, 71, 72, 73, 74,
75, 76
1901, 8, 13, 22, 23, 27, 29,
31, 32, 34, 36, 44, 50, 51,
56, 58, 65, 66, 68, 69, 70,
72, 74, 75, 76
1902, 8, 13, 22, 23, 27, 29,
31, 32, 34, 44, 50, 51, 56,

58, 65, 66, 68, 69, 70, 72,
74, 75, 76, 77, 78
1903, 8, 13, 22, 23, 27, 29, 31,
32, 34, 36, 44, 50, 51, 56,
58, 65, 66, 68, 69, 70, 72,
74, 75, 76, 77, 78, 79
1904, 8, 13, 22, 23, 27, 31, 32,
34, 36, 44, 50, 51, 56, 58,
65, 66, 68, 69, 70, 72, 74,
75, 76, 77, 78, 79
1905, 8, 13, 22, 23, 27, 31, 32,
34, 36, 44, 50, 51, 56, 58,
65, 66, 68, 69, 70, 72, 74,
75, 77, 78, 79, 80, 81
1906, 8, 13, 22, 23, 27, 31, 32,
34, 36, 44, 50, 51, 56, 58,
65, 66, 68, 69, 70, 72, 74,
75, 77, 78, 79, 80, 81, 82,
83, 84, 85, 86
1907, 8, 13, 22, 23, 27, 31, 32,
34, 36, 44, 50, 51, 56, 58,
65, 66, 68, 69, 70, 72, 74,
75, 77, 78, 80, 81, 82, 83,
84, 86, 87, 88, 89, 90
1908, 8, 13, 22, 23, 27, 31, 32,
34, 36, 44, 50, 51, 56, 58,
65, 66, 68, 69, 70, 74, 75,
77, 78, 80, 81, 82, 83, 84,
87, 89, 90, 91, 92, 93
1909, 8, 13, 22, 23, 27, 31, 32,
34, 36, 44, 50, 51, 56, 58,
65, 66, 68, 69, 70, 74, 75,
77, 78, 80, 81, 82, 83, 84,
87, 89, 90, 91, 92, 93, 94,
95, 96, 97, 98, 99, 100, 101,
102
1910, 8, 13, 22, 23, 27, 31, 32,
34, 36, 44, 50, 51, 56, 58,
65, 66, 68, 69, 70, 74, 75,
77, 78, 80, 81, 82, 83, 84,
87, 89, 90, 91, 92, 93, 94,
95, 97, 99, 100, 102, 103

1911, 13, 22, 23, 27, 31, 32,
34, 36, 50, 51, 56, 58, 65,
66, 68, 69, 70, 74, 75, 77,
78, 80, 81, 82, 83, 87, 89,
90, 91, 93, 94, 95, 97, 99,
102, 103, 104, 105, 106,
107
1912, 13, 22, 23, 27, 31, 32,
34, 36, 50, 51, 56, 58, 65,
66, 68, 69, 70, 74, 75, 77,
78, 80, 81, 82, 83, 89, 90,
91, 93, 94, 95, 97, 99, 102,
103, 104, 105, 106, 107, 108,
109, 110, 111, 112, 113, 114,
115
1913, 13, 22, 23, 27, 31, 32,
34, 36, 50, 51, 56, 58, 65,
66, 68, 69, 70, 74, 75, 77,
78, 80, 81, 82, 83, 89, 90,
91, 93, 94, 95, 97, 99, 102,
103, 104, 105, 106, 108, 109,
111, 113, 114, 115, 116, 117,
118, 119, 120, 121, 122
1914, 13, 22, 23, 27, 31, 32,
34, 36, 50, 51, 56, 58, 65,
66, 68, 69, 70, 74, 75, 77,
78, 80, 81, 82, 83, 89, 90,
91, 93, 94, 95, 97, 99, 102,
103, 106, 108, 111, 113, 114,
115, 116, 117, 118, 120, 121,
123, 124, 125
1915, 13, 22, 23, 27, 31, 32,
34, 36, 50, 51, 56, 58, 65,
66, 68, 69, 70, 74, 75, 77,
78, 80, 81, 82, 83, 89, 90,
91, 93, 94, 95, 99, 102, 103,
106, 108, 111, 113, 114, 116,
118, 121, 123, 124, 126, 127,
128
1916, 13, 22, 23, 27, 31, 32,
34, 36, 50, 51, 56, 65, 66,
68, 69, 70, 74, 75, 77, 80,

81, 82, 83, 89, 90, 91, 93,
94, 95, 99, 102, 103, 106,
108, 111, 113, 118, 123, 124,
126, 127, 128, 129, 130, 131,
132, 133, 134, 135
1917, 13, 23, 27, 31, 32, 34,
36, 50, 51, 56, 65, 66, 68,
69, 70, 74, 75, 77, 80, 81,
82, 83, 89, 90, 91, 93, 94,
95, 99, 103, 106, 108, 111,
113, 118, 123, 124, 126, 128,
129, 130, 132, 133, 134, 135,
136
1918, 13, 27, 31, 32, 36, 50,
51, 56, 65, 66, 68, 69, 70,
74, 75, 77, 80, 81, 82, 83,
89, 90, 91, 93, 94, 95, 99,
103, 106, 111, 113, 118, 123,
124, 126, 128, 129, 130, 132,
133, 134, 135, 136, 137, 138,
139
1919, 13, 27, 31, 32, 50, 56,
66, 69, 70, 74, 75, 77, 80,
81, 82, 83, 90, 91, 94, 95,
99, 103, 111, 113, 118, 123,
124, 129, 132, 134, 137, 138,
139, 140, 141, 142, 143, 144,
145, 146, 147
1920, 13, 27, 31, 32, 50, 56,
69, 70, 74, 75, 77, 80, 81,
82, 83, 90, 91, 94, 95, 99,
103, 111, 113, 118, 123, 124,
129, 132, 134, 136, 137, 138,
139, 140, 141, 143, 144, 145,
146, 147, 148, 149, 150, 151,
152, 153, 154
1921, 13, 27, 31, 32, 50, 56,
69, 70, 74, 75, 77, 80, 81,
83, 90, 91, 95, 99, 103, 113,
118, 123, 124, 132, 134, 136,
137, 138, 139, 140, 141, 143,
144, 145, 146, 147, 150, 151,

152, 153, 154, 155, 156, 157,
158

1922, 13, 27, 31, 32, 50, 56,
69, 70, 74, 75, 77, 80, 81,
83, 91, 99, 103, 118, 123,
124, 132, 134, 136, 137, 138,
139, 140, 141, 143, 144, 145,
146, 147, 150, 151, 152, 153,
154, 155, 156, 157, 158, 159,
160

1923, 13, 27, 31, 32, 50, 56,
69, 70, 74, 75, 77, 80, 81,
83, 91, 99, 103, 118, 123,
124, 132, 134, 136, 137, 138,
139, 140, 143, 144, 145, 146,
147, 150, 151, 152, 154, 155,
156, 157, 158, 159, 160, 161

1924, 13, 27, 31, 32, 50, 56,
69, 70, 74, 75, 77, 80, 81,
83, 91, 99, 103, 118, 123,
124, 132, 134, 136, 137, 138,
139, 140, 143, 144, 145, 146,
147, 151, 152, 154, 155, 156,
157, 158, 159, 160, 161, 162,
163, 164

1925, 13, 27, 31, 32, 56, 69,
70, 75, 77, 80, 81, 83, 91,
99, 103, 118, 132, 134, 136,
137, 138, 139, 140, 143, 144,
145, 146, 147, 151, 152, 154,
156, 157, 158, 159, 160, 161,
162, 163, 164, 165, 166, 167

1926, 13, 27, 31, 32, 70, 74,
75, 77, 80, 81, 83, 91, 99,
103, 118, 132, 134, 136, 137,
138, 139, 140, 143, 144, 145,
146, 147, 151, 152, 154, 156,
158, 159, 160, 161, 162, 163,
164, 165, 166, 167, 168

1927, 13, 27, 31, 32, 70, 74,
75, 77, 80, 81, 83, 91, 99,
103, 118, 132, 134, 136, 137,

138, 139, 140, 143, 144, 145,
146, 147, 151, 152, 154, 156,
158, 159, 160, 161, 163, 164,
165, 166, 168, 169, 170, 171

1928, 13, 27, 31, 32, 70, 74,
75, 80, 81, 83, 91, 99, 103,
118, 132, 134, 136, 137, 138,
139, 140, 143, 144, 145, 146,
147, 151, 152, 154, 156, 158,
159, 160, 161, 163, 164, 165,
166, 169, 170

1929, 13, 27, 31, 32, 70, 74,
75, 80, 81, 83, 91, 99, 103,
118, 132, 134, 136, 138, 139,
140, 143, 144, 145, 146, 147,
151, 152, 154, 156, 158, 159,
160, 161, 163, 164, 165, 166,
169, 170, 172, 173

1930, 13, 27, 31, 32, 70, 74,
75, 80, 81, 91, 99, 103, 118,
132, 134, 136, 138, 139, 140,
143, 144, 145, 146, 147, 151,
152, 154, 156, 159, 160, 161,
163, 164, 165, 169, 173, 174,
175, 176, 177

1931, 13, 27, 31, 32, 70, 74,
75, 80, 81, 91, 99, 103, 118,
132, 134, 136, 138, 139, 140,
143, 144, 145, 146, 147, 151,
152, 156, 160, 163, 164, 165,
169, 173, 174, 175, 176, 177,
178, 179

1932, 13, 27, 31, 32, 70, 74,
75, 80, 81, 91, 99, 103, 118,
132, 134, 136, 138, 139, 140,
143, 144, 145, 146, 151, 152,
156, 160, 163, 164, 165, 169,
173, 174, 175, 176, 177, 178,
179

1933, 13, 27, 31, 32, 70, 74,
75, 80, 81, 99, 103, 118, 132,
134, 136, 138, 139, 140, 143,

144, 145, 146, 152, 156, 160,
163, 164, 165, 169, 173, 174,
175, 176, 177, 178, 179, 180
1934, 13, 27, 31, 32, 70, 74,
75, 80, 81, 103, 118, 132,
134, 138, 139, 140, 143, 144,
145, 146, 152, 156, 160, 163,
164, 165, 169, 173, 174, 175,
176, 177, 178, 179, 180, 181,
182, 183
1935, 13, 27, 31, 32, 70, 74,
75, 80, 81, 103, 118, 132,
134, 136, 138, 139, 140, 143,
144, 145, 146, 152, 156, 160,
163, 164, 165, 169, 173, 174,
175, 176, 177, 178, 179, 180,
181, 182, 183
1936, 13, 27, 31, 70, 74, 75,
80, 81, 103, 118, 132, 134,
136, 138, 139, 140, 143, 144,
145, 146, 152, 156, 160, 163,
164, 165, 169, 173, 174, 175,
176, 177, 178, 179, 180, 181,
182, 183, 184, 185, 186
1937, 13, 27, 31, 70, 74, 75,
80, 81, 103, 118, 132, 134,
136, 138, 139, 143, 144, 145,
146, 152, 156, 160, 163, 165,
169, 173, 174, 175, 176, 177,
178, 179, 180, 181, 182, 183,
184, 185, 186
1938, 13, 27, 31, 70, 74, 75,
80, 81, 103, 118, 132, 134,
136, 138, 139, 143, 144, 145,
146, 152, 156, 160, 165, 169,
173, 174, 175, 176, 177, 178,
179, 180, 181, 182, 183, 184,
185, 186, 187, 188, 189, 190
1939, 13, 27, 31, 70, 74, 75,
80, 81, 103, 118, 132, 134,
136, 138, 139, 143, 144, 145,
146, 152, 156, 160, 165, 169,

173, 174, 175, 176, 177, 178,
179, 180, 181, 182, 183, 184,
185, 186, 187, 188, 191
1940, 13, 27, 31, 70, 74, 75,
80, 81, 103, 118, 132, 134,
136, 138, 139, 143, 144, 145,
146, 152, 156, 160, 165, 169,
174, 175, 176, 178, 179, 180,
181, 182, 183, 184, 185, 186,
187, 188, 192, 193, 194
1941, 13, 27, 31, 70, 74, 75,
80, 81, 103, 118, 132, 136,
138, 139, 143, 144, 145, 146,
152, 160, 165, 169, 174, 175,
176, 178, 179, 180, 181, 182,
183, 184, 186, 187, 188, 192,
193, 194, 195
1942, 13, 27, 31, 70, 74, 75,
80, 81, 103, 118, 132, 136,
138, 139, 143, 144, 145, 146,
152, 160, 165, 169, 174, 175,
178, 179, 180, 182, 183, 184,
186, 187, 192, 193, 194, 195
1943, 13, 27, 31, 70, 74, 75,
80, 81, 103, 118, 132, 136,
138, 139, 143, 144, 145, 146,
152, 160, 165, 169, 174, 175,
178, 179, 180, 182, 183, 184,
186, 187, 192, 193, 194
1944, 13, 27, 31, 70, 74, 75,
80, 81, 103, 118, 132, 136,
138, 139, 143, 144, 145, 146,
152, 160, 165, 169, 174, 175,
178, 179, 180, 181, 182, 183,
184, 186, 187, 192, 193, 194,
196, 197, 198
1945, 13, 27, 31, 70, 74, 76,
80, 81, 103, 118, 132, 136,
138, 139, 143, 144, 145, 146,
152, 160, 165, 169, 174, 175,
178, 179, 180, 181, 182, 183,
184, 186, 187, 192, 193, 194,

196, 197, 198, 199
1946, 13, 27, 31, 70, 74, 75,
  80, 81, 103, 118, 132, 136,
  138, 139, 144, 145, 146, 152,
  160, 165, 169, 174, 175, 178,
  179, 180, 181, 182, 183, 184,
  186, 187, 192, 193, 194, 196,
  197, 198, 199, 200
1947, 13, 27, 31, 70, 74, 75,
  80, 81, 103, 118, 132, 136,
  138, 139, 143, 144, 145, 146,
  152, 165, 169, 174, 175, 178,
  179, 180, 181, 182, 183, 184,
  186, 187, 192, 193, 194, 196,
  197, 198, 199, 200, 201, 202
1948, 13, 27, 31, 70, 74, 75,
  80, 81, 103, 118, 132, 136,
  138, 139, 143, 144, 145, 146,
  152, 165, 169, 174, 175, 178,
  179, 180, 181, 182, 183, 184,
  187, 192, 194, 196, 197, 198,
  199, 200, 201, 203, 204, 205,
  206, 207
1949, 13, 27, 31, 70, 74, 75,
  80, 81, 103, 118, 132, 136,
  138, 139, 143, 144, 145, 146,
  152, 165, 169, 174, 175, 178,
  179, 180, 181, 182, 182, 184,
  187, 192, 194, 197, 198, 199,
  200, 201, 203, 204, 205, 208,
  209, 210, 211
1950, 13, 27, 31, 70, 74, 75,
  80, 81, 103, 118, 132, 136,
  138, 139, 143, 144, 145, 146,
  152, 165, 169, 174, 175, 178,
  179, 180, 181, 182, 183, 184,
  187, 192, 194, 197, 198, 200,
  201, 203, 204, 205, 208, 211,
  212, 213
1951, 13, 27, 31, 70, 74, 75,
  80, 81, 103, 118, 132, 136,
  138, 139, 143, 144, 145, 146,

152, 165, 169, 174, 175, 178,
179, 180, 181, 182, 183, 184,
187, 192, 194, 197, 198, 200,
203, 204, 205, 208, 211, 212,
213, 214, 215
1952, 13, 27, 31, 70, 74, 75,
  80, 81, 103, 118, 132, 138,
  139, 143, 144, 145, 146, 152,
  165, 169, 174, 175, 178, 179,
  180, 181, 183, 184, 187, 192,
  197, 198, 200, 203, 204, 205,
  211, 212, 213, 214, 215, 216,
  217, 218
1953, 13, 27, 31, 70, 74, 75,
  80, 81, 103, 118, 138, 139,
  143, 144, 145, 146, 152, 165,
  169, 174, 175, 178, 179, 180,
  181, 183, 184, 187, 197, 198,
  200, 203, 204, 205, 211, 213,
  214, 215, 216, 217, 218, 219,
  220, 221, 222
1954, 13, 27, 31, 70, 74, 75,
  80, 81, 103, 118, 138, 139,
  143, 144, 145, 146, 152, 165,
  169, 174, 175, 178, 179, 180,
  181, 183, 184, 187, 197, 198,
  200, 203, 204, 205, 211, 213,
  214, 215, 216, 217, 218, 219,
  220, 221, 222, 223, 224
1955, 13, 27, 31, 70, 74, 75,
  80, 81, 103, 118, 138, 139,
  143, 144, 145, 146, 152, 165,
  169, 174, 175, 178, 179, 180,
  181, 183, 184, 187, 197, 198,
  200, 203, 204, 205, 211, 214,
  215, 216, 217, 218, 219, 220,
  222, 223, 224
1956, 13, 27, 31, 70, 74, 75,
  80, 81, 103, 118, 138, 139,
  143, 144, 145, 146, 152, 165,
  174, 175, 178, 179, 180, 181,
  183, 184, 187, 197, 198, 200,

203, 204, 205, 211, 214, 215,
216, 217, 218, 219, 220, 221,
222, 223, 224, 225
1957, 13, 27, 31, 70, 74, 75,
80, 81, 103, 118, 138, 139,
143, 144, 145, 146, 152, 165,
174, 175, 178, 179, 180, 181,
184, 187, 197, 198, 200, 203,
204, 205, 211, 214, 215, 216,
217, 218, 220, 221, 222, 223,
224, 225, 226, 227, 228, 229
1958, 13, 27, 70, 74, 75, 80,
81, 103, 118, 138, 139, 143,
144, 145, 146, 152, 165, 174,
175, 178, 179, 180, 181, 184,
187, 198, 200, 203, 204, 205,
211, 214, 215, 216, 217, 218,
220, 221, 222, 223, 224, 225,
226, 227, 228, 229
1959, 13, 27, 70, 74, 75, 80,
81, 103, 118, 138, 139, 143,
144, 145, 146, 152, 165, 174,
175, 178, 179, 180, 181, 184,
187, 198, 200, 203, 204, 205,
211, 215, 216, 217, 218, 220,
222, 223, 224, 225, 226, 227,
228, 229
1960, 13, 27, 70, 74, 75, 80,
81, 103, 118, 138, 139, 143,
144, 145, 146, 152, 165, 174,
175, 178, 179, 180, 181, 184,
187, 200, 203, 204, 205, 211,
215, 216, 217, 218, 220, 222,
223, 224, 225, 226, 227, 228,
229
1961, 13, 27, 70, 74, 75, 80,
81, 103, 118, 138, 139, 143,
144, 145, 146, 152, 165, 174,
175, 178, 179, 180, 181, 184,
187, 200, 203, 204, 205, 211,
215, 216, 217, 218, 220, 222,
223, 224, 225, 226, 227, 228,

229, 230, 231, 232
1962, 13, 27, 70, 74, 75, 80,
81, 103, 118, 138, 139, 144,
145, 146, 152, 165, 174, 175,
178, 179, 180, 184, 187, 200,
203, 204, 205, 211, 215, 216,
217, 218, 220, 222, 223, 224,
225, 226, 227, 228, 229, 230,
231, 232, 233
1963, 13, 27, 70, 74, 75, 80,
81, 103, 118, 138, 139, 144,
145, 146, 152, 165, 174, 175,
178, 179, 180, 184, 200, 203,
204, 205, 211, 215, 216, 217,
218, 220, 222, 223, 224, 225,
226, 227, 228, 229, 230, 232,
233, 234, 235, 236
1964, 13, 27, 70, 74, 75, 80,
81, 103, 118, 138, 139, 144,
145, 146, 152, 165, 174, 175,
178, 179, 180, 184, 200, 203,
204, 205, 211, 215, 217, 218,
220, 222, 224, 225, 226, 227,
228, 229, 230, 232, 233, 234,
235, 236, 237
1965, 13, 27, 70, 74, 75, 80,
81, 103, 118, 138, 139, 144,
145, 146, 152, 165, 174, 175,
178, 179, 180, 184, 200, 203,
204, 205, 211, 215, 217, 218,
220, 222, 224, 225, 226, 227,
228, 229, 230, 232, 233, 234,
235, 236, 237, 238, 239
1966, 13, 27, 70, 74, 75, 80,
81, 103, 118, 138, 139, 144,
145, 146, 152, 165, 174, 175,
178, 179, 180, 184, 200, 203,
204, 205, 211, 215, 217, 218,
220, 222, 224, 225, 226, 227,
228, 229, 230, 232, 233, 234,
235, 237, 238, 239, 240
1967, 13, 27, 70, 74, 75, 80,

81, 103, 118, 138, 139, 144,
145, 146, 152, 165, 174, 175,
178, 179, 180, 184, 200, 204,
205, 211, 215, 217, 218, 220,
222, 224, 225, 226, 227, 228,
229, 230, 232, 233, 234, 235,
237, 238, 239, 240, 241, 242,
243

1968, 13, 27, 70, 74, 75, 80,
81, 103, 118, 138, 139, 144,
146, 152, 165, 174, 175, 178,
179, 180, 184, 200, 204, 205,
211, 215, 217, 220, 222, 224,
225, 226, 227, 228, 229, 230,
232, 233, 234, 235, 237, 238,
239, 240, 241, 242, 243, 244

1969, 27, 70, 74, 75, 80, 81,
103, 118, 138, 139, 144, 146,
152, 165, 174, 175, 178, 179,
180, 184, 200, 204, 205, 211,
215, 217, 220, 222, 224, 225,
226, 227, 228, 229, 230, 233,
234, 235, 237, 238, 239, 240,
241, 242, 243, 244, 245, 246,
247, 248, 249

1970, 13, 27, 70, 74, 75, 80,
81, 103, 118, 138, 139, 144,
146, 152, 165, 174, 175, 178,
179, 180, 184, 200, 204, 205,
211, 215, 217, 220, 222, 224,
225, 226, 227, 228, 229, 230,
233, 234, 235, 237, 238, 239,
240, 241, 242, 243, 244, 245,
246, 247, 248, 249, 250, 251,
252, 253, 254, 255, 256, 257,
258, 259, 260, 261, 262

1971, 27, 70, 74, 75, 80, 81,
103, 118, 138, 139, 144, 146,
152, 165, 174, 175, 178, 179,
180, 184, 200, 204, 211, 215,
217, 220, 222, 224, 225, 226,
227, 228, 229, 230, 233, 234,

235, 237, 238, 239, 240, 241,
243, 244, 245, 246, 247, 248,
249, 250, 252, 253, 254, 257,
258, 260, 261, 263, 264, 265,
266, 267, 268, 269, 270, 271,
272, 273, 274, 275, 276, 277,
278, 279, 280

1972, 27, 70, 74, 75, 80, 81,
103, 138, 139, 144, 146, 152,
165, 174, 175, 178, 179, 180,
184, 200, 204, 211, 215, 217,
220, 222, 224, 225, 226, 227,
228, 229, 230, 233, 234, 235,
237, 238, 239, 240, 243, 244,
245, 246, 247, 248, 249, 250,
252, 253, 254, 257, 260, 264,
265, 266, 270, 271, 274, 275,
278, 279, 280, 281, 282, 283,
284, 285, 286, 287, 288, 289,
290, 291, 292, 293, 294, 295,
296, 297, 298, 299, 300, 301,
302, 303, 304, 305, 306, 307,
308, 309, 310

1973, 27, 74, 75, 80, 81, 103,
138, 144, 146, 152, 165, 174,
175, 178, 180, 184, 200, 204,
211, 215, 217, 220, 222, 224,
225, 226, 227, 228, 229, 230,
233, 234, 235, 237, 238, 239,
240, 243, 244, 245, 246, 247,
249, 250, 252, 253, 254, 257,
260, 264, 265, 266, 270, 271,
274, 275, 278, 279, 280, 281,
282, 284, 285, 286, 287, 288,
289, 290, 292, 293, 294, 295,
296, 297, 298, 299, 300, 301,
302, 303, 304, 305, 306, 307,
308, 311, 312, 313, 314, 315,
316, 317, 318, 319, 320, 321,
322, 323, 324, 325, 326, 327,
328, 329, 330, 331, 332, 333,
334, 335, 336, 337, 338, 339,

340, 341, 342, 343
1974, 27, 74, 75, 80, 81, 103,
138, 144, 146, 152, 165, 174,
175, 178, 180, 184, 200, 204,
211, 215, 217, 222, 224, 225,
226, 227, 228, 229, 230, 233,
234, 235, 238, 239, 240, 243,
244, 245, 247, 249, 250, 253,
254, 257, 260, 264, 265, 270,
271, 274, 275, 278, 279, 280,
281, 282, 284, 285, 286, 287,
288, 289, 290, 292, 293, 294,
295, 297, 298, 299, 300, 301,
302, 303, 304, 306, 307, 308,
311, 312, 313, 316, 318, 319,
321, 323, 324, 325, 327, 328,
329, 331, 332, 333, 336, 340,
341, 342, 344, 345, 346, 347,
348, 349, 350, 351, 352, 353,
354, 355, 356, 357, 358, 359,
360, 361, 362, 363, 364, 365,
366, 367, 368, 369, 370, 371,
372, 373, 374, 375, 376, 377,
378, 379, 380, 381
1975, 27, 75, 80, 81, 103, 138,
144, 146, 152, 165, 174, 175,
178, 180, 184, 200, 204, 211,
215, 217, 222, 224, 225, 226,
227, 228, 229, 230, 233, 234,
235, 238, 240, 243, 245, 249,
250, 253, 254, 257, 260, 264,
265, 270, 271, 274, 275, 279,
280, 281, 282, 284, 285, 286,
287, 288, 289, 290, 292, 293,
294, 297, 298, 299, 303, 304,
307, 308, 311, 313, 316, 318,
319, 321, 323, 324, 325, 327,
329, 331, 332, 333, 336, 341,
342, 344, 345, 346, 347, 349,
354, 355, 356, 358, 360, 361,
362, 363, 364, 365, 366, 367,
368, 369, 370, 371, 375, 376,

378, 380, 381, 382, 383, 384,
385, 386, 387, 388, 389, 390,
391, 392, 393, 394, 395, 396,
397, 398, 399, 400, 401, 402,
403, 404, 405, 406, 407, 408,
409, 410, 411, 412, 413, 414,
415, 416, 417, 418, 419, 420,
421, 422, 423, 424, 425, 426,
427, 428, 429, 430, 431
1976, 27, 75, 80, 81, 103, 138,
144, 146, 152, 174, 175, 178,
180, 184, 200, 204, 211, 215,
217, 222, 224, 225, 226, 227,
228, 229, 230, 233, 234, 235,
238, 240, 243, 244, 245, 249,
253, 254, 257, 260, 264, 265,
270, 274, 275, 279, 281, 282,
284, 285, 286, 287, 288, 289,
290, 293, 294, 297, 298, 303,
304, 307, 308, 311, 313, 316,
318, 319, 323, 324, 325, 327,
331, 332, 333, 341, 344, 345,
346, 347, 349, 354, 355, 356,
358, 360, 361, 363, 364, 365,
367, 368, 369, 370, 371, 380,
382, 383, 384, 385, 386, 390,
391, 392, 393, 395, 396, 397,
398, 399, 403, 404, 405, 406,
407, 408, 409, 410, 411, 412,
413, 414, 415, 416, 417, 419,
420, 422, 425, 428, 429, 430,
432, 433, 434, 435, 436, 437,
438, 439, 440, 441, 442, 443,
444, 445, 446, 447, 448, 449,
450, 451, 452, 453, 454, 455,
456, 457, 458, 459, 460, 461,
462, 463, 464, 465, 466, 467,
468, 469, 470, 471, 472, 473,
474, 475, 476, 477
1977, 27, 80, 81, 103, 138, 144,
146, 152, 174, 175, 178, 180,
184, 200, 204, 211, 215, 217,

222, 224, 225, 226, 227, 228,
229, 230, 233, 234, 235, 238,
240, 243, 244, 245, 253, 254,
257, 264, 265, 270, 274, 275,
281, 282, 284, 285, 286, 287,
288, 289, 293, 294, 297, 298,
303, 304, 307, 308, 311, 313,
316, 318, 319, 323, 324, 325,
327, 331, 332, 333, 341, 344,
345, 347, 349, 354, 356, 358,
360, 361, 363, 364, 365, 367,
369, 370, 371, 380, 382, 383,
384, 385, 386, 390, 391, 393,
395, 396, 397, 398, 399, 403,
404, 405, 406, 407, 408, 409,
410, 411, 414, 415, 416, 419,
420, 422, 425, 428, 429, 430,
432, 433, 434, 435, 438, 439,
440, 442, 443, 446, 448, 449,
450, 451, 452, 455, 456, 457,
458, 459, 461, 462, 469, 470,
473, 474, 476, 477, 478, 479,
480, 481, 482, 483, 484, 485,
486, 487, 488, 489, 490, 491,
492, 493, 494, 495, 496, 497,
498, 499, 500, 501, 502, 503,
504, 505, 506, 507, 508, 509,
510, 511, 512, 513, 514, 515,
516, 517, 518, 519, 520, 521,
522, 523, 524, 525, 526, 527,
528, 529, 530,-532, 533, 534,
535, 536, 537-9
1978, 27, 80, 81, 103, 138,
144, 146, 152, 174, 175, 178,
180, 184, 200, 204, 211, 217,
222, 224, 225, 226, 228, 229,
230, 233, 234, 235, 238, 240,
243, 244, 245, 257, 264, 265,
270, 274, 275, 282, 284, 285,
286, 287, 288, 289, 293, 294,
297, 298, 303, 304, 307, 313,
316, 318, 323, 324, 325, 331,

333, 344, 345, 347, 349, 354,
356, 358, 360, 361, 363, 364,
369, 370, 371, 382, 383, 384,
385, 386, 391, 393, 395, 396,
397, 398, 403, 404, 405, 407,
408, 409, 410, 411, 414, 415,
416, 419, 425, 428, 429, 430,
432, 433, 434, 435, 438, 439,
440, 442, 443, 446, 448, 449,
450, 451, 452, 455, 456, 457,
458, 459, 461, 462, 463, 469,
470, 474, 476, 477, 480, 481,
482, 483, 484, 487, 488-94,
497, 498, 499, 501, 502, 503,
504, 506, 509, 511, 512, 514,
516, 517, 519, 520, 522, 523,
526, 529, 530-2, 534, 536,
537-42, 543-95
1979, 27, 80, 81, 103, 138, 144,
146, 152, 174, 175, 178, 180,
184, 200, 204, 211, 217, 222,
224, 225, 226, 228, 229, 230,
233, 234, 235, 238, 240, 245,
257, 264, 265, 274, 275, 281,
282, 284, 285, 286, 287, 288,
289, 293, 297, 298, 303, 304,
307, 316, 318, 323, 324, 325,
331, 333, 344, 345, 349, 354,
358, 360, 363, 364, 369, 370,
382, 383, 384, 385, 386, 393,
395, 396, 397, 398, 403, 404,
405, 407, 408, 409, 410, 411,
414, 416, 419, 428, 429, 430,
432, 433, 434, 435, 438, 439,
440, 442, 443, 446, 449, 450,
451, 452, 455, 457, 458, 459,
462, 463, 469, 470, 474, 477,
480, 481, 483, 484, 487,
488-94, 499, 501, 502, 504,
511, 514, 516, 517, 519, 520,
522, 523, 526, 529, 530-2,
534, 536, 537-42, 544, 545,

547-9, 553, 555, 556, 557,
559-61, 562-7, 568-72, 574,
577, 579, 580, 583-5, 588,
589, 592, 595-638
1980, 27, 80, 81, 103, 138,
144, 146, 152, 174, 175, 178,
180, 184, 200, 204, 217, 222,
224, 225, 226, 228, 229, 230,
233, 234, 235, 238, 240, 245,
257, 264, 265, 274, 275, 281,
282, 284, 285, 286, 287, 288,
289, 293, 297, 298, 303, 307,
316, 318, 323, 324, 325, 331,
333, 344, 345, 349, 354, 358,
360, 363, 364, 369, 370, 382,
383, 384, 385, 386, 393, 395,
396, 397, 398, 403, 404, 405,
407, 408, 409, 410, 411, 414,
416, 419, 428, 429, 430, 432,
433, 434, 435, 438, 439, 440,
442, 443, 446, 449, 450, 451,
455, 457, 458, 459, 462, 463,
469, 470, 474, 477, 480, 481,
484, 487, 488-94, 499, 501,
502, 504, 511, 514, 516, 517,
519, 520, 522, 523, 526, 529,
520-2, 534, 536, 537-42, 544,
545, 547-9, 553, 556, 557,
559-67, 568-72, 574, 577,
579, 580, 583-5, 588, 589,
592, 595, 596, 598, 600-607,
609-13, 615, 616, 620-2, 624,
627-30, 632, 634, 636, 638-84
1981, 27, 80, 81, 103, 138,
144, 146, 152, 174, 175, 178,
180, 184, 200, 217, 222, 224,
225, 226, 228, 229, 230, 233,
234, 235, 238, 240, 245, 257,
264, 265, 274, 275, 281, 282,
285, 286, 288, 289, 293, 297,
298, 303, 307, 316, 318, 323,
324, 325, 331, 333, 344, 345,

349, 354, 358, 360, 364, 369,
370, 382, 383, 384, 385, 386,
391, 393, 395, 396, 397, 398,
403, 404, 407, 408, 409, 410,
411, 414, 416, 419, 428, 429,
430, 432, 433, 434, 435, 438,
439, 440, 442, 443, 446, 449,
450, 451, 455, 457, 458, 459,
462, 463, 469, 470, 474, 477,
480, 481, 484, 487, 488-94,
501, 502, 511, 514, 516, 517,
519, 520, 522, 523, 526, 529,
530-2, 534, 536, 537-42, 544,
545, 547-9, 553, 557, 559-67,
570-2, 574, 579, 580, 583-5,
588, 589, 595, 596, 598, 600,
601, 603, 604-606, 609-13,
615, 616, 620-2, 624, 628,
629, 632, 634, 636, 638-40,
646-8, 650-61, 664-7, 669-72,
675-83, 685-815
1982, 27, 80, 81, 103, 138, 144,
146, 152, 174, 175, 178, 180,
184, 200, 217, 222, 224, 225,
226, 228, 229, 230, 233, 234,
235, 238, 240, 245, 257, 264,
265, 274, 275, 281, 282, 285,
286, 288, 289, 297, 298, 303,
307, 316, 318, 323, 324, 325,
331, 333, 344, 345, 349, 354,
358, 364, 369, 370, 382, 383,
384, 385, 386, 391, 393, 395,
396, 397, 398, 403, 404, 407,
408, 409, 410, 411, 414, 416,
419, 428, 429, 430, 432, 433,
434, 435, 438, 439, 440, 442,
443, 446, 449, 450, 451, 455,
457, 458, 459, 462, 463, 469,
470, 474, 477, 480, 481, 484,
487, 488-94, 501, 502, 511,
514, 516, 517, 519, 520, 522,
523, 526, 529, 530-2, 534,

536, 537-42, 544, 545, 547-9,
553, 557, 559-67, 571, 574,
579, 580, 583-5, 588, 589,
596, 598, 600, 601, 603, 605,
606, 609-13, 620-2, 624, 632,
634, 636, 638, 640, 646-8,
650, 653-61, 664-7, 669-72,
675-83, 685-93, 695-9,
701-26, 728-31, 733-50,
752-77, 779-810, 812-50

1983, 27, 80, 81, 103, 138,
144, 146, 152, 174, 175, 178,
180, 184, 200, 217, 222, 224,
225, 226, 229, 230, 233, 234,
235, 238, 240, 245, 257, 264,
265, 274, 275, 281, 282, 285,
286, 288, 289, 297, 298, 303,
307, 316, 318, 323, 324, 325,
331, 333, 344, 345, 349, 354,
358, 364, 369, 370, 382, 383,
384, 385, 386, 391, 393, 395,
296, 397, 398, 403, 404, 407,
408, 409, 410, 411, 414, 416,
419, 428, 429, 430, 432, 433,
434, 435, 438, 439, 440, 442,
443, 446, 449, 450, 451, 455,
457, 458, 459, 462, 463, 469,
470, 474, 477, 480, 481, 484,
487, 489-94, 501, 502, 511,
514, 516, 517, 519, 520, 522,
523, 526, 529, 530-2, 534,
536, 537-42, 544, 545, 547-9,
553, 557, 559-61, 563-7, 571,
574, 579, 580, 583-5, 588,
589, 596, 598, 601, 603, 605,
606, 609-13, 621, 622, 624,
632, 634, 636, 638, 640,
646-8, 650, 653, 655, 661,
664, 667, 669-72, 675-80,
682, 683, 685-91, 693, 695-9,
701-708, 710-19, 721-6,
728-31, 733-9, 741-50,

752-77, 779-810, 812-20, 822-
39, 841-90

1984, 27, 80, 81, 103, 138, 144,
146, 152, 174, 175, 178, 180,
184, 200, 217, 222, 224, 225,
226, 229, 230, 233, 234, 235,
238, 240, 245, 257, 264, 265,
274, 275, 281, 282, 285, 286,
288, 289, 297, 298, 303, 307,
316, 318, 323, 324, 325, 331,
333, 344, 345, 349, 354, 358,
364, 369, 370, 382, 383, 384,
385, 386, 391, 393, 395, 396,
397, 398, 403, 404, 407, 408,
409, 410, 414, 416, 419, 428,
429, 430, 432, 433, 434, 435,
438, 439, 440, 442, 443, 446,
449, 450, 451, 455, 457, 458,
459, 462, 463, 469, 470, 474,
477, 480, 481, 484, 487, 489-
94, 501, 502, 511, 514, 516,
517, 519, 520, 522, 523, 526,
529, 530-2, 534, 536, 537-42,
544, 545, 547-9, 553, 563-7,
571, 574, 579, 580, 583-5,
588, 589, 596, 598, 601, 603,
605, 606, 609-13, 621, 622,
624, 632, 634, 636, 638, 640,
646-8, 650, 653, 655, 658,
661, 664, 667, 669-72, 675-80,
685-91, 693, 695-9, 701-708,
710-19, 721-6, 728-31, 733-9,
741-50, 752-77, 779-810, 812-
20, 822-7, 829-39, 841-51,
853-7, 859-63, 865-920

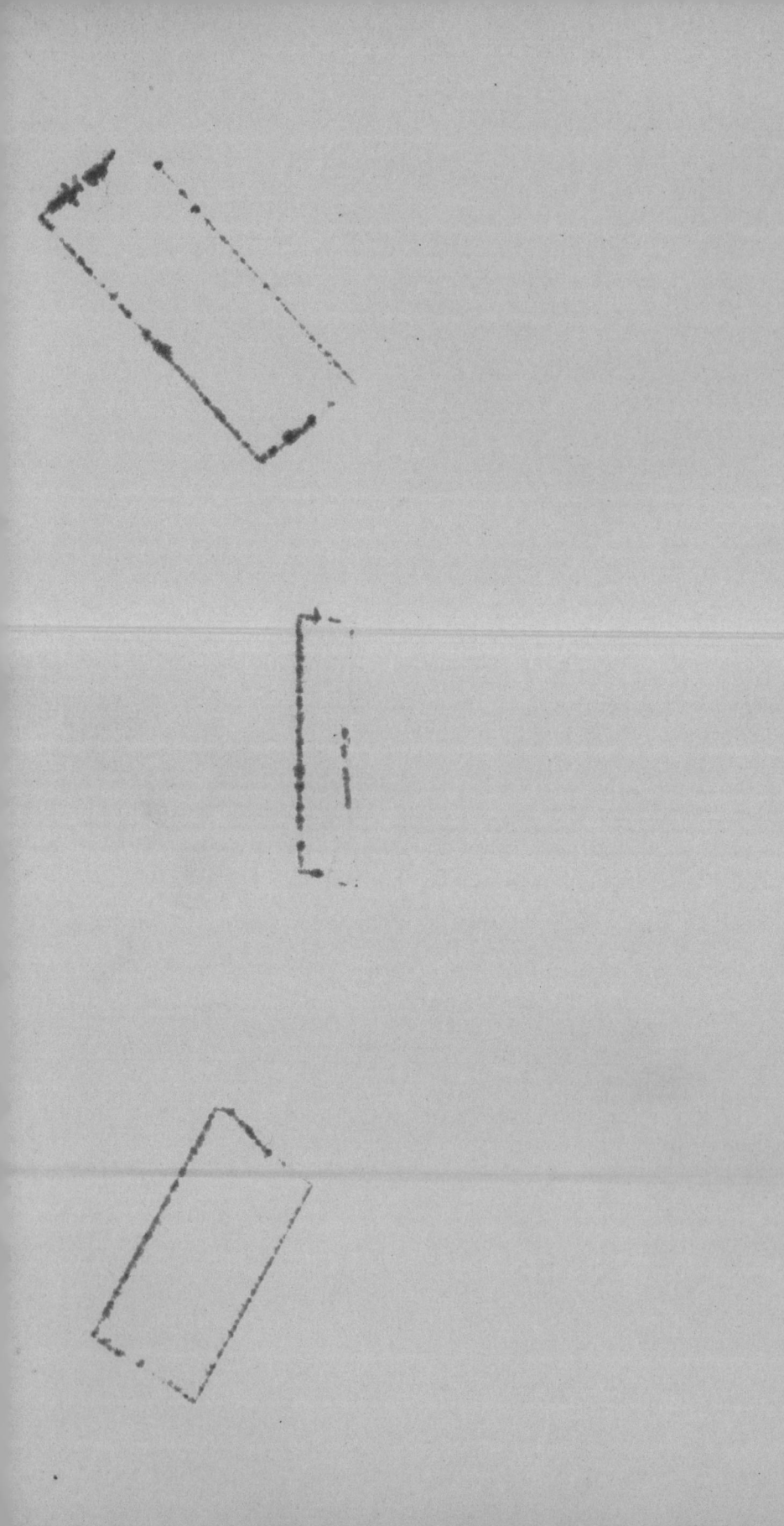